Confessions
of an
Igloo Dweller

Confessions
of an
Igloo Dweller

James Houston

A Peter Davison Book

HOUGHTON MIFFLIN COMPANY

BOSTON • NEW YORK

For information about permission to reproduce selections from
this book, write to Permissions, Houghton Mifflin Company,
215 Park Avenue South, New York, New York 10003.

For information about this and other Houghton Mifflin trade
and reference books and multimedia products, visit
The Bookstore at Houghton Mifflin on the World Wide Web
at http://www.hmco.com/trade/.

ISBN 0-395-78890-0
CIP data is available.

Printed in the United States of America

QUM 10 9 8 7 6 5 4 3 2 1

_All the drawings in this book were
created by James Houston._

*To Inuit and other Arctic friends
who made this possible*

Contents

Author's Note

In earlier Arctic days, the subject of this book, the word "Eskimo" was recognized and respected around the world. That term recently seems to have fallen out of favor. Now "Inuit" (plural) and "Inuk" (singular) are used in Canada in the place of "Eskimo," though they are not yet in all our English dictionaries. I worry about the confusion in other countries where these remarkable Arctic people are known as "Eskimo."

"Inuit," which simply means "the people," literally separates humans from animals, animals that Inuit understand and respect so well. "Inuk," meaning "the person," and "Inuit" have long been used by these people to describe themselves in their language of Inuktitut. "Eskimo" is perhaps of Algonquin Indian origin and is said to mean "eaters of raw meat," though that remains unclear.

I expect that the Canadian use of the word "Inuit" will increase and that the use of "Eskimo" will decline. For that reason, although the terms were never used in English during the time I was in the North, I have used "Inuit" and "Inuk" almost exclusively throughout this book.

Confessions
of an
Igloo Dweller

I

Northward

George Charity was a somewhat shy man from South Porcupine, not usually given to flinging open doors at 6:00 a.m. and calling, "Hey, Houston, you want to go flying this morning?"

I sat bolt upright, looked at him and then at my watch. Why was this bush pilot asking me a question like that?

"Flying? You bet!" I answered. "Where are we going?"

"Last night, a Hudson's Bay post in the Arctic relayed a broken radio message by Morse key down here to Moose Factory. They can't make voice contact this far south. There's been some kind of an accident and the surgeon here, Dr. Harper, is going to try to get up there."

I scrambled out of my sleeping bag.

"If you're coming, you've got to help me woggle the gas and haul in at the landings. If that's okay, we'll take you with us. Free."

Free! That was the word I needed to hear.

"Come on fast!" he said. "The doctor's already up. He's milking the coffee urn. Summer's over and the light's going down up north. Bring only your sleeping bag, your sketch books, and a few warm clothes, and be prepared to pump gas and haul anchor. You agree to that?"

"Damn right I do!"

"Then let's go!"

In an instant I was up, rolling my sleeping bag. I had spent the last month in James Bay, that southern dip beneath Hudson Bay, making drawings, mostly of Swampy Cree Indians. But I had never dared to hope that I would reach the Arctic, to me a dream country like Xanadu. The Arctic, the treeless country, began 1,200 kilometers north. No existing roads or rails, and no scheduled boats or planes went there. Here was my one and only chance to get there – free!

I ran out of the Hudson's Bay Company staff house where I had been staying with the 1948 crop of young clerks fresh out from Scotland, bound for Indian country, along with a few young Canadian nurses. To hell with coffee. I ran down to the little floating dock, my sleeping bag and sketch books flapping like wings.

The stubby, single-engine Norseman rested in the water on her floats. I grabbed the pump that George had stuck into the waist-high barrel of fuel and I started woggling, as the Air Force liked to call it, woggling back and forth at breakneck speed while George directed the battered gasoline funnel into one of the plane's three tanks, making sure its old felt filter didn't fall into the river. We wanted no muck-ups to delay this Arctic flight. We were going almost as far north as Toronto, my home town, was to the south, and that was a world away.

Together we rolled a spare drum of gas up a wooden ramp into the small cabin space. Dr. Harper hurried down with his little black medical bag, his wife in tow to see him off. She was a kindly, plump, red-cheeked motherly woman who had on occasion invited me to dinner at their small government house on Moose Factory Island, because, she said, she thought I had a hungry look. She couldn't help sensing my excitement that morning. She may even have encouraged George and her husband to make this free journey possible for me.

As we started to get into the plane, she kissed her husband, then me. "Take care of them," she called to George.

I untied the rope that held the plane, climbed in, and slammed the door. George gunned up the rugged old Austin Airways plane and she trundled out into the center of the Moose River like a heavy war horse decked out in oil-streaked armor. There weren't any "Fasten Your Seatbelts" signs or "No Smoking" warnings, none of that newfangled stuff. There were no seat belts, and the ashtray was overflowing. The question was, were we too heavily loaded, with both wing tanks full and all the other necessary Arctic freight aboard, to take off and still clear the trees?

The Norseman wheezed and coughed, then roared as we went lumbering along the gutway throwing spray. The floats at first refused to leave the water. Oh, Lord, I thought, these trees ahead of us are getting too close. Come on, baby, lift! The violent spray off the floats was deafening. I tried to lift her with my stomach muscles. I could see the old doctor smoking like a chimney and gulping for air. Lift, lift, you stubborn bastard, lift!

Norseman on Floats

The plane hit a small wave and lurched into the air. We were off and clear, skimming low over the island's trees. The doctor lit another cigarette off the butt of his first and I lit up as well, then leaning forward looked out the pilot's window at James Bay spreading out like a huge, blue-gray map of a dream. George turned his head, smiled and nodded, then set his course up the east side of James Bay to Hudson Bay.

Instead of crawling up front with George, the doctor and I sat back in the smoky haze and hollered in each other's ears. It was difficult to talk in those old planes for they made a wicked amount of noise.

"A child got badly bitten by some dogs," Dr. Harper explained. "I don't know the details. Dogs rushed into an Eskimo tent and grabbed a baby out of its mother's hood and started to eat it. The woman fought back and got the child away from them. It was still alive last night. That's what Ron Duncan was able to read off the Morse key."

"How long will you stay up there?" I asked, thinking of my chances to draw or paint. Ever since I'd got out of the Canadian army at the end of the war I'd been trying my hand as an artist, first in France, most recently in Quebec. The idea of the Arctic as my subject was terrific.

"Can't tell from here," he shouted in my ear. "I'll give the baby some penicillin and sew it up, if it lives. We may wait there three or four days to see if its temperature goes down. The sutures I'll use are the kind that dissolve by themselves. It's not a good idea to bring a baby south unless you have to because it may be a year or even two before you can be sure to get it back and find its mother again. And then you might discover that whole camp has moved away, God knows where. These families are nomad hunters, they move with the animals."

"Sounds great!" I shouted. "Four days! I ought to be able to get lots of drawings and watercolors done by then."

The doctor crawled forward and sat by George. I leaned against the cold red barrel of fuel, staring out the small, blurry window as the east coast of the Bay unfolded beneath me. The timber was thinning. No signs at all of any human habitation.

The doctor came back after an hour and I eased forward into the co-pilot's seat. George handed me a large, tattered map and pointed to the mouth of the George River. "We'll land there, gas up, and leave some stuff," he said.

Fort George was the first place I had seen in Canada where the Indians were still using old smoke-blackened teepees constructed around a bundle of long, thin tent poles with a wind flap protruding from the top to control the smoke.

Cree teepee

"This place is famous for its beaver," George told me as we woggled in more gas. "The fur auction houses agree that the Cree people here stretch and scrape a beaver pelt until it's as clean and white as the finest table linen. That's what makes the big Fort George beaver pelts so highly prized by furriers in Montreal, New York, London, Paris."

The doctor called to the beautiful new nurse, standing beckoning to us on the riverbank. "Sorry, we can't visit your new nursing station now, my dear. Maybe later, on the way back!"

She waved goodbye. Everyone knew we had to make our next stop in good light.

We made it and stayed overnight in Great Whale River (now renamed Poste de la Baleine). I'll tell you something strange about that place later. On this visit I was struck that there were only two buildings: a small red-roofed trading post and the pale, flaking Anglican mission, huddled on either side of a rickety wind-charger used to churn up enough electricity to charge batteries for relayed radio messages, such as the brief one received the day before at Moose Factory. When the wind blew hard, it would even light up the twenty-watt bulb that hung in the trader's kitchen.

When we left there and flew north again next morning, I saw huge bald patches of rock and tundra appearing beneath us. The dwarfed, wind-blasted trees were leaning, crouching, all but gone. Although it was still September a northwest wind had scattered fine, thin drifts that curved like snow snakes inland toward the Labrador. The vastness of it all was impossible for me to grasp. This gigantic Arctic region, a part of my own country – so remote it had remained unknown to almost all North Americans.

Sometime later, George leaned over and shouted, "I'm going to put down in Richmond Gulf. We've got some gas cached near a German trader's hut. He's a short old guy. His wife is with him, living here with the Indians. There's no one else."

The Norseman glided down and landed, its momentum carrying us toward the tiny trading post surrounded by a dozen tents. The trader came down and led George and the doctor up to his house. The Indians there seemed inclined to keep away from me. As I woggled in the gas, I watched one of them holding a flaming torch above his head, running hard, letting out yips as he wove in and out among their tents. Fortunately he gave me and my open barrel of gas a wide berth.

"What's he doing?" I asked the gnomelike German lady when she came down to the plane wearing a babushka and beaded moccasins.

She gave me a piece of her hot, raisin-filled bannock, smiled and shrugged. "Chasing off some sickness maybe, or some spirits that's bad. I got coffee here. You want some?"

"Sure!" I gasped.

She held the cup to my mouth while I continued to woggle, for the others were already returning.

We three lit up, climbed in, waved and taxied off. Richmond Gulf is huge, with endless waters. George could take his time to become airborne.

Now that we were north of the treeline, all hints of green had disappeared and the whole world beneath us had turned into an endless expanse of gray granite laps and folds containing shining lakes and ponds beyond all counting. This northern end of the Laurentian Shield, I was later told, is a geologist's paradise, one of the world's earliest rock formations, utterly stripped of the usual overburden of earth and timber.

As we passed along the chain of Nastapoka Islands, George pointed down to a cove with white lumps on the shore.

"Old ice?" I asked.

"No, that's a cluster of five Eskimo tents, a hunting camp. They probably don't live there. They'll be on the move before the heavy snows."

For a long time there were no other human signs until George pointed north to the Portland Promontory and the mouth of the Inukjuak River. Out beyond it drifted huge, shattered jigsaw puzzles of broken ice.

"Ice down from the north," he explained, "not calved off glaciers."

Many of these flat, floating islands were larger than a city block, with nine-tenths of their mass hidden beneath the water as they spumed off smaller pieces. All of it was ice drifting south to melt and die in the relative warmth of Hudson Bay, that most southern of the Arctic seas. Most people can hardly believe it but the Bay is so big that more water flows into it from its rivers than flows into the Atlantic and Pacific oceans combined.

"We're going north of the Inukjuak and on to some place near Canso Bay. Watch the coastline for some tents."

George saw them first, dipped his wing and turned. The doctor and I lit up cigarettes as we prepared for landing. Such rough, uncharted waters with their hidden rocks could make any pair of greenhorns nervous. But we landed smoothly between the rock-bound coast and the drifting ice as near the tents as George could manage, turning the Norseman's snubby nose toward the tight clutch of people who had gathered on the shore to show us the best place to come in.

I wore an almost knee-high pair of elkskin mountain boots with nails for climbing. I clanked cautiously out along the metal float with rope in hand. Seeing rocks, I hopped into clear, shallow water that turned out to be well above my boot tops to about crotch-deep. It was nippy!

Inuit hunters waded out and grabbed the floats, pushing back to keep the Norseman off the rocks. One man took the heavy doctor with his leather medical grip and carried him ashore on his back. Fortunately, there was no wind and the water was still. The tide was rising. George stayed on one float, putting out his pike pole to protect the plane's tail end from rocks. A few people quickly led the doctor up to one particular tent. The rest of them seemed to cluster around me.

Old men and women, and younger people with their children, all were dressed in clothing never seen by me before – knee-high sealskin boots, with duffel stockings. Many wore sealskin parkas and mitts. Mostly the women wore sailcloth parkas, fashioned like a well-fitted tent, with enormous, fur-trimmed hoods, an infant staring out of each. Each of these worn yet brightly trimmed garments had a round, apronlike form in front and a long, wide, almost ankle-length tail dangling elegantly behind. This, anyone could see, would greatly improve the prospects of sitting comfortably on stony ground or in snowy places.

But these Inuit costumes, though impressive, were nothing at all compared to the people wearing them. They were short, strong, and deeply tanned. The women wore their jet-black hair in two tight braids, while the men had ragged bowl haircuts. Their eagerness to shake hands, their wide smiles and friendly way of laughing, their gruff singsong voices, excited me. I had never dreamed of seeing people like these unknown countrymen of mine.

I glanced toward the tent where the doctor had disappeared and then at George. "I guess you want your sketch books!" he called. Opening the plane's back door, he got out my folio and, leaning off the float, handed it to me. I looked around at the barren rocks and tundra with the few tents graying with age and weighted down against the wind, and I took in the steel-blue sea and the biggest ice that I had ever seen and then the tanned, smiling people. I could scarcely breathe. I thought, *This is the place that I've been looking for and now I've found it. I'm here!*

I opened the sketch book and grabbed a 6B pencil from my too-thin parka pocket. Right there and then I started to draw the most interesting person near me – an elderly, particularly hardy-looking woman who was smoking a pipe with one of those metal wind protection tops that I've rarely seen since. When I completed my first fast sketch of this woman, a man removed the sketch book and the pencil from my hands and began a drawing of me, with everyone seriously watching his work.

Stone-bowl pipe

What manner of people are these? I asked myself. I'd been drawing soldiers during the war, models in life classes at schools and later in London and Paris, but not one single person had ever taken my pad to make a drawing of me. I leaned over to glance at his sketch several times. It was coming along fine – big chin, round eyes, and my hair in what my mother in Toronto called a shameful criminal cut.

Suddenly, I looked up to see Dr. Harper hurrying down toward the plane. He was carrying an infant in his arms, and a young woman with torn parka sleeves, brown from dried blood, was hurrying after him.

As he passed me, he shouted, "Get a move on, Houston. We're leaving right now. This child has got to get to hospital. I'm taking it to the Royal Victoria in Montreal."

That was two thousand kilometers away, much more than a thousand miles on the route he'd have to go.

"I'm not going," I said.

"What the hell do you mean you're not going?" Dr. Harper shouted as he stepped into the water and up onto the float.

"I'll never have another chance like this. I'm staying here."

"What will your mother say?" the doctor bellowed at me.

"She won't care," I answered. "She's used to it. I was away for five years in the war."

The doctor with the child followed by its mother got inside the plane. George passed my sleeping bag ashore, and climbed into the pilot's seat and warmed up the engine. He waved to me in a somewhat secretive way as they roared off. Soon the plane was just a humming dot to the south and the people around me were talking quietly in their tongue.

I tried to get my sketch book back from the man who had it, but he was unwilling to give it up since he had not yet finished his drawing. A sharp wind was beginning to rise. I looked around again and began to wonder if I'd really done the right thing. I didn't know anyone's name, of course, and only the two words of Inuktitut that everyone knows, "igloo" and "kayak." These people spoke no other language. Soon the man doing the drawing finished my profile and handed back my pad. The likeness was good, I thought.

Together they led me up to their tents. There was a lot of discussion. I imagine it was centered on the subject of where I'd sleep. Finally, a kindly, smiling man took me by the arm. I followed him and his wife, ducking in through their waist-high, leather-hinged doorway to their oval-shaped tent. It was rock-weighted and billowing on the west side like a sail.

All who could get in crowded after me. They pointed to the corner of the tent beside the door where on the gravel lay a pile of fish and other red meat. I didn't feel hungry at that time. I was given a battered enamel mug full of hot tea poured from a blackened kettle. That soon drove me outside, for I desperately needed to spring a leak. This brought some younger sightseers out, to check, I guess, making certain that everything was normal.

Once back in the tent again, I couldn't think of what to say or do, so I began another drawing. Many huddled close around my back to watch the process. After a while, someone put their arm across my shoulders and someone else did the same from the other side. There was lots of gentle, rhythmic talk mixed with good-natured laughing. I finished that drawing and made another of a girl before the sketch book was gently taken away from me again and an elderly man made a drawing of his neighbor. No laughter this time, just careful watching. When it was done, the women of the tent unrolled my sleeping bag behind me.

I lay back, thrilled to be in such a place with such people. Imagine, no roads, no cars, no trains, no planes anywhere near me. I was exhausted. The whole back half of this tent, too low for me to stand, was taken up with one wide, total bed. This meant that the gravel spread beneath for drainage was covered with various skins – sealskins, tattered bear skins, caribou skins – and worn Hudson's Bay blankets. I didn't care. I had found the place that I'd been looking for. People lay down close on either side of me and we all went to sleep.

2
Inukjuak – 1948

In the light of early morning, there was much stirring around and coming and going from the tent, but to my surprise, almost everyone came back inside, drank tea, then went back to sleep. There was too much wind for hunting on the sea that day, which, of course, I didn't fully understand.

When I did wake, I shared a half-melted chocolate bar I had with the three kids and ate a piece of raw but gutted fish, which I like to think was fresh, cutting away, as directed, one mouthful at a time. The neighbors came in again and I unslung two sketch books, one for me and one for them. I was serious. After a while, I drew a person I was sure was one of the visitors' wives and when I was finished, her husband carefully tore it from my sketch book and neatly folded her picture into four. She seemed pleased.

Soon the man disappeared and I went outside again to catch a breath of air and wet the rocks. Before I could go back inside, this same man came up to me and held out his closed fist. Alarmed, I thought that this kind of drawing could lead to trouble, perhaps a punch in the nose. But no. He opened his hand and inside it he held a small stone carving of a caribou.

Next day, after the drawings, I was given two more small carvings and encouraged to keep them. Were these carvings something old, I asked myself, perhaps made by their grandfathers or handed down over many generations? I had seen such ancient ivory carvings in the Royal Ontario Museum with my father and later in museums in London and in Paris. Two of these carvings seemed as robust and powerful as the small objects I had seen from the caves of Europe that had been carved as many as 15,000 to 20,000 years ago, following Europe's last ice age.

About midday, I was encouraged by some of those hunters and their sons to walk with them to the Inukjuak River, which, as I had seen when flying over it, was wide and fast. The weather was miserable, with fog, wet sleet, and snow. For part of the war, I had trained others in the hardy art of the route march. I thought I was reasonably fit. But I can tell you for sure that Inuit can walk over rocks and spongy tundra much faster than soldiers can march! As we crossed a hill, I watched with admiration as the boys leapt, sure-footed as mountain goats, from one rock to another. Slowly through the mists, I could make out the red roofs of a small Hudson's Bay Company house and, closer to the river, the trading post. My new-found friends herded me on toward the freshly painted white-walled store and followed me inside. There I found Norman Ross, the post manager, his clerk, Ralph Knight, and their interpreter, Tomasi Palliser from the Labrador. Here I was on a small island of civilization with the vastness of the Arctic spread around us. We all shook hands, exchanging names.

"Houston, you look kind of gaunt," Ross said. "Ralph, will you go up to the house and ask Frances to put on tea?" He smiled. "Are you planning to stay around here?"

"I certainly hope so," I answered. "If that's possible."

He stared at me, but did not answer.

I'd been in a Scottish regiment for the five war years and I was well adjusted to austere Scottish ways, which was a good thing if you were going into the Arctic in those days. You would meet very few Canadians. The outsiders you would encounter were mostly Scots and Newfoundlanders who had been recruited from that crown colony of Britain which was just about to join Canada and become the tenth province.

To break the silence between us, I reached into my pocket and unwrapped my handkerchief to produce the three small carvings.

"When do you think these were made?" I inquired breathlessly.

Norman and the interpreter glanced at them, then back at me.

"Oh, sometime this past week, maybe last night, or even this morning early," Norman said.

"You mean they're *new*?"

"Aye, they're new. Probably just made for you." They both agreed. Norman added, "You should see the ivory cribbage boards they make up at Lake Harbour. These people around here are no good at that saleable kind of work. We don't buy carvings here."

Well, I thought, *imagine that. These three carvings are not old at all and these men say they were probably carved for me.* To trade with me, I guessed. One art for another. I was thrilled with their answer. I wasn't interested in ivory cribbage boards or ashtrays, but I loved the look and feeling of the two best carvings in my hands.

As Norman led me up to tea, I said, "I've got to find a way to stay around in this country."

He looked at me and said, "That may not be as easy as it sounds."

When we entered the house, it was full of the wonderful smell of baking bread. Norman introduced me to his tall, elegant red-headed wife, Frances, and their small son, Billy Ross (now, since the world is full of coincidences, the Toronto lawyer for my publisher). I tried not to wolf down the small sandwiches like an animal, but the food was good!

"You could stay here with us, for a day or so," said Norman.

"No, I'll go back with the others," I said, "but I'll come over again soon. I'm anxious to talk to you about how to stay – I mean, for quite a long time."

I rejoined the hunters and their sons and in the dark we all walked back to their camp across the hills. The snow had turned to rain, then stopped. The moon was running through the breaking clouds. Behind us near the river, I could hear sled dogs howling in a seemingly endless chorus. Later, as we drew near the tents, I could hear other dogs howling, which I had already begun to think of as our own. That night, I lay awake thinking. With nothing but a sleeping bag and sketch books, how could I ever manage to winter in this country?

Next day, I went on drawing and dreaming and being given a few more small carvings. I was amazed at the ongoing warmth and hospitality of the people. Their style of eating meat, which they were more than willing to teach me, was to stretch a chunk between your teeth and your hand and cut off a chewable-sized piece with a jackknife or any other sharp instrument that was handy. Even the smaller kids were good at this, using their mother's moon-shaped *ulu* knife, cutting upwards close to their noses. (Perhaps it's sometimes just as well to have no language between you. Today, I try to go to good foreign films and ignore the captions where I don't understand the language. There it often seems to me that I am free of language and can keep close watch on the look of faces and scenes during the flow of action. I find that this can be a very worthwhile experience, and it reminds me of my early days among "the people.")

Ice was forming on the ponds. The tents had little heat, only that coming from the stone seal-oil lamps tended carefully by the women who were expert at keeping each foot-long cotton wick burning evenly, melting the seal fat that flowed into it. *Good Lord, I thought, if this tent is this cold now, what will it be like in the dead of winter? Igloos must be a whole lot colder than any tent.*

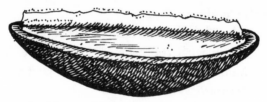

Lighted stone seal-oil lamp

Next day, a boy came in to me with a note that he had for some reason folded smaller than his thumb. When I opened it, I read, "James Houston, come over here when you get this letter. I have news for you." It was from Norman Ross. It was almost dark and I spent part of that night wondering what his note could be about.

I was up at first light and with two teenagers, a boy and a girl – *uvikait*, they're called – we hurried back across the hills to the river that flowed beside the Hudson's Bay post. It was no accident on my part that I arrived just in time for breakfast.

"We got a message on the key night before last. George is planning on flying up again before the river freezes tight. There's a piece of equipment gone haywire across the river at the new weather station and they've sent out for a replacement part. Radio conditions are rotten around James Bay, and they say they'll have to wait for the new part to come in on the train to Moose Factory. It's a toss-up this time of year, but I think George might get in. Come on, bring your tea. Let's go down to the store."

It was freezing cold inside that building, colder than our tent, for at least the tent contained the lamp and the heat that humans generate. Unheated buildings are the worst. There was absolutely nothing in the store that would freeze. White-fox trapping hadn't started yet that season and it was expected to be a poor year. The items the Company traded for fox- and sealskins were usually tea, tobacco, sugar, flour, rifles, cartridges, rope, fish hooks, accordions, tartan shawls for women, knee-length socks and rakish sailors' hats with Hudson's Bay Company badges for the men, and lots of Scottish duffel cloth. The shelves were well stocked with all of them.

"Do you still feel you'd like to come back here?" Norman asked me.

"Absolutely," I said. "This is just the kind of place that I've been looking for."

"Then I'd suggest that if George gets here, you go back outside with him and try to make some arrangements. It's interesting that you're so taken with this country and the carvings here. Do you think that others outside might consider buying them?"

"Yes, I do," I told him.

Norman smiled, believing, I think, that I was crazy. "I've no idea how you could work that out, but I hope you do go south and try to sell someone on your idea. We could use something like that here. I'd like to see you come back again."

"Is there a dictionary for this language?" I asked.

"No, only a Moravian dictionary. It doesn't work."

I hurried back to the comparative warmth of the tent and drew small pictures of various objects and wrote down phonetic versions of what I took to be the words for them. Everything was new to me and I was never for an instant bored. It seemed that these people around me possessed a cheerful, fatalistic view of life and death and had armed themselves with an abundance of native ingenuity and skills. But even then, in the late forties, one could sense that the juggernaut of civilization was grinding steadily toward this ancient world of theirs. It was, after all, only in 1939 that the Canadian government had assumed formal responsibility for these nomadic people, and now, just nine years later, I felt that I was visiting them at the end of an era.

Summer tent

Then about 3:00 p.m. one afternoon, I heard the Norseman. I ran out of the tent and there she was, stubby as a bumblebee against the darkening sky, heading for Norman's post. I checked my sketch book for my small drawing of a plane and the word beside it, "*Kungataju!*"

"*Kungataju takoviit?* Airplane see you?"

"*Ayii.* Yes."

"*Tuavi, tuavi!* Hurry, hurry!"

I dodged inside the tent and found my host's wife rolling up my sleeping bag and crying – or was she tearfully laughing, with relief? I didn't stop to analyze just which; I carefully rolled the dozen carvings I had been given in my extra woolen pants and gave away my sweater along with anything I'd bought at the post. I bundled up my sketch books and lumbered out through the tent's low door.

Everyone from the camp who was spry enough trotted over with me to the post. It wasn't often that they saw a plane, which by that time was anchored in the river.

When I went into the Hudson's Bay house, I found George sitting in his stocking feet on the sagging sofa, eating a piece of cake. He smiled shyly at me.

"The Rosses are going to let me sleep right here tonight," he said, pointing at the sofa. "I'll give you a free ride south with me tomorrow, if the weather's any good."

And that's the way it happened. Alf Mansel, the Mountie, came across in a canoe with Johnny, the balloon man from the weather station, and Freddy Woodrow, the radio operator, came along the river with his daughter, Freddie, who had grown up in the Inuit world, and Bill Kerr, an ex-policeman with the Baffin Trading Company. There was a crowd of Inuit and southerners around the plane as we said goodbye and climbed in with the government mail sacks, and then George took off into the river's estuary to get a quick lift out of the icy blast of west wind.

"Good to be flying with you again," I shouted to George.

"And you," he nodded, handing me the map. "I'm all gassed up and we've got no load. We'll try to make it to Great Whale River before dark. Freddy Woodrow heard on the key that the weather's clearing to the south."

We made it all right, and on the next day we arrived at Moose Factory. Not many of our friends were left at the staff house. Most of the new Scottish apprentice clerks and a few nurses had been shipped off to Cree Indian posts around James Bay: Attawapiskat, Keniapiskow, Winisk, and Rupert's House, established by the company from 1670 onward, few of them familiar place names in Canada, then or now.

When I saw Dr. Harper, he said, "I got that baby and its mother into hospital in Montreal and I hear they're doing fine. But your mother, I got in touch with your mother, and she gave me hell for leaving you up there. I'm glad you got the chance to get out. You tell her that your staying was entirely your fault, not mine!"

The once-a-week Ontario Northland train came into Moosonee next day and turned around for its journey back the following day. Being October, snow was gathering in the bush. My fellow passengers were mostly Finnish loggers, who drank a lot of rye and cursed the engineer when he stopped his puffing engine and got out of the train to hunt spruce grouse. He came back with a huge handful of dangling birds and yelled back happily at the passengers, telling them what they could do.

I called my mother in Toronto when the train arrived in Cochrane, Ontario, to tell her I was safe and on the way back to my recently built log studio in Grand'Mère, Quebec, where I lived and was the art director of a small agency we'd started called Valley Advertising. There I worked with a Shawinigan printing company that had a likeable young fellow named Jean Chrétien make deliveries on his bike. That same young man was later the best Minister for Northern Affairs Inuit and Indians ever had. Even later, long after I had left the Arctic, he was, in my opinion, doing a great job as Canada's Prime Minister.

When I got back to the studio, I put my carvings along the mantelpiece. Everybody wanted one. It was good to be there for Christmas, but I felt restless for the north and spent too much time staring out my window at the freshly frozen St. Maurice River, wondering how I'd ever manage to get back to Arctic Quebec again.

My neighbor, who had many connections in Montreal, suggested that I make an appointment at the Canadian Guild of Crafts and go to see Jack Molson, the president, and Alice Lighthall, the vice-president. (They seemed to change places every second year.) They invited me to tea and we got along so well that when I told them where I'd been and showed them my newly acquired carvings, they asked me straightaway if I would go in again in the spring on the Guild's behalf. I jumped at the chance!

The Guild was the oldest, most respected, non-profit organization of that kind in Canada, founded at the turn of the last century. Jack Molson got in touch with the Hudson's Bay Company, first at Beaver Hall Hill in Montreal and then at their offices in Winnipeg. As Norman Ross had suggested to me, we developed a credit line, a chit system, between the HBC and the Guild, where I would be able to write the amount to be paid for a carving and give it to the carver and he would in turn be able to trade that amount at any HBC post any time. Remember, this was years before any system involving money was used in the eastern or central Arctic. It seems to me in retrospect remarkable that the whole enterprise worked so well. To my knowledge, every single slip I wrote out to a carver, weaver, or seamstress was traded for the goods they wanted, sometimes as much as a whole year later.

3

Companions

As soon as the ice opened in the river, enough to make a float-plane landing possible, I went back with George to Inukjuak. That turned out to be one of the most enjoyable and carefree summers I have ever known. I bought a new rifle at the Company store, and a young hunter I had known before showed me the best place near the falls where I could fly fish for enormous speckled trout. (The French had invented a spinning reel, but the habit had not yet spread to Canada.)

I wanted to be able to move around the country in my quest to know more carvers, and to do that I needed shelter. From the Company I bought ropes and thread and canvas, and I had a small tent sewn to measure by two clever older seamstresses. They rounded the corners of my tent igloo-style so that instead of resisting, it would bend with the winds. This tent had a small, wooden door, stamped "B.C. apples," to outwit mosquitoes. It was held in place by sturdy, rawhide hinges. Inside that glowing summer tent, I had one of my first real encounters with Inuit life.

This young man about my age had taken me on as his hunting companion, the main difference between us being that he had a lively, attractive young wife and I had none. He tried in many ways to convince me that I needed one.

Early one summer morning, perhaps 3:00 or 4:00 a.m., my friend and his wife arrived at my tent door laughing and joking together quietly, not wishing to wake others in the camp. They sat down by my sleeping bag and she leaned over me to take my kettle and put it on the Primus stove to make tea. When we had finished, the husband stretched and smiled at me. "You go back to bed. I'm going hunting."

"I'll go with you," I said.

"No, no," he said, "you stay here. Let me borrow your new rifle."

"Sure," I nodded.

He rose and ducked out through the door. I sat awkwardly for a while, then stepped outside. I could see him paddling down the estuary. He stopped, looked back, then waved at me.

When I went inside again, his wife had pulled off her parka and was examining a hole in one of my long, thick duffel stockings. I sat down closer to her this time. "Comb, have you?" she asked as she began to unbraid her hair, slowly spreading its shining blackness over her shoulder. I knew it was an intimate thing for a woman to do outside her family.

I moved closer.

She had that beautiful, human, female smell that I find more alluring than any other perfume in the world. Passion is an overwhelming force and I excitedly prepared for action.

Not too much later, she left the tent, her undone hair well hidden in her hood. She walked smoothly over the rough ground, swinging my duffel stocking and admiring the soft, still morning as any thoughtful seamstress might do.

My hunting companion came back toward evening, returning my rifle and a fair share of his catch. Life was like that in those days. We three remained good friends, forever.

4

The Walrus Hunt

An unexpected Norseman on floats arrived at Inukjuak in midsummer 1949. I was then visiting with Akiaktasuk, a plump, cheerful hunter who had the overall appearance of a hard, brown leather football and who, I believe, was the first major carver whose work was widely recognized. (He was the best of all the carvers trading into Inukjuak, at a time when important men like Sywooli, Johnny Inukpuk, Amidilak, and Isa Smiler were busy revealing their talents with every new carving that they created.) I ran with Akiaktasuk down to the plane. There was never any permanent dock at these Arctic places because the high tides or the moving ice would sweep them away.

Rusty Blake was one of Austin's pilots then. "The weather's looking not so good," he said, eyeing the sky out over Hudson Bay. "But I'm going to try going north. George told me if you were here that you might like a ride up to Povungnituk."

"I sure would," I said. "Hold on a minute until I get my stuff." I raced back to the little empty house that the Anglicans had loaned me. I rolled my sleeping bag, grabbed my sketch books, stuffed some clothing into my pack, and tied my rifle into its canvas sleeve.

Rusty had been up to the post for something to eat and we met again hurrying down the bank toward the plane. "George tells me you're used to woggling gas into a Norseman. But you're safe today. This one's just been filled. Let's go."

We jumped into the canoe owned by Tomasi Palliser, the Hudson's Bay interpreter, and he took us out to the anchored aircraft.

"Tadlo," he called me, which means chin. "When are you coming back?"

"I don't know," I answered. "But not with this plane. I'll just wait there and see what happens."

Rusty gunned up the engine. We waved goodbye and he took off. There was nothing unusual about the flight north or the long, stark coastline we flew over except for the sighting of three oval tents. We saw no other sign of life, nothing but worn-out folds of gray rock that seemed as old and wrinkled as an elephant's back.

"There it is," said Rusty, pointing at the single red roof of a building and a tiny outhouse. "I wonder where the tents are. And where the hell's the boat?"

He landed on the bay and taxied in to shore. I got out, clutching the royal mail bag.

"I don't like to leave without seeing anybody here," Rusty said. "You never know what might have happened. Strange, nobody's down to meet us."

I hurried up to the house while Rusty stayed with the plane, holding it just offshore with his paddle. I pushed open the door and called, "Anybody home?"

No answer. I saw there was a kitchen with a bedroom off it, and a trading place attached to the back. On the homemade table, I found a note. It read:

> Hello, whoever you are. I've gone south in the Peterhead to pick up the post supplies. I'll be back. I'm not sure when.
>
> Irving
>
> P.S. Don't turn the damn place upside down!

I hurried back to the plane. "It's all right. Irving has gone down to Inukjuak and I guess the Inuit are off hunting. They'll be back."

"Yeah?" said Rusty, looking half amused. "You sure you don't want to go back with me?"

"Not now. I'll wait," I said. "Look, I've even got a house to stay in. I'm all set. But will you pick up those cases of carvings that we have packed in Inukjuak and take them south with you?"

"Sure. Good luck. I've got to go," he said. "I still don't like the look of that sky."

I stood on the shore and watched the Norseman rise after taking the shortest run I'd ever seen on floats. After all, she had nothing in her now except the pilot.

When I reached the house again, I put down my kit and slowly walked around. Apart from the wind charger and a shed, the house stood alone with a silence all around it that made me stand in wonder, listening. Not a sound. I waited. Still no sound. No bird to chirp, no leaf to rustle. Nothing. True isolation, a situation that I would almost never know again.

I went into the silent house and sat down at the table. Slowly at first, then growing stronger, I felt an immense sense of loneliness gather around me. No clock ticked. No wind blew. I was alone.

To hell with this, I thought. I can't just sit here. The house was cold. I crumpled up some pages from a mail-order catalogue and stuffed them in the stove, put kindled box wood on top, and lit it. I left the stove lid off until the smoke turned into fire. Then I reached into the coal bucket and laid a dozen pieces on the rising flames. When I replaced the stove lid, the burning wood continued to make a comforting crackling sound. I looked out the window at Hudson Bay stretching away to the far horizons north and west like a vast pool of molten metal reflecting in the afternoon sun.

I watched about a hundred snow geese fanning out and setting their wings to land near the post. Stepping outside, I racked a shell into the breech, picked the second bird and ran my thin, iron sight to the end of the beak. I swung with him but did not fire. "Aw, what the hell's wrong with some bully beef and a hardtack biscuit this evening?" I said aloud, though I'd been warned against talking to myself in the Arctic. The geese may have heard me, for they called back "kungo, kungo, kungo" and I waved at them and answered "kungo, kungo, kungo." Now that's not talking to yourself, it's imitating bird calls, and that's considered all right.

I went and pulled back the curtain that concealed the remains of Irving's last year's mess of food. Not much. But still I didn't need a goose – or the embarrassment of missing one. I thought I'd just relax and enjoy the isolation.

I lay down on the sleeping bag and folded it half over me and thought about the pocket book by William Blake that I had in my kit. I let the memory of his proverbs from *The Marriage of Heaven and Hell* rise up one by one inside me until I fell asleep.

When I awoke, I had no idea what time it was. The sun was high and I asked myself if I could have slept only for a few minutes or perhaps the whole night through, and I called out loud, "Who cares?" And then I didn't say anything more aloud because it sounds bad when you're alone. And if anyone does happen to come near and hear you talking to yourself, they'll assume that you've gone round the bend. A little singing aloud is all right, perhaps, but go easy on the talking. That is a rule I've tried to keep, for I am not usually afraid of utter silence – I mean the kind of silence when you hear a snowbird chirp outside and you can't imagine how far away it is.

Next morning I heard the sound of distant voices and the heavy flapping of canvas. I got out of my sleeping bag and went to the window. Not far off, two women and a younger girl were busy putting up a tent with an old man who drew the long lines tight, tying them to heavy rocks. Beyond them at the water, I could see some hunters with women carrying up a large green freight canoe. They had been about a day's travel north on the Povungnituk River fishing for char.

I went out and the Inuit shook hands with me, though they may have wondered how I had gotten there. But probably they had heard the plane. They asked me if I was in the *companykut*, family of the Company. It puzzled them when I said, "*Kitapik*, a little bit."

I had brought five good carvings with me from Inukjuak which I hoped to show. I arranged them on a flour sack on top of a fuel drum. When you have so little of the language, it's always helpful to have something to point at and to try to talk about along with a sketch pad.

We got on very well and one man, who seemed more interested than the others, sent a woman to the place where they were setting up a tent. She returned with a finger-length carving of distinction. *Ahh*, I thought, *Norman could not say they made this one just to trade with me.* They, of course, knew nothing about the slips of HBC paper I could give in trade for carvings. But I wanted to do something to impress them.

This man, named Siroapik, seemed to be more or less offering this stone carving of a hunter bent over a seal hole to me. I reached into my pack and produced a pair of U.S. war assets pilot's goggles that I had purchased to try out against the Arctic glare. These goggles were of a type that could be adjusted with a small hand screw, so that the lenses changed subtly from clear to yellow to blue to red, then darkened to blue-black. They were designed for pilots who needed to see enemy fighters coming at them out of the sun. The glasses had probably cost a lot of money to make, but were no longer needed or expensive.

Now, however, these hunters saw them as a wonder that would adjust against the incredible glare of the spring sun off snow. Siroapik and the others could not believe that I was offering him the goggles in trade for a single stone carving. That transaction spoke louder than any words, and the story was probably passed that there was some sort of a crazy man who was passing out wonders in trade for carvings. Everyone scattered, running to find stone.

I don't believe I had any other thing with me that I could sensibly have traded. In my bid to win their friendship, I became overgenerous with my tin of tobacco and cigarette papers and then found myself, as my new friends had been, without any. Now that could have been a desperate situation! A few days later I felt a sense of relief when I heard the children calling out and pointing to the sail on an approaching Peterhead boat. These sturdy little vessels were common in the North, named after the Scottish home port of many of the fishing boats on which they were all based.

Irving Gardner came ashore from the *Kungo* with Joni POV, the man who helped him run the post. His name, pronounced as letters, P-O-V, was his well-known nickname from the word "Povungnituk." They were returning with the Company's annual supplies from Inukjuak. We all shook hands.

The Povungnituk hunters with Irving had their minds on walrus, those great safety nets against human starvation at the end of winter, meat that was the necessary fuel to run their vital dog teams.

In the week before their planned walrus hunt, I received enough carvings to fill two strong wooden ammunition cases. I was absolutely delighted with the best of them. Siroapik, Joe Talirunili, Kopikolik, and Kalingo, I believed, would come to be recognized as great carvers.

On the morning we had hoped to leave, there was a strong offshore breeze. We raised *Kungo's* sail and set out about 5:00 a.m. for the Ottawa Islands, almost a hundred miles straight to the west on Hudson Bay. With occasional help from the tired, old engine, we managed to arrive in the lee of the Ottawas at dark and anchored in a cove. The island known for walrus was lower than our stubby mast and offered little protection.

At dawn, we moved out and began our search around the edges of the island.

"*Tippiouvit?* Do you smell them?"

"*Kenukiak?* What is it?" I asked.

"*Aivait.* Walrus," the hunter answered as he lowered himself into the hold and began passing up a dozen walrus harpoons and *avataks*, big, bearded sealskin floats.

As the Peterhead moved upwind, there was tremendous action on deck. Four men were kneeling, blowing with all their might, puffing at the plug holes in the rectums of the sealskin floats to fill them up with air. Kopikolik was busy arming the ivory shafts, attaching the separate harpoon heads with their inch-long arrow points of sharpened steel embedded in their ivory tips, then drawing the harpoon lines tight and lashing them to the thick, wooden harpoon shafts.

"*Tiaka tiaka!* Look, they are!" called Kumalik, and they hurriedly lined up the harpoons and the attached floats, six along the starboard, six along the port bow.

"Be careful not to get your feet caught in those damned lines," Irving warned me.

I joined the others in drawing my rifle out of its canvas sleeve.

"Don't even think of firing until one of these guys fires first," he said. "They know exactly when. We don't."

I could hear deep grunting as the pigpen smell intensified. Walrus were lying like giant potato sacks on a smooth-worn rock. I tried to count them. There were perhaps thirty or forty animals with half a dozen big bulls among them. They kept rearing their heads high, their curved tusks flashing white as they sensed or perhaps smelled us approaching.

"We're in range," I whispered to Irving.

"Hold your water," he said. "You'll see how it goes."

Kumalik cautiously turned the rudder so our boat would pass them at the perfect distance.

"*Niakok kisiani,* heads only," Kopikolik called. "*Angiukuk sivordlukpak,* the bosses first."

We leveled our rifles and I heard him fire. One of the largest walrus collapsed. I aimed and made a head shot. Down it went. I racked the rifle and carefully took another shot. The awful sound of a bullet's deadly smack as it pierces through flesh and bone sticks in the memory so much more than the mere discharge of a rifle. The killing went on for only a minute or maybe two before that part of the shooting was over. Half a dozen dead walrus remained on the rock. The rest of the herd had heaved themselves into the water and were bobbing their basketball-sized heads up, then under, their breaths steaming in the cold.

"Don't shoot!" Irving warned. "You don't want to sink them, lose them in deep water. Wait!"

Joni POV held a harpoon ready and when a walrus rose within striking distance, he arched his body back and cast it like a javelin thrower, striking the leathery hide that encased a muscular, thrashing ton of meat. The walrus dove and the skin line uncoiled, then jerked the blown-up float into the water. When the walrus reappeared, it was immediately shot in the head and killed. Its body quickly sank, but was not lost to us because of the harpoon's line and float.

Harpoon and float

Kopikolik harpooned another in that same fashion.

"*Watsiou!* Wait!" Kopikolik called as we saw the herd before us turn into a fairly shallow bay.

"*Atai!* Now!" the hunters shouted, and racked their rifle bolts.

We could shoot to kill, and did. In another minute or two, the entire hunting phase was over.

"*Taimak, illawak,* enough, plenty!" Kopikolik called, and I could hear all our cartridges being carefully ejected from the rifles.

The majority of the herd, perhaps thirty animals, swam off, spreading out and disappearing in the low mist that covered the water. We didn't follow them, but turned our attention to those that hung from the harpoon floats or lay dead on the bottom, their huge carcasses shimmering blue-green beneath the clean, clear waters of the shallow bay. The canoe that had lain across the deck in front of the small engine housing was unlashed and pushed off into the sea. Two of the hunters leapt aboard.

Lashing a harpoon and line to a long pike pole customarily used to ward off ice, the canoe men peered down into the waters until they were over a dead walrus. They drove the long shaft downward, impaling the carcass, then drew it easily upward to the surface and passed the line back to the boat. We suspended a block and tackle from the mast and to it the walrus was attached. Because of the huge weight of the meat once it was out of the water, they cut the animals in half while they were still on the surface, and were careful to secure the second half from sinking.

We combined our strength to haul the first half walrus in. I believe Inuit developed their cleverness in so adroitly handling huge weights of meat from the American and Scottish whalers who had hunted here in square-rigged ships, relying on the help of Inuit little more than a half century earlier. When each half carcass was on deck, it was quickly cut into quarters and swung down into the hold, all too near my two boxes of best carvings. During the next seven or eight hours, I worked harder than I'd ever worked in all my life as we stored the precious meat!

When we had all the meat retrieved from the bottom of the shallow bay, we returned to the original walrus rock and began to butcher and take aboard the animals that had been killed there. When all but a few were in our hold, Joni POV took me by the shoulder and pointed across the low, flat island at a thin line of white water that stretched along the western horizon.

"*Anowavingaluk!* A huge wind! *Audlalungivosi,* we're going!"

I looked at the last bull walrus lying dead before us and thought, *We can't just go and leave behind that last great animal we've killed.* But the anchor was being hauled up fast and in no time the hurricane hit us with a rising force that frightens me even to remember. The first great smashing wave that engulfed the Peterhead broke and carried away the two halves of the canoe. I wished to God then that we had seen no walrus and had run instead for safety. I wished that we'd never come on this perilous hunt.

It was all I could do to hang on, then slide open the fo'c's'le door and fall down the ladder in a torrent of water along with Kumalik and Kopikolik. We were soaked to the skin. My sleeping bag was floating, but I was too frightened to feel the cold.

During the entire storm, I never laid eyes on Irving Gardner again or even knew whether he and the others were still aboard. The engine had cut out or they had stopped it. Fortunately, Kalingo and Irving, at the last moment, had been able to storm-tie the helm and set the sail, though it was torn by morning.

Up in the fo'c's'le, I was most alarmed by the perilous swinging of the lantern, which I felt might spill kerosene and cause a fire. I turned it out, but I heard wails and moans of protest in the utter blackness and soon someone struck a match and relit the lantern. Inuit were used to sleeping by the light of a seal-oil lamp all winter and the rest of the year had the long, white night of summer to light their tents. They did not trust the darkness. I noticed a small clump of little finger-length, ivory knives tied together with a twisted piece of sinew which rattled against the heaving bulkhead. They had been put there, Kumalik said, to help cut the weather.

Small knives to cut the weather

What a hellish night that was, with the bulkhead trickling red with walrus blood from the hold! I'm grateful for the fact that I don't seem to be able to get seasick. But some Inuit can.

There was no map aboard. Inuit didn't use maps. But the wind and waves had eased enough by dawn that we could risk putting our heads up through the fo'c's'le to empty the urine can. I was desperate to see where the winds had carried us. Behind me lay the low, ominous, whalelike backs of the rocky King George Islands. Somehow we had come blindly charging through them without knowing they were there.

Far off our bow among low scudding clouds and thin curtains of blowing snow, I could see other long, black rock forms that appeared then disappeared in the violent surf. Oh God, I thought, we're sure to hit one of those. I tried yelling as hard as I could to the low engine housing. No one answered. Was there anyone in there to hear me? The helm was still rope-tied. Our stubby sail was torn, but helping still. I ducked inside again and slammed the hatch as a big wave came sweeping over *Kungo's* stern. Oh Jesus, I thought, dare we risk going out on that slippery, pitching deck and try to take the helm? The very thought of going between the reefs and islands without anyone even trying to steer made me feel sick. But nobody could have lived on that deck, so with no one at the helm, that's exactly what we did.

Once inside of the islands, the power of the sea diminished. We three in the fo'c's'le crawled out and, clutching hold of anything we could, we made our way astern and hammered on the engine hatch.

Irving stuck out his head, his face as pale as a ghost. "Oh, you're all there! That's good!" Irving groaned.

A wave sloshed icy water into the engine room, but it didn't matter. The engine hadn't worked throughout the storm.

Kalingo, who Irving said had knelt and prayed throughout the night, now pulled a fisherman's yellow slicker over his parka. He got out and had the courage to unlash the helm and tie himself in position. Everything was getting better now. We had passed safely through the north end of the Nastapoka Island chain. Somehow, the hunters recognized a pair of stone cairns ashore on a hill. We got into a nearby bay and waited until the surf died down. Then they got the engine going, rigged the sail, and headed north along the coast toward Inukjuak. We arrived at night, still shaken. According to the maps, we'd traveled a hundred miles west, then been blown southeast more than a hundred miles off course, a journey of more than four hundred kilometers.

Irving, with the *Kungo* and her crew, was anxious to go north again and cache their walrus meat before it got too high. From under the bloody meat already in the hold we had a helluva job digging out the two sturdy ammunition boxes filled with what I thought to be Povungnituk's best carvings, vintage 1949.

As they left, I remember shouting, "I'll come up by dog team and visit you this winter!"

"What's the matter?" Irving yelled back. "You don't like traveling by sea?"

5

Sold Out

I flew south again with George Charity. Most of the carvings had gone before me to Montreal. We at the Guild had all thought that a thousand dollars of credit would be more than enough for my second trip north, but we were wrong. I wrote an additional check of my own for five hundred dollars to the HBC, Winnipeg, through Norman, but that still was scarcely enough. Those people were hungry for action and the honestly earned trade goods that carvings would bring to them.

Those were wildly exciting days at the Guild in Montreal. I was young and strong then, and was glad to carry the boxes of stone carvings from one floor to another. Alice Lighthall and Mrs. Peters would often come and help me unpack them, unwrapping the crumpled pages of the Scottish newspapers, squealing with delight as each carving came into view. As they appeared, one by one, for me it was like seeing old friends again.

Word got around and reporters from the *Montreal Star*, the Montreal *Gazette*, and other newspapers came to see these new carvings. What caught my attention was that these press people all wanted to buy one. No one had expected to see so many highly saleable carvings come in and by the time we had arranged the pre-Christmas exhibition and sale, there was already a lot of interest. No one at the Guild, least of all me, was prepared to see these carvings purchased at such a rate. We were essentially sold out in three days. The Guild gladly returned the additional five hundred dollars I had added for the purchasing of carvings, although I myself was paid no salary at all during that time in the Arctic or outside. Just think what those carvings would have been worth now, nearly a half century later, if I had decided to keep them. But I wanted much more to have the public see them, buy them!

The press was eager to take photographs of these new Canadian Inuit carvings that the public, like myself, had not known existed. Photographs taken by the *Montreal Star* and the National Film Board were all carried by Canadian Press across the country. We chose to show the splendid early carvings of Akiaktasuk, Siwooli, Joni Inukpuk, Amidilak, and others. This quickly drew into the Guild that first passionate collector, as I had the honor to name him, Ian Lindsay, along with Harry Handel, a Montreal bookseller. Harry's wife, Esther, called me to say, "Mr. Houston, if you see my husband in the Guild trying to buy more carvings, would you please not sell him any more? He's got our dining room table covered with them." It was true. Harry was busy setting up his ultimate retirement benefit, though none of us, not even Ian Lindsay knew it at that time. Harry's great collection (which he continued to amass over twenty years) is now safely in the Art Gallery of Ontario, thanks to that other enthusiastic collector, Sam Sarick. And Ian Lindsay's collection is now in the Winnipeg Art Gallery, together with their other major collections. What could be better?

One morning in November 1949, when I was busy in the Guild's gallery in Montreal trying to arrange a carving display, a friend dropped in to visit. "Hello," she called.

"Forgive me, Jill," I answered without looking back at her, "I've got to concentrate on what I'm doing. I'll see you later."

"When?" she asked.

I turned around and there beside her stood the most beautiful girl I had ever seen.

"Don't disturb yourself, we could come back later, maybe," said this tall, dark-haired creature as she turned away to examine one of the carvings more closely.

"This is Allie Bardon," said my friend. "She's a new reporter for the *Montreal Star*. She's supposed to write something for the paper about Eskimo art and you."

We shook hands.

"Maybe we could do it another time," the smooth-skinned beauty suggested.

"No, no, let's do it today," I said. "Let's talk it over during lunch. Just us."

"Where? What time?" she asked.

"The restaurant in the Mount Royal Hotel, one o'clock."

I was living there. It was less than a block from the Guild. The hotel was new and very spiffy then, with quite a few young ex-air force, army, and navy types also billeted there. Some were waiting for their outpatient hospital treatment, others just whooping it up while they tried to settle down and decide what they should do with the rest of their lives. I hoped that they would all be in the dining room for lunch that day to see this incredibly elegant-looking girl whom I had been clever enough to find.

I began to discover that aside from being so well dressed and handsome, she was also bright and intuitive. Allie had grown up in Nova Scotia, worked with the navy at H.M.S. Cornwallis during the final two years of the war, and had then become a school teacher, before becoming a journalist. When she asked questions, she didn't need to take notes about the Arctic and Inuit/Eskimo art. She remembered everything. I learned later that she had no handy little book of telephone numbers, appointments, or addresses. She simply kept all of that in her head.

When we had finished our coffee and it was time to go, I said, "No intelligent girl would even consider going into a country like the Arctic. Would they?"

"I'm not so sure of that," she said.

We looked cautiously at each other. Thinking back, I believe that the die was cast right there at the end of that first lunch.

I lived that winter in Grand'Mère in my log studio and drew

political cartoons for a syndicate of newspapers. I made many trips to Montreal, helping the Guild and preparing to go north again. I gave a lecture here and there and continued courting Allie. But I had definitely and irrevocably been bitten by the Arctic bug.

6

Historical Move

In ancient times, probably before 2500 B.C., the ancestors of the present-day Inuit migrated from Asia, slowly spreading across Alaska and the whole of Arctic North America to Greenland. Their culture, which archaeologists call Pre-Dorset, lasted until approximately 800 B.C., when it evolved into Dorset culture, which flourished until A.D. 1300. Today, most Dorset art still lies hidden in the permafrost, below the earth's surface, though archaeologists have uncovered a number of carefully incised implements and some small, lusty carvings of animals and humans in ivory, antler, stone, and wood. These were probably shamanistic amulets to aid families in the search for polar bear. The white bear has always figured prominently in Inuit art and seems to have been closely entwined with religion. It has long been believed that the bear, especially with its skin removed, most closely resembles the human in anatomy.

Another migration from Alaska to Greenland about A.D. 1000 produced the vigorous Thule culture, which replaced the Dorset. The inventive Thule developed dog teams, kayaks, bow-drills, and, perhaps, the igloo. They also carved animal and human figures, but in a larger and cruder style. One popular subject frequently carved from walrus teeth was a goddess, half seal and half woman, her hair tied in a topknot, a figure used in a magical game.

In the nineteenth century, American and Scottish whalers, keen to supply the world's need for whale oil, sailed along the edges of the Inuit world. But with the discovery of petroleum, large-scale whaling stopped. Left behind on the beaches were scattered piles of century-old whalebone, perfect for the carver's ax.

Inuit migrations were followed by the arrival of explorers, adventurers, traders, missionaries, and finally government with police, schools, and nursing stations. Today settlers are coming from the South. Businesses are springing up as Nunavut, an exciting new Inuit division of the Northwest Territories, promises to come into being. A similar development occurred in the North American west during the past century, perhaps providing us and thoughtful Inuit with some lessons.

7

Great Whale River

In February 1950, I was off and running north again on the east coast of Hudson Bay. I took the train to Cochrane, then to Moosonee, and flew with George Charity to Great Whale River.

"You can see it down there now," the pilot said. "Over there on the left bank." He was pointing a bit east from the frozen river's mouth.

The sky over Hudson Bay was black with winter fog. I looked at my watch. It was still early, but it was growing dark. At first, I could see nothing except white snow and a few windswept rocks on the huge, flat plateau above the curving bank that marked the edge of the river ice. On the south side of the river were the last of a few scraggly tamarack trees, permanently bent by the winds. All else was snow.

We two were alone in the single-engine Norseman, its four passenger seats folded up and the whole back jammed with freight and a few government mail sacks. This World War II aircraft used to be called the work horse of the north. It was built strong and stubby for skis or floats and it took forever to take off or to land.

The red roof of the trader's house attached to his small store stood near the warehouse and the whirling wind charger. Beyond that, we could see the brindle-colored mission church, with its small steeple and the tiny missionary's house. It was what we called a trading post in those days . . . no school, no nursing station, no police, just a trader and a mission, and a few igloos or winter tents impossible to see against the snow from the air. This was Great Whale River in 1950, now known as Poste de la Baleine on all the maps.

George banked the plane. As the Norseman coughed and sputtered, then rode the air bumps down toward the river ice, George craned his neck, searching for the longest blue-gray shadows that would hint at the height of the major drifts. Avoiding those that might flip us up, he eased the aircraft down. Her skis skipped gingerly at first, then hard enough that a big drift threw us back into the air. Then we were down again, pounding across the hard, meringue-pie drifts until George eased her to a halt. Both of us were puffing strongly on our cigarettes. In those days, it would never have occurred to us to put them out for landing or for takeoff. After all, a quart-sized fire extinguisher was aboard.

We climbed stiffly out of the battered freight plane. Pulling out the canvas engine covering, we struggled with it in the wind. Then, after anchoring it in place, we paused and gazed along the high riverbank.

Not a soul appeared.

George said, "We're not going anywhere else tonight. I should have buzzed them."

We started to unload the Great Whale part of the freight onto the snow-covered ice. George took the ice chisel and made three V-shaped cuts in the ice. Then, with strong ropes attached to the cuts, we tied down the tail and each wing of the Norseman. It was now about 2:20 p.m. and the afternoon gloom was closing in.

We studied the riverbank again. Still, no one.

"Maybe they're both dead," said George. "You can never tell what's happened in one of these isolated settlements."

We pulled our hoods forward against the sharp wind that sent swirls of snow at us along the frozen river. On top of the riverbank, we saw a moving sled. It turned and came plunging down toward us at such a speed that it overran the dog team and began to drag its half dozen yelping dogs behind it. When the sled reached the ice, its Inuk driver jumped up and booted his dogs back into their places. Then they raced straight at us like a pack of hungry wolves in a horror story.

I could see the driver sitting cross-legged on the sled. He was short, dressed mostly in Eskimo clothes: knee-high sealskin boots, caribou windpants, a high-pointed, canvas parka with a doghair trim and faded, tattered braid.

"Awooh!" the driver called to his team. The dogs stopped and immediately sat or lay down.

"Is that you, Scottie?" George asked, for the light was growing poor.

"Aye, 'tis me," he said, and coming forward shook our hands. There was an awkward pause before the trader said to George, "I hope ye brought that part for my friggin' wind charger! I've had no power since the damn thing broke."

George opened the rear door and pointed with his moosehide mitt at a small, wooden crate. "Looks like it there."

"I hope ye're right," said the trader. "Mean damned wind out here. We'll throw on the freight and ye can come up to the house for the night."

Those were the words we'd been listening for.

"Scottie, could you have your man dig out three barrels of Av-gas from our cache?" George shouted, for the wind was rising. "Have him haul them to the plane tonight or by first light in the morning."

The trader nodded. We lashed on the load along with our two sleeping bags and two small packs, then trotted beside the sled and made our way up the river's bank. By the time we were on top, we were warm again. We followed Scottie to the small white building that served both as his living quarters and the trading store.

He jerked open the storm porch door. It squealed in the cold. He bumped the second door with his hip and we followed him into his small kitchen. The cast-iron coal stove was letting off sickening waves of heat. We stepped back into the cold porch and stripped off our hats, parkas, and extra sweaters, and stepped out of our wind-pants. But I left on my old sealskin boots and George his beaded moosehide moccasins. Together, these lightly tanned hides let off a rich smell in the hot kitchen whose walls were painted a revolting shade of pea-soup green. A faded, three-year-old calendar of a nearly naked woman answering a telephone hung on the wall. A wide bread board and rolling pin to roll the dough sat on the counter nearby.

"Tea?" Scottie asked us. "Or have ye gone American and yearn for coffee?"

"Coffee would go best with this," said George unrolling his sleeping bag and handing the trader a large bottle of overproof rum.

When the coffee was poured, Scottie uttered a long sigh of plea-sure as he drew the cork and topped off our half-filled enamel cups. He adjusted his kerosene lamp, and we settled down around the kitchen table. After the second pouring, the trader went into his mess room and returned with six thick, square pilot biscuits and a large five-pound tin of bully beef from Argentina. He fanned out the biscuits like playing cards. Then, in Inuit fashion, he laid the tin of corned beef on its side, not bothering with its key, and used a meat clever to cut the tin in half. As we each dug a portion of the meat out with the points of our jackknives, Scottie went to the cupboard and brought back some plates.

The pilot biscuits, as thick as your thumb, were pale and hard as plaster wallboard, and they probably would have tasted like that before we soaked them in rum and coffee. That made all the dif-ference.

"These are good," George told him. "We didn't have any lunch."

"Hell," I said, "we didn't have any breakfast either."

Turning my head, I saw a tall, shadowy figure coming across the snow. It had to be the Anglican missionary, the only other white man in the tiny community. George had told me he had sometimes stayed with him overnight. He was struggling now across the drifts, breaking a new path from his house to the trader's door. He had on high sealskin boots, overall pants, and a tattered brown work parka cover, its hood rimmed with a shaggy wolverine trim. He wore a purple wool knit hat that he must have fancied from a mission bale. Pulled down snugly over his ears, it looked like a British tea cozy.

We three watched him until he reached the outer storm porch. The trader then leaned back in his chair and casually turned the key, locking the inner door.

We could hear the missionary inside the snow porch struggling with the door handle, then bumping it with his hip. When it did not budge, he realized that it was locked. He knocked, paused, then hurried outside and around to the frost-rimmed kitchen window. Face almost touching the glass, he tapped with his bare red knuckle. Peering in, he smiled at the three of us and waved.

"I haven't laid eyes on the Reverend in more than a year," said George, half rising to let him in.

"Nor shall ye. Not in this house while I am here," the trader said sternly. "Ye can enjoy him there through that fuggin' window or sleep over at his place if ye wish." He took a long drink of the rum and coffee and shifted his chair, turning his back on the pained face in the window.

The pilot rubbed the back of his neck and smiled at the missionary, then studied the worn oilcloth pattern on the kitchen table.

The missionary remained outside, nodding and smiling at George and me, beckoning us with his bare hand. I lacked the moral courage to stand up in the trader's house and unlock his door. Slowly, the missionary realized that he was not about to be allowed inside. He waited, crouching on the high drift for some time, staring in disappointment at the two of us before he turned and trudged away toward his mission, which had now disappeared in the Arctic gloom.

I went upstairs to the loft and spread my sleeping bag on the floor.

"Careful of yer head, Houston," Scottie called to me. "I mean when ye're coming down on the morrow. And watch out for that long, last step at the bottom or it will surely cast ye low!"

He had a strong West Highland accent. Soon, I could smell the delicious odor of the second part of our dinner, dried macaroni boiling and sprouted onions frying on the stove. When I came down, George was nodding by the stove, for we had put in a long day, and among the three of us we had half finished the rum.

"Robert Flaherty, have you ever heard of him?" Scottie asked me. "He lived here during most of one winter," Scottie said. "He's that Irishman who made the first real moving pictures up here, *Nanook of the North*, ye'll recall. This house used to have a ladder up to the loft, but that wasn't good enough for him. He built those stairs himself," said Scottie, "when this house still belonged to Revillon Frères, the French fur traders from Paris. That was in 1920 or '21. Many a man's bloodied his head on that low board or sprung his crotch on that last high stair tread. It's dark in that damned hall. That's Flaherty's wee piano in the factor's parlor. Can ye play us a tune?"

"No, I wish I could," I groaned, still clutching my sprung crotch.

"I warned ye, didn't I?" he laughed, and shuffled the onions around the pan as I came into the kitchen. "Do ye know that grand piper's tune called 'Over the Sea to Skye'? Sit ye doon here, lad, it will soothe yer pain. Just ye keep an eye on the onions for me and I'll have a go at that piano myself. Ye can sing along if ye've a mind to. I grew up on the Isle of Skye," he said. "It's a grand piece of turf. Let's have a touch more rum. No need to wake George. I'll take care of whatever ye politely leave behind."

Next morning, the house creaked in the deadly cold, but it didn't matter. There were no water pipes or toilets to freeze. As I hurried into my clothes, I could hear Scottie down below rattling the cinder grate, then crumpling paper and breaking slats of packing boxes across his knee. A sprinkling of Welsh coal went tumbling from his scuttle. George was already talking to Scottie.

I ducked my head low as I started down the stairs, but I forgot the missing bottom step and went crashing once more into the opposite wall.

"That long drop to the last tread is a real bugger for anyone who's stayed here, especially after getting brained by the one, then failing to remember the other."

I felt my head to check for blood or broken bones, then dizzily pulled on my parka and groped my way outside, following the narrow snow path until I reached the Company fur shed. Light was rising in the eastern sky through a crack beneath the heavy winter overcast. Some aggressive sled dogs came too close to me and I made that inhuman growling sound in my throat, forming the Inuktitut word *"uu-naa-luk!"* That means, "Watch out or you're going to get it!" The wolf-eyed dogs ran off.

I stood there wetting the snow, staring in surprise at a battered tin bathtub whose outside was painted green, the inside a peeling, white enamel. It was tipped crazily, half buried in the snow, and was pierced through with three finger-sized bullet holes. There were even marks where someone had thrown a harpoon through the tub. I had heard earlier about that famous bathtub, recently taken from the Company's fur shed, for it was considered just another of Flaherty's many extraordinary eccentricities. Imagine that man having the temerity to bring a bathtub and a piano this far north with him, loading them onto the Revillons' little herring smack called *Laddie*. Seeing that stabbed tub made me think of the large painting hanging in the Louvre in Paris of Marat murdered by Charlotte Corday in his bath during the French Revolution.

Remembering the power of that picture and trying to button up my fly, I heard, "Psst! Psssst!"

I turned my head. There in the dawn stood the missionary, carefully hidden from the trader's window by the corner of the fur shed. He beckoned to me and I hurried toward him. We shook hands and then he turned and led me past his mission house to the entrance of the small mission church. He stood there waiting for me, his broad shoulders hunched in the cold, his bare hands thrust deep into his parka sleeves like a northern Chinese mandarin.

When I reached him, he seemed to come awake and started to kick away at the heavy snowdrift that blocked the entrance. When he bumped his hip against the church's plywood door, it bent inward before its cold hinges yielded.

"Pity you hadn't come on Sunday," he said. "I could have held a special service for you."

The church was bleak and gray inside, frigid with the cold. The tall, narrow windows had no frost, for there had been no heat inside this building since the day that it was built.

The missionary dropped to one knee and bowed his head, then led me up the narrow aisle between a dozen backless, wooden benches. One side, by custom, was strictly reserved for men, the other side for women. Heaped before the altar lay two huge mounds of snowy, feathered ptarmigan. There must have been three or four hundred of those birds, each looking like a small, white chicken. All of them were frozen stiff. Not far away was another pile, this one made up of lake trout, glazed with frost and stacked like cord wood.

"These are welcome gifts from my parishioners," he said with pride. "Of course, they have no money for the collection plate." He laughed. "Truth is, they don't even know what money is. Still, the trappers always bring in some food for me from the camps when they come this way to trade. I had piles of gull eggs and of eider eggs in late summer, but they don't last. Both Inuit and Cree women say they worry about me. They say I'm growing much too skinny for their liking." He laughed nervously. "All my parishioners are away hunting caribou at this time or trapping foxes for that stingy lout whose house you're using this time."

"Well," I said, "it's good to meet you. I've read a lot about you in the press in connection with those murders on the Belcher Islands."

"The press made an awful hash of that," he sighed. "It wasn't my fault. Would you like me to tell you the truth about it?"

"I've got to be getting back," I told him. "George and I are leaving just as soon as we can woggle the wing tanks full of gas."

He sniffed and wiped his prominent, red nose against his parka sleeve. "Going north then, are you, to Inukjuak? You're the lucky one. I'd go anywhere these days to get away from that brute over there." He nodded toward the old Revillon trading post. "Now, Mr. Norman Ross is up there where you're going. He's a proper, decent Hudson's Bay trader, an experienced Arctic and Cree country man. I've known him for a long time and always admired him. He's not a religious man, mind you, but he's worth talking to, nothing like that unsociable beast who sits over there brooding by himself.

"But what I called you over for was, well, first to meet you and say hello." He pulled his large hands nervously from his sleeves. "But mainly to ask if you would take some of these best-tasting, Great Whale River ptarmigan up to Mr. Ross. Tell him they're a gift from me."

He reached down into the waist-high pile of birds and carefully selected four. These did not seem to be the largest, but perhaps they were the best.

"Don't worry about space," I told him. "The plane's half empty now. I'll be glad to take as many birds as you'd care to send him." He eyed me narrowly, then cautiously picked out two smaller, bloody-feathered birds.

Just as he was about to pass the six ptarmigan to me, he drew his left hand back, returning two of the plumper birds to the pile.

"I imagine those four will be enough for Mr. Ross. He's a lean man. Not a heavy eater, I would guess. Yes, four birds should do him very nicely. Let's say two for Mr. Ross and two for Ralph, his clerk. Yes, please give my blessings to them both." He smiled, his broad shoulders and heavily-hooded pale blue eyes reminding me of some distant Viking heritage.

"Sure, I'll be glad to give him these." We shook hands again.

"Forgive me, but I won't come down to see you off today," he said. "Send-offs and arrivals have always been the cause of our worst troubles." He nodded bitterly toward the red-roofed house. "Say goodbye to George for me. Tell him if he's got the space next time, I'd be grateful for a free ride north or south with him. I've managed to get a sled ride as far north as Inukjuak some years."

"I've got to run for it now," I said. "I see George is heading down to the plane."

"Safe journey," he called, and turning, went back inside the church.

8

Dog Team to Povungnituk, 1950

When I stepped out of the Norseman onto the river ice at Inukjuak, I had the warm feeling of being home again. Crazy as that may sound in weather that was thirty below, I felt that I was exactly where I belonged.

Dog team travel and anything related to it was something that I longed to do. I asked Tomasi Palliser, the Company interpreter, how I should make a journey to Povungnituk, two sleeps north of Inukjuak in normal traveling weather. Tomasi arranged that his son, Epikudluk, and another young man named Itok would handle the team and give me the chance to learn how.

Loaded dogsled

I had brought in a military parka with a hood and large pockets that had been developed in World War II. It was reversible with a white camouflage lining inside and gray khaki outside, nothing in between. I had thick, lined mitts over gloves and a heavy, woolen, Cowichan Indian sweater that my father had gotten in British Columbia. It had a thick, shawl collar. I thought that with long, fleecy, trap door-type underwear, thick wool pants, and a heavy woolen shirt and a knitted balaclava hat my sister, Barbara, had made, all of this would be enough for any winter journey. I had been warned by Norman Ross, who had sledded at Arctic Bay, that I should walk or run, not be content to just sit on the *kamotik* and allow myself to freeze solid so early in the game.

Footwear was the most important thing, Ross had stressed. So I had a beautiful, sinew-sewed pair of knee-high sealskin boots made for me with moccasinlike white *kiaktok* soles. I was told the going price for these was one or two dollars, depending on the fit. That seemed reasonable enough even in those far-off days. *Kiaktok* meant that the fat had been bleached out of the skin in the cold and strong spring sunlight; when the black outer layer of skin peeled away and the soles turned pure white it meant they were bleached of oil and would not conduct the cold. Under these light, thin, winter boots, we wore socks, thigh-high caribou-skin stockings with thick hair, and over them snug, sealskin slippers.

Man's and Woman's sealskin boots

A small clutch of people came to see us off. I wore a scarlet, finger-woven belt that a girl there had made for me. I tell you I thought I looked spiffy and I felt like Dr. John Rae, the explorer, taking off to search for Sir John Franklin. This image was spoiled a little when all the young kids jumped aboard the sled as if on a hayride, clinging on through the rough ice, and only dropping off one by one as they got cold stares from the driver.

We had twelve dogs in that team. Out on the flat, snow-covered ice, a smart wind was whipping out of the north straight at us. Run, walk, sit, shudder, run again. I could not keep warm. The thin military parka was no good without any fur around the hood, and drafts blew miserably down my neck. No matter what I did, I could not get warm.

The driver pointed back at my left cheek. "*Kakuktok*, white. *Kouaklokasaktok*, almost frozen."

I snatched off one mitt and felt an area of my cheek that was hard, with no feeling. He showed me how to hold my bare hand over the cheek to warm it while holding my other mitt over the bare hand. He looked back again and I showed him my face.

"*Oupuktopapik*, it's red now." But he could see that I was cold.

They stopped the sled and unlashed the covering canvas, then pulled out a thick, caribou parka and a pair of knee-length wind pants. I pulled them on over what I wore and soon I felt as if I were getting off a plane in Florida. Real warmth surrounded me and to my surprise the pants and parka were so well cut for this purpose that I found it easy to run.

Epikudluk smiled at me as if to say, "You southerners may know some things, but you don't know anything about traveling in the cold."

I will refrain from recounting the details of that first journey, except to say that we built two igloos on our way and visited two camps. The first had an old woman and a young girl tending a seal-oil lamp. The men, they said, were away hunting at the floe edge. That igloo was smoked dark gray inside, was cold, and had a gloomy atmosphere, like the inside of an old, ice-encrusted freezer with its light burned out.

The next one was a larger, permanent igloo, larger than I had imagined them to be, with a complex of wind porches, and meat and entrance porches, and an ice window. Off the sides of this igloo were smaller igloos – rooms, I was told by the family, for additional relatives or guests when they could no longer fit in the wide, family bed.

I showed them two small stone carvings that had been made by two different Inukjuak carvers. Everyone examined them with care. I looked at their hand-shaped walrus ivory harpoon heads, knife handles, and the oval, often decorated, ivory buttons that every mother wore on the front of her *amautik* to support the carrying strap that helped her carry the child in her hood. These were wide-faced, cheery men and women with tight brown skin drawn over their glowing cheeks. For families who had never eaten any fruit or vegetables and who lived on a constant diet of meat, fish, and eggs in season, they were a remarkably strong and healthy people.

We arrived at Povungnituk in the early evening as an almost full moon was rising. Dozens of dogs raced out from their places near the four igloos around the post and engaged our dogs in a massive fight which I imagine was enjoyed by all. After the dogs had all been kicked apart by drivers from both sides, everyone stepped forward for a handshake. That is one of the Arctic's most embarrassing moments. Far worse than the absence of any kind of toilets is the moment when we foreigners must pull off a mitt and extend an almost-frozen claw. The worst part of this is the shock of feeling the warm, soft hand of the hunter or his wife. Their hands are always soft because they do their work in mittens, and their hands are warm, I think, because they're Inuit born and raised in the country and have more or less mastered the cold.

Irving Gardner, the HBC man in charge of this outpost whom I had missed the first time, was there with Ralph Knight, who was up there helping him, perhaps just to break up the isolation. We went inside and I stripped off my heavy clothing, for it seemed intolerably hot inside the little house.

"Are you hungry?" they asked me. "We've got some fresh caribou meat."

"I'm starving," I told them as I unrolled a large bottle of whisky that I'd kept tucked safely in my sleeping bag. Their eyes widened, for a full bottle of Scotch was as rare as gold in this remote place with so many moons between winter and next summer's shiptime and when, just to celebrate the ship's departure, such treasures would ordinarily have been consumed.

Irving got out the jelly jars that he used as glasses when he had company. He thought them much more elegant than chipped enamel mugs. We drank the whisky and ate delicious caribou, and finally half of a small English fruitcake that had been saved. Then, as I remember, we tried a few Gregorian chants until Ralph dropped off to sleep in his chair.

"He's been asking me to give him a haircut for weeks," said Irving. "Let's do it. I've always thought he looks like one of those early monks. I'll start cutting and you get the razor and that bar of yellow soap. We'll give him a proper trim."

By the time I had the razor and soap ready, Irving had sheared away the hair at the center of Ralph's head in a neat tonsure. He certainly didn't mind. He was still sound asleep. When I had the center area nicely finished, we headed for our sleeping bags.

"Ralph," Irving called, "are you going to sit there all night?"

Ralph woke and stepped outdoors as we had, letting in a blast of white steam as the hot and cold air mixed. He got in his bag and slept.

We had breakfast in the morning and talked to Joni POV, the Inuk assistant on the post, and his cheerful wife, Akinasi. Later, we heard a shout when Ralph first tried to comb his naked head. We laughed and Ralph reminded us that it would be many months before he met anyone who cared a damn about hairstyles. Akinasi wove him a hat, a decorated scarlet skull cap with a dangling tassel to cover his naked crown.

The hunters trading into Povungnituk had among them some very talented carvers who made a distinctly different kind of carving from the people trading into Inukjuak. There was really no common subject matter for either area. The carvers at Inukjuak melted down old black phonograph records to insert in deeply incised lines and spots on tattooed ivory faces that they embedded in their stone carvings. They had stopped doing that by the mid-fifties. The Povungnituk carvers started to carve bases as a part of their carvings, something they had never done in earlier times. Inuit carvers were always striving to be original. They wanted to create new ideas, new ways to portray animals and humans and the mythology that continued to be important to them, something I hope they never lose.

9

A Stitch in Time

Ralph Knight, who became a lifelong friend, once showed me while we were in Povungnituk his idea of a good way to pass a stormy day. He believed that it showed signs of growing bushy just to sit and stare at the window when it was so thickly glazed with frost no one could see out.

Ralph handed me an old mail order catalogue from Eaton's department store. It had been published several years before. The photographs were all black and white, but they were not used much in such catalogues. Most of the items shown were painfully accurate illustrations.

First, we skipped past the hernia trusses and found the ladies' corset section. All of these illustrations were bland and disappointingly unsexy. Then he flipped to his favorite item – leather boots. He had ordered a pair a year earlier and they had finally arrived at shiptime in the annual mail. They proved unsatisfactory for the Arctic because tanned leather lets in the wet and if you greased them, they were cold. Ralph didn't care. He said he'd wear them in the south when he went out on leave the following year.

What he suggested that day was to have me take a pencil and carefully count the number of stitches in the catalogue's illustration while he did a comparative count along the side of one of his real mail-order boots. When we both finished counting, to our surprise the number of stitches matched exactly. All the same, Ralph insisted we should double-check to make certain. We counted again. Yes, they were the same.

"What would you have done if they had been different?"

"Oh, I don't know," he said, "but you can't be too careful. After all, the Hudson's Bay Company and Eaton's are in competition." He took his boot off the table. "Gosh, look how the time has flown! Let's put on the tea."

10

Akulivik

I asked Ralph Knight about Akulivik and Ivuivik, more northern places I wanted to visit, and he offered to go with me. As soon as the weather cleared, we set out with Tomasi Kumalik, who was a joy to be with on this whole trip, and his team. We had fine weather on our journey north and visited all the camps. On the way, we crossed fresh tracks of a large bear, but it had gone out beyond an upheaved tidal crack and disappeared.

We arrived at the small post at Akulivik (also called Cape Smith) after dark. Al Sigvaldason and his wife, June, were there alone. They were of Icelandic descent, but living in a country much colder and more forbidding than their ancestral home. After dinner, I dried the dishes while the two Bay men listened to the daily radio sked which came in by Morse Key. They had no message to send out and none coming in, which was usual for such an isolated post. But their acknowledgement on the sked was an important check to see that everyone was alive.

As she washed the dishes June listened to other messages passed along on the Morse Key. She laughed and said, "Listen."

I listened.

"Dot-dot-dit-dot-dit-dit." June said, "They've decided to build a big Indian hospital at Moose Factory – the clerks down there – are delighted – more nurses will come into the country, they say."

She could wash dishes, talk to me, and at the same time "read" the dots and dashes off that key. She told me it was just as easy to read the keying of the various operators, hearing just the way their fingers touched the key, as it would be to distinguish their hand-writing.

"You should be careful of the messages you send over the air up here," she warned me. "Everyone along the line is listening."

She was right. In the evenings, there were so few things that newlyweds could do.

As a hobby, the Sigvaldasons had raised an enormous and beautiful-looking husky, their favorite from a new batch of pups. June had hand-fed this dog on seal liver, which they didn't eat, and all their table scraps. The dog had been protected by them from the normal fights and discipline that keep team dogs in line, so he was bold and fearless.

When I was returning to the house early next morning after a quick trip outside, this huge animal frolicked up to me. I was one of the first non-Inuit strangers he had ever encountered. He came right up close in front of me, the way no ordinary husky would dare, and sniffed at me, then started jumping up and snapping his jaws toward my face. I hoped he was playing. But when I reached out to try and pat him, he snarled. A dozen other huskies, some of them from our team, had gathered close around him.

This was potential trouble. By now the big dog, raised as an indoor pet, had grown bold. Probably he would not have harmed me. But if I had slipped and fallen, that could have been fatal. Inuit dogs were not pets. No one should have any doubt that an excited team will grab a person who goes down, and can even kill him. People living in the North know that all too well.

When the situation seemed to be growing worse, I pulled off my sealskin mitts and threw one in each direction. All the dogs lunged after them, fought over them, and ate them. In the meantime, I slipped into the house.

We discovered only one very clever carver at Akulivik. That was Danialik, a crippled man who made splendid ivory carvings of birds and continued to do fine work for the rest of his life. So my trip was proving instructive as I built up a picture of the prospects for a trade in art.

The weather was changing on us again, so we decided to try to race up to Ivujivik and sit it out up there. But the going turned grim, then grimmer. Halfway there, we decided we'd had enough of the windchill driving straight in our faces and of pointing out each other's frost patches, so we turned south again. What a comfort! It wasn't snowing, of course. Hell, it was too damned cold to snow! We were in the middle of a tremendous ground drift that was sweeping the fine snow up and whirling it around like a sand storm.

Kumalik, who knew a lot about such storms, stopped the team and urged us to stand up on top of the grub box as he had done. When I stood on the waist-high box I found to my utter amazement that my head was just above the drift and the visibility was clear, with a blue evening sky and Jupiter twinkling in the west. The whole top of that miserable ground drift was tinted slightly pink. I climbed back down into the darkness of the swirling storm, discouraged.

Ralph took my place and looked. When he came down, he said, "I'll tell you, Houston, I am never, ever, going to make another dog team trip!"

We agreed we were never going to suffer like this again. We went on and on until finally we came to a long, hard drift formed by this new storm. We stopped there and built our igloo for the night.

It's important to find a drift deep enough to allow you to carve straight down for your snow building-blocks. You never want to touch bare, frozen ground, which is murderously cold. Sleeping on top of cellular snow is, by comparison, warm. And, of course, igloos built of ice were rare. I saw only one in all my life, at Gjoa Haven, and it was used not to live in, but as a cache for meat. Ice igloos were only built in desperation when hunters were out on the ice and no good, hard snow was to be found.

Finally, we got back to the post at Povungnituk. We flung off our outer clothes and Irving poured the whisky. He waited until we'd had a couple of drinks, then asked, "How was it?"

I was amazed to hear myself say, "Oh, not too bad."

And Ralph readily agreed with me.

It is said that if we could truly recall the taste of, say, caviar or maple syrup, there would be no need to ever eat those delicacies again. The same is true of dog-team traveling. You could say that, but the desire to see strange new places was still strong in me. I dog-teamed back to Inukjuak, enjoying relatively uneventful conditions. The snowbirds were returning and the ptarmigan were flocking, the males flashing the scarlet patches above their eyes and calling, "Come here, come here." And the female ptarmigan were answering, "Get-a-bible, get-a-bible." It was good to be thumping across the hard, blue-shadowed drifts of snow knowing I'd soon be among old friends again. Every sign seemed to point to the coming of spring. How long, I wondered, could I manage to stay in this almost unknown country?

11

Igloo

One of the most difficult tasks for any Arctic archaeologist to determine is anything about the origins and early use of igloos built of snow. We know that ice igloos were occasionally built and used by Inuit as meat caches, for dogs found them impenetrable. Ice igloos were never favored as human dwellings – they are cold! Igloos used by humans were made of relatively dry, hard, wind-packed snow.

Since an igloo by the very nature of the elements will reduce itself to a few pails of water, the best clue we could have of the early existence and source of igloos would be, for example, an engraving of one scratched into walrus or mammoth ivory. No such discovery has been made in Alaska, Canada, or Greenland. Most experts believe that igloos were first conceived somewhere in the vastness of the Canadian Arctic where man was faced with a treeless expanse and was forced to invent and dwell with his family in that small monument to human genius in the face of adversity, the household dome of snow.

I believe these east coast Inuit in what is now Arctic Quebec were among the best snowhouse builders in the world. Toward the end of winter there in 1950, I saw not a single family (except the Hudson's Bay interpreter and the Royal Canadian Mounted Police special) living in anything but an igloo throughout the winter.

An igloo built as an overnight structure for one human traveler alone will sometimes be no bigger than a dog house. Yet igloos can be very large – *ugas*, dance houses, are made to accommodate up to forty persons. I remember their curved domes in Igloolik were so high that the ingenious builders, who did not yet have the invention of the ladder, had to climb the cross pieces on their long sleds to complete the dome from the interior.

When used as family dwellings, igloos need not have only one room under a central dome. The older ones used to bristle with long, complicated entrance passageways and blocks of snow set up and adjusted as a baffle against the prevailing wind. Often there were side apartments used to house in-laws or visiting relatives, or simple meat caches where the family could protect their fortune against the ravages of a wandering bear or their own dogs.

The entrance to the igloo's interior was built with care. It was fully realized that heat rises and cold falls. The entrance to the snowhouse was built well above floor level, thereby preventing the coldest dead air from penetrating into the house. If it did, the parents would inform you that the coldness inside had been created by children playing, running in and out of the house, drawing in behind them freezing drafts of air.

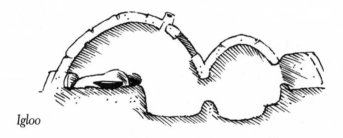

Igloo

The igloo usually had an air vent over the entrance called the nostril, which was stuffed with a mitten at night. Beneath it was traditionally the only window, made of a clear or almost clear slab of four- to six-inch-thick lake ice. Salty sea ice is too murky. The whole dome of a snowhouse lets in light, important during winter when there is so little natural light. However, in the lower part of the dome around the sleeping bench, the snow wall is doubled on the outside to prevent unwanted drafts.

Inuit also recognized that eating enough food and getting exercise were the best methods of driving out the cold. Of course, they did not mean bending or stretching exercises, or walking on a treadmill. They meant useful work.

The whole family slept side by side, heads toward the entrance passage, on a wide sleeping platform that reached from wall to wall. It was about knee-high above the floor. This platform was made of solid snow. In Arctic Quebec they covered this bed with stunted willows each as slender as a child's finger, loosely shaped into thin mats. Inuit gathered these small branches growing close to the ground during their caribou hunts on the sub-Arctic inland plains. The only other household articles in an igloo were one or, better, two stone seal-oil lamps in which caribou back fat was also burned, and a squarish stone pot suspended from a tennis racketlike drying rack for boots and mittens. Meat for more immediate use was kept in the entrance tunnels to protect it from the dogs.

These houses intended as more or less permanent dwellings were built in the deepest snowbank one could find. And during the course of the winter some of them were partly drifted in by snow. I know this because once, while walking along the bank of a frozen river admiring the opposite side, I fell through the roof of an igloo and landed hard on an icy floor. I could not imagine what had happened until I sat up, trying to feel my coccyx bone, to see if it was broken. Before me was a sleeping platform and on it sat a very old woman, whom I had never seen before.

"*Itiriit*," she said to me. "Enter." In the circumstances it was a very polite thing to say.

I looked up at her and wondered if I still could rise.

"*Teetilauvit*," she said, inviting me to have some tea.

I struggled to my feet and sat down in the only place I could, beside her on the bed. She was small and frail, with sunken cheeks, and thin wisps of hair protruding from her parka hood. Her legs were thrust straight out before her in a way impossible for our old folks who sit on chairs at tables. Her sealskin boots were large, stuffed with long caribou stockings and probably several pairs of sealskin slippers.

I looked up through the hole I'd made in her snowhouse roof and wondered who I'd send to mend it. She lit her pipe and offered me tobacco and the only little book she had. I pulled out a page and rolled it clumsily into a cigarette. We sipped our tea and smoked together for a while. She explained that one son and his wife took care of her.

She showed me a package of tea, nodded at the tobacco, and, feeling around in her sealskin bag, pulled out a small box of fifty .22 cartridges given to her by the trader.

"I give all of these to a young hunter, and tell him to bring me *akikigik kolit*, ten ptarmigan," she explained, spreading the fingers of both hands. "I tell him that he can eat or give away all the other birds he gets as long as he brings me my ten."

"What if he doesn't get that many birds?" I asked her.

"Oh, he'd better get them or I'll give these *sekoapiks*, little bullets, to someone else who is a better hunter."

That's what took the place of an old-age government pension in those days.

12

Moving House

The failure of the Baffin Trading Company was locally acknowledged in the summer of 1949. Its three eastern Arctic trading posts at Inukjuak, Salluit (Sugluk), and Kingait (Cape Dorset) were closed down, but not forgotten. At Inukjuak, the Hudson's Bay Company bought the local post building. The house and store combined were only a little bigger than a garage. No wonder, larger spaces were costly to heat, and local wood was non-existent north of the treeline. Building supplies were very expensive, since they had to be shipped in a very roundabout way of several thousand miles, a voyage that would take months.

Norman Ross, the experienced HBC man, wanted that abandoned trading house to use as his additional Company warehouse. But how to move the damned thing? It could not be taken apart because of the excessive amateur over-nailing of the tongue-and-groove boards. It could not be hauled across the landscape because of the impossible, roadless, rock-strewn terrain. There was certainly no local ark on which to sail it!

The only option was to wait until the sea ice formed and move it in the spring of 1950. Then the sea would make a wide, flat highway. But what would power the movement of a whole house? Norman decided to try dogs. I arrived back from Povungnituk about that time, and Siwooli and Inukpuk and a number of other hunters with good-sized teams had come in from distant camps to trade, so the time was right.

This was a carefully planned operation. Eager to imitate Leonardo da Vinci's drawings of architectural and warring devices, I helped Norman by making sketches before tackling the leveling problems of this mechanical feat. Then Norman took the role of Ghengis Khan about to lead his nomadic tribesmen into battle with their strong, well-trained ponies that he hoped would triumph over the Arctic elements.

With twenty men helping to hand-lever it, lifting the building proved not too difficult. Sliding eight sleds under it caused much more grunting and groaning on our part. Each of the eight drivers, with the help of their sons and nephews, gathered their dogs, about a dozen in each team, hitching each animal to a long, single skin line from its shoulder harness to the eight strongly-braided *ipitoks* attached to the individual sleds beneath the house. There were nearly a hundred dogs involved. Then with the dogs pulling, we had to ease the old post house around the largest rocks and down the perilous slope, struggling to get it through the ice barrier that the winds and tide had heaved ashore. Once we were through that, we paused on the main body of salt ice, essentially one enormous, drifting mass that daily rose and fell throughout the endless months of winter.

"This is going to be a long, slow haul," Norman sighed, "even if the sleds don't break down."

I agreed.

"If we run into any rough ice," he said, "they'll probably find bits of this broken house and the sleds floating in the rivers of Russia."

Ready for the start, the eight dog teams fanned out in front of the house, singing, yelping, howling, eager to put their muscle into their best loved game of pull.

"*Atai*, go!" the drivers yelled. The dogs uncurled their tails, a sure sign that they were pulling hard, and their chests and bellies pressed down until they touched the ice. With every human pushing and grunting at the house, the gluelike stick that forms between iced sled runners and hard snow broke. Suddenly the house jerked free. At first, it moved slowly forward, but then faster, in a way that we had not expected. The house behind the dogs was shuddering, moving now so fast that we had to trot beside it. It was gaining speed. I stayed close, but not too close, for fear the damned house might swerve and tip over on me.

I'm convinced the dogs were running scared, frightened that the looming, slithering monster behind would overtake them. Under normal conditions, the drivers, with the rest of us, would have leapt onto each of the fast-moving sleds and had a hell of a ride, but all the sleds were hidden under this swaying house that was quickly pulling away from us.

Soon we, the drivers and enthusiasts who had rigged this mad event, were falling far behind, unable to curb the wild enthusiasm of the running teams. The dogs, who usually know just what they're doing and will bring you home in a blinding storm, continued to travel along the coast as though we were still in charge. Now, to us, the house looked like a battery-powered toy that was heading for God knows where.

But, fortunately, in the distance we saw the dogs turn eastward as they instinctively ran into the frozen mouth of the Inukjuak River and halted exactly where their drivers would have ordered. We could hear the women and children screaming and laughing with delight at the sight of this new house arriving on its own, having escaped from its human movers, who were still staggering far behind it on the sea ice!

13

Family Allowance

Family allowance was not given out to Inuit families until two years after it had been authorized to all Canadian families living further south. This fault occurred, perhaps, because there was a great deal of discussion in the House of Commons and in the Canadian press for and against an issuance of family allowance to Inuit, who did not operate in a money economy. Finally, authority was given by the government for the traders to give out not only the current family allowance in trade, but all of the two-year backlog that Inuit had not received. At that time, Inuit had no idea what on earth this incredible treasure being tossed to them across the counter of a usually tight-fisted trader was all about. And, although it was as if your local bank manager was handing out suitcases full of money to passersby, no one seemed too anxious to explain it to them.

The annual shiptime had brought in all this abundance and soon it was being given out like the usual trader's fall debt to the hunters. They were used to that system, where the trader in effect staked you to get you through winter, and you repaid him with furs, but this new thing was not fall debt. It was free, a windfall for every Inuit family. The more children, the more stuff. Had the trader lost his mind? How could it be? No need to bring any fur, just walk into the store. And they would give you Hudson's Bay blankets, flour, tea, sugar, kettles, cooking pots, rifles, ammunition, ice chisels, new tent canvas, everything a hunting family could have ever dreamed of. Some families had five or six children. Two years' worth of family allowance released to them seemed nothing short of madness!

I watched as whole families stepped shyly into the trading post. They took what they were given and staggered out and cached their treasures under rocks, then hurried back to get the rest. The Inuit believed that the traders and the police had temporarily gone insane and they should hurry to get all that was being given away, afraid that their wits would return at any moment and they would close the store.

Those few, panic-driven days marked the end of a rational era for eastern Arctic Inuit who lived where no winter dwelling was used except a pure snow igloo. Beforehand, the Government of Canada had not dealt directly with Inuit except in the persons of the doctor and dentist, and the other men sent around on the annual supply ships. But now the old Department of Mines and Resources became the Department of Indian and Eskimo Affairs, and then acquired the new name, Department of Northern Affairs. The names kept changing over the years as the government's activities in the Arctic increased, and the traders' once overwhelming importance began to fade. Eventually, territorial government would be handled in Yellowknife, and later in Iqaluit for eastern Arctic matters.

It will remain an arguable question as to whether Inuit fared better in the earlier, calmer period of the trader, or in the later period when government took greater control. Certainly, during both periods a unique hunting lifestyle was fading away, with no attempt to hold back or regulate what can be called "progress." During the middle period when I asked a number of Inuit who they preferred, the *policikut*, the *Companykut*, the *missionarymiut*, or the *governmentimiut*, they would think about that for a while, then almost all would answer, "*Companykut*." I think they preferred the Company because life in those times seemed more carefree, more exciting.

14

Kayak Dreams

Left-handedness seems rare among Inuit, but perhaps that is because we encounter people in their communities in such small numbers.

An old man named Saumi, Left-Handed, had died and his elegant kayak rested on its stone rack near his grave by the Inukjuak River. The rack was to protect the skin boat from the teeth of dogs, who in the North will eat anything. His widow had seen me admiring it and when she noticed that I, too, was left-handed, she decided to give me his kayak. This I discussed with Norman Ross, and then gratefully gave her a gift in exchange.

The sealskins on Saumi's kayak were worn and opening along the seams. The many bent, wooden ribs needed to be retied with sealskin lashings and the whole kayak frame needed recovering. The old woman offered to organize the new sewing, and I contributed a skin or two, which was the custom.

Old-fashioned, perhaps shamanistic rules took over when it came to sewing the kayak. All men were warned by the women to keep away during the whole skin-covering process which, because of tradition or for practical reasons, had to be completed between dawn and dark. I was very eager to see the kayak repaired, so, using binoculars, I watched from a distant place among the rocks. What a disappointment! The women have lost the art, I thought. What would I do with a soggy-looking kayak-covering like that?

I was totally wrong. In the morning breezes, the scraped kayak skins soon dried and tightened to drumhead smoothness and the early slanting sunlight made the kayak partly transparent, showing its slender inner ribs in a golden glow.

Kayak rack

This long, sleek kayak had a fully rounded cockpit in the style of Arctic Quebec, that is to say it was formed by a strong piece of wood soaked and steamed, then bent between a strong man's teeth into an oval, then snugged tight by the skin deck cover. There were no nails or pegs. Everything was lashed together so that during storms it could stretch and bend with the waves instead of breaking.

Naomialook made me a new double-ended paddle with typically narrow blades, no wider than your palm and strongly tipped with bone. These blades were narrow, some Inuit say, because wider wood was almost never available and they learned to use the thicker narrower blades to great advantage, since they were strong when hunters needed to fend off ice.

Kayakers warned against allowing your boots to carry even the slightest amount of sand into kayaks, saying that the tiny grains would grind beneath the ribs and wear holes in the skin. They showed me a place called *kavuvavak* where the kayakmen carried their vessels out from shore by stepping on an irregular arrangement of stones. There they floated their kayaks in deeper water before swishing their feet clear of sand, then easing themselves inside.

Old men showed me how to paddle in the safety of the river, how to hold a paddle high if you wanted speed, how to place a piece of seal fat on the cockpit's gunnel and how to roll the double-ended paddle on it to ease your arms on longer journeys. This kayak was steady enough to allow another person to lie on its back deck. Only one girl I knew ever volunteered to take that chancy crossing with me in the driver's seat.

With your paddle rolling on the piece of blubber you can paddle somewhat mindlessly, enjoying the incomparable pleasures of drifting through glassy calm waters with big ice resting nearby. A ringed seal may rise up silently almost within touching distance of your paddle and stare round-eyed at you, undisturbed by the sound or smell of a thrashing engine.

When I left Inukjuak, I shipped my kayak north to Kingait. When it arrived, its round cockpit was broken. The *Kingaimiut* gladly fixed it, but, alas, they gave it a flat back, in the Baffin style. Finally, in a joint effort between Jack Molson and myself, that kayak found a home in the McCord Museum in Montreal. Perhaps we can now think of that slim, perfect vessel as representing the old migration between Arctic Quebec and the Baffin Island world.

15

Post Inspection

My return in July to Montreal was brief, just that necessary swing around Hudson Bay. I headed north again, this time to the west coast of the bay, taking the train from Winnipeg to Churchill. My objective was to continue to buy carvings to sell at the Guild, my expenses paid by a grant from the Department of Mines and Resources.

Churchill, on the southern edge of the Arctic and the west side of Hudson Bay, could be a difficult place to stay in 1950. There was a military base where civilians were not welcome unless they were girls on a Saturday night. Apart from that, it was a huge grain elevator and a few houses. There was no place to eat breakfast or have an evening meal unless you managed to beg it. At noon, an unpainted shambles of a house that looked more like a small barn, locally called the Dewdrop Inn, served bacon and eggs with a chunk of bread. I ate all I could get at that daily lunch, feeling like a camel taking on water before crossing a desert. One of the most interesting things about Churchill at that time was old Mrs. McIver, an elderly Scottish lady – or so she seemed to me when I was in my twenties – who would sometimes draw back her curtain and wave me in for a cup of tea and thin cheese and pickle sandwiches with oatmeal wedges for a treat. I usually trudged pitifully back and forth in front of her house before this happened.

The only Churchill attraction was a tiny, private museum run by Brother Jacques Volant, OMI. The Oblate Order was made up almost exclusively of Europeans: French, Belgian, and Italian priests. Brother Volant was a blessing, for he was very keen on his new museum and proud to lead anyone around to see his collection of small ivory, bone, and stone Inuit artifacts, the oldest being from the Dorset culture, perhaps 1,000 to 2,000 years old, others from the Thule culture, 500 to 700 years old, and a few from the nineteenth-century whaling period. The age was roughly guessed at because radio carbon dating was not well established in those days. These objects had been collected by OMI missionaries on the west coast of Hudson Bay, Baffin Island, and in the central Arctic as well.

Brother Volant told me that the OMI had purchased a mine sweeper and renamed the vessel *Regina Polaris* and that she was about to set out in an attempt to resupply their missions. I bought my passage north.

Captain Bannerman, master of *Regina Polaris*, was an old Scot who had scarcely been ashore during all the dangerous North Atlantic crossings throughout the war. He seemed to want to talk to somebody and invited me onto his bridge, but I didn't seem to help his constantly downhearted mood. When two missionary priests tapped on the bridge door, he waved them angrily away in spite of the fact that they owned the ship.

I was excited when we entered and almost filled a tiny but protective harbor. The two appropriately rugged-looking fathers who had their mission there came paddling out to greet us, as did the young Hudson's Bay Company manager in his canoe. He invited me to stay with him, so we went ashore.

What a wonderful, rarely visited place this was. The older people had wide, welcoming smiles and facial tattoos, and almost everyone wore skin clothing: boots, pants, and rather shabby caribou summer parkas turned inside out. Their hair was usually long. Everything about them seemed to make them worth knowing, worth drawing.

When the trader ushered me inside the company post, I was amazed to find every room was stripped bare. There was not a chair, sofa, table, rug, picture, fancy lamp, or drapery. Almost nothing.

"How long have you been here without a clerk?" I asked him.

"More than a year," he said. He was thin, shy, and by nature a sensitive sort of a person.

A young woman came into the kitchen and he spoke to her in excellent Inuktitut. She smiled, shook hands with me, and went outside.

"Don't tell me the Company couldn't get the furniture in here because of ice! Is yours out aboard the *Regina Polaris* to be delivered this trip?"

"No, no," he said, seemingly annoyed with the question. "It's all out in the warehouse, in the cases still packed up."

"Why?" I asked him.

"Well, I don't want to wear it out or get it dirty. It belongs to the Company. Forget the furniture," he said. "I'll make some tea. We can stand up at the kitchen table if you want, or sit on the floor. I heard that you might be coming. I imagined you'd be coming in with the Company inspectors."

"I don't know them," I answered. "When are they coming?"

"Tomorrow, next day, maybe. Lord, it makes me twitchy having this first inspection here." He stood staring at the kettle. "The fathers say the Company bosses raise the devil if everything is not kept exactly right on the post."

"Where are they going to sleep?"

"I don't know. Maybe they'll come in the morning and fly on to Igloolik toward night. There's still good light. Bill Calder's their man up there, he's used to inspections." He laughed again.

"Forget that," I said. "They're probably going to stay right here and they'll need beds. Believe me, inspectors are not the kind to lie around on floors in a Company house. They're not like pilots, for God's sake, or missionaries or mounted policemen."

"What'll I do? The fathers have no space. The inspectors are supposed to be in Eskimo Point tonight."

"Okay," I said. "You round up two men and we'll carry up the furniture tomorrow morning and hang the curtains."

"I hate to take it out of the boxes," he said. "Get it all messed up."

"You'll hate it a lot more if they arrive here and find you've been sitting on the floor while living in their empty house."

I spread my sleeping bag and slept well, glad not to be rolling around in that old minesweeper's iron bunk. I spoke of our moving plan next morning as we stood eating our oatmeal porridge and staring out the kitchen window. When he saw a boy passing, the trader stepped outside to call him. The boy turned and ran to an Inuit tent and soon a man and his son came up the path toward the house.

"*Teetilauvit?*" the manager asked them, smiling warmly, then giving each a cup of tea while he explained to them the craziness of having to bring up *sinukviks*, beds, to sleep on, and *isivouts*, chairs, to sit on while the house already had a warm, comfortable floor.

While we were bringing up the furniture, he continued a long conversation with the older man.

"Where did you learn to speak Inuktitut like that?" I asked him, green with envy.

"From the father." He nodded toward the mission house. "He's really good at it."

"Interesting that he'd teach a Company man so well. Are you Roman Catholic?"

"I wasn't when I came here, but I am now. There are some Catholic Inuit here. I was orphaned as a baby, so I never knew which religion I belonged to."

"Oh, well, that explains it," I said. "Don't forget the rolls of carpeting for the living room. They'll expect that, and floor lamps even if your wind charger's not working. These will be very civilized English businessmen."

The *Regina Polaris* squeezed out of the bathtub-sized harbor and headed north into heavy, drifting ice. I went that morning to visit the mission. The Inuktitut-speaking missionary was an admirable-looking man, with that kind of large, splendidly proportioned French nose so well worth drawing. Both he and the brother with him wore long black cassocks beneath their parkas and warm, well-stuffed sealskin boots that peeked out from their skirts with every step.

The fathers sociably produced a bottle of their own homemade wine. It was very good indeed, and so were the feelings inside that dark, gray-brown little mission. The Oblates take a vow of poverty. They are not sent into the Arctic or elsewhere, I am told, to teach, but simply to live there making converts when they can.

When we heard the Inuit shout, "*Tingmiak! Tingmiak!*," we ran outside. It was the Company plane, a small flying boat that landed just outside the little harbor and taxied in. The manager and his native clerk pushed off excitedly in their freight canoe and plucked off the three passengers. Even from shore, anyone could tell they were executives. They wore business suits, fedoras, raincoats, and carried briefcases. They climbed into the canoe like persons who know in advance that they are about to fall downstairs.

Don't get smart-assed, I told myself, *you're no Inuk hunter yourself. These men coming ashore are your people, Southerners, simply wearing knee-high, rubber boots and looking just as awkward as you usually look to the people who live here.*

The Hudson's Bay executives shook hands with me on the beach in order of rank and formally invited me up to the post with them as though I had not slept there for two nights. Their man on the post kept a respectable pace behind them as did their pilot and myself. Then with much stomping and scraping of wet boots, we entered the house.

"Well, young man, congratulations. You've kept everything looking as good as new," said the second in command, a sociable sort of man.

"We'll want you to get a radio message out to head office, Winnipeg, telling them that we've arrived," said the top man, taking off his rimless glasses and polishing them as he settled in a brand new chair.

"Where's your lavatory, lad? We'll all need to wash up. It's been a bumpy trip."

"In there,sir, but I forgot to put the pail inside the toilet can. You can just go around the back of the house for now. I'll have the can in by morning – when you'll need it most."

The top man looked horrified. He was English and knew nothing of such informalities. However, he followed the others out into the rising mist, returning in a better frame of mind.

To maintain this feeling, the head of personnel rustled around in his ditty bag and fished out a towel-wrapped bottle of 1670 Hudson's Bay Company Scotch. "This is our gift," he said, handing it over like a bag of gold as they sat down on the shimmering, nylon green sofa and the overstuffed, matching chair. "Would you like me to open it up? We could all use a drink. It's been a long, hard day and it's awfully damp and chilly out there."

"Can't you find a chair, Mr. Houston?" asked the sociable,

middle-management man. "I'm sure our host would like you to share a drink with all of us."

The pilot, a silent man, rolled his eyes at me and cursed silently. A pilot never drinks when he's flying the Company's higher brass.

I pulled up one of the two indestructible Canadian maple chairs that I had brought up myself that morning. I heard the girl come in on soft skin boots, pour a bucket of water into the neatly painted Imperial 45-gallon fuel drum that stood beside the stove, heard her slide the kettle on and go out again. It was five o'clock, the time most Northerners, if they have a house, prepare to serve the dinner.

I looked at the manager, who popped his eyes at me and we both took a drink from the new glasses. It was the Company's finest whisky. I kept quiet, enjoyed it, and listened. This was to be an important Company evening, preceding the annual inspection, which could not always be annual because of ice.

"You are a good housekeeper," said the head man. "You keep things looking almost new. Will that young woman be here to help with breakfast?"

The Company's higher brass was always interested in the sex lives of their unmarried men on a post. After all, they had been carefully monitoring northern love life for three hundred years. Love has always played an influential role in the Northern fur trade. In posts where Company men quite often failed to survive the winter, how could much else matter? A warm-blooded female bedmate possessing perfect local knowledge, one who knows how to laugh at winter, can change your entire view of the world inside or outside of a sleeping bag. But higher management may not always approve of that simple fact.

I was mulling over thoughts like that while I cut into a huge, iron frying pan thick slices of bacon the inspection team had brought in and cracked into the other pan the dozen eggs that the pilot had left beside the stove. We were cooking on a coal stove. Given a good, swift kick, it would usually brighten up. It was, of course, the only heat source in the house. As I laid the dishes around on the kitchen table, I noticed the young girl who normally helped standing on tiptoe, peeking in the window, apparently too awed to take any part in such a high-level affair.

In the morning, I walked down with the head of Arctic personnel to the old HBC house which had recently been demoted to a warehouse. That house had the right old Arctic look to it, including a spacious armchair made of local walrus ivory tusks.

"Well, I see the Company's making good progress up here," the personnel man said. "Everything in that house is spick and span. Personnel in the old days," he confided in me, "used to recruit in Scotland, always on the lookout for young Scots or Newfoundland lads they thought would fit in well at our southern chain of stores: Winnipeg, Moosejaw, Saskatoon, Calgary, Vancouver. That was our standard reqirement in those days. But experience has sharpened our thinking lately. We've started to consider the misfits, you know, the somewhat unsociable chaps who don't like to work with other people, sort of hermit-types who don't give a damn about an unheated store in winter, men who detest the very thought of vacationing in southern California or the West Indies. The older Scots who used to trade in all these posts for us, and for Revillon Frères and Baffin Trading, they said they deplored the idea of a vacation once every three years. They swore it took a year to come into the country and settle down, three years to enjoy the life here, then the fifth year to pack up again and go back to the old country on leave.

"The man of ours here told me almost that same thing after dinner last night. Said he dreads going out next year and thinks we should reinstate the old idea of a vacation every five years. Says it would be more than enough leave for him."

That wonderfully interesting young manager, with all his honesty and eccentricities, did not remain with the Company for long. He went south again, and using his high intelligence and language skills, was working on his Ph.D. thesis when I last saw him.

That old community that I had the good fortune to visit has changed dramatically, like so much else in the North. I wonder if the beluga still make their marvelous birdlike chirping sounds as they seem to make a game of rolling over the harbor's reef on summer mornings.

16
Showing the Flag

In Ottawa, I attended a meeting where there was a large display of aerial photographs of Arctic Canada spread across a wall.

"Do you know who photographed all those separate sections of this aerial map?" the director, who had been a colonel, asked. "The American Air Force. They're the ones who bloody-well did it. They flew very fast over the whole country during World War II. They made their military survey maps – everything from Alaska across Canada to east Greenland, then north to Ellesmere and all our other islands of the Arctic archipelago. They gave these maps to us as a present, a little sign of friendship, they said, to the second-biggest country in the world!"

"I've heard that only a handful of people, including Eskimos, have ever even seen this country," one chief of a division said, waving his hands at the vast expanse of stark black-and-white photos with huge jigsaws of ice. "Most Canadians think our provinces are somewhere due south of Alaska. That's what strong U.S. publicity can do."

"We've got to fly the flag more widely on all the outer edges of these huge territories of ours." The director ran his pointer over the map. "This is all Canada, all right. It's ours and we've got to pay attention if we want to keep it. Here's how. Up to now we've barely had any impact on the people who live up there as nomads. The new plan will change that and we'll build local schools, put in some male nurses and one- or two-bed nursing stations. Then a scientific station here, an ionospheric station there. Seed it with a few government administrators and spread the Royal Canadian Mounted Police around in two-man detachments. None of that will cost us much. Schools about the size of your average swimming pool. Those dots spread over the landscape will serve to occupy this whole territory, and the settlements will draw the people together to make it a lot easier to service them. Yes, I know that it'll have an impact on that whole nomadic hunting society, but we can't afford to have them wandering around, perhaps starving, and our government people out in planes looking for them. It gets us nothing but bad press."

"Why do we want all that desolate northland?" a new civil servant asked.

"I'll tell you why," the colonel said. "If we give away this territory or let it get taken away from us, the bloody place will turn out like Oklahoma. We'll find it's loaded with oil, minerals, and natural gas, and we'll be standing down here with egg all over our face."

17
Ready – Set – Go

Returning from the west coast of Hudson Bay, I was met by Allie at the Montreal railway station. We decided that same evening that we would become engaged and marry. Before doing that, she insisted we must visit her family in Nova Scotia. After that, and back in Grand'Mère, I was in my studio again, high up with its wonderful view over the St. Maurice River. But the magnetic pole had turned its drawing power on me. I thought of little except getting married and hurrying back into the Arctic to stay. Allie in Montreal seemed just as keen as I to go.

We went to my mother's home in Beaverton, an early Scottish settlement, a district where parts of our family had lived for several generations. Eight miles away at Port Bolster on Lake Simcoe, our family had had a summer cottage where I had gone for the first time, my mother said, when I was two weeks old. In Beaverton, we heard through the Guild and government that I might get a flight to Baffin Island on the monthly run the Royal Canadian Air Force took from Montreal to their Arctic base at Frobisher Bay, now Iqaluit. If I missed that flight, all plans would have to be postponed.

No one flew to other places on Baffin Island except Air Force Search and Rescue, based in Greenwood, Nova Scotia, and then only on some life or death emergency. So we decided to get married then and there with family in the small church in Beaverton. It was the end of December.

After a joyous celebration, my best man and youngest uncle, Douglas Barbour, drove us to our closed cottage in Port Bolster. It was freezing cold with lots of snow and the cottage was heated only by a large fireplace. But I assured Allie that she should start to grow accustomed to conditions a lot colder and more difficult. I didn't know myself how much more difficult that would be, but we would soon find out!

We were both young and strong then, in our twenties. I insisted that we walk the eight miles from Port Bolster to Beaverton to visit my mother, then walk back again the same day. That was like an infantry route march. I was used to that. But Allie? I was delighted that she did it cheerfully and well.

We returned to Montreal and bought our Arctic kit: long, yellow, woolen, winter underwear and heavy underclothing, a parka, wind pants, and boots for Allie. Serious clothing for the trail we would arrange for once we were in the country. After all, who could know more than Inuit women about cold weather clothing?

Jack Molson, who had become a good friend, was an enthusiast about so many things and had cheerfully made all the transportation arrangements with the Royal Canadian Air Force. He drove us out to their air base at St. Hubert near Montreal, gave us a gallon of maple syrup made from his own trees, slapped me on the back, and kissed Allie goodbye.

Allie and I were almost alone in the back of the military aircraft, with piles of lashed-down freight around us. We got off when the plane turned around at Goose Bay, Labrador. There we were told that nothing was going north for a week or two. I must say we both had a wonderful time at the Goose Bay Air Force base and made a lot of friends, Canadian and American pilots, mostly fresh out of European bases. They were eager to help us in any way they could. But the commanding officer told us that no matter what authority I had, he was not going to allow us to fly further north to Baffin Island. He said that the military there were under Canadian–U.S. joint command and that he would not allow a woman on that base, Crystal II. He told me we should return to Montreal. He was not friendly or unfriendly about this. It was simply his decision not to let us go.

When we explained the turn of events that night to friends in the mess, both Canadian and American pilots, they laughed. "Screw him!" the pilots shouted in that united spirit that helped to win the war. One suggested, "We'll drive you over to the American side of the airstrip tomorrow morning. The Yanks will take you up to Frobisher."

And that's exactly how it happened. We gathered our kit together and in the darkness before dawn, one of the Canadian fighter pilots took us on a hair-raising dash in a Jeep across the airstrip, an illegal passage at any time and especially when an aircraft was approaching. It was common to know wild risk-takers in those days when governments had just stopped giving them medals for being wild.

In the back with us on this flight were several other U.S. military personnel and lots of freight. When our still-camouflaged prop aircraft landed on the airstrip at the head of Frobisher Bay, we stepped out into a cold blast of wind and held our breaths. In the distance stretched the bleak white reaches of the frozen bay, and beyond was a blue-shadowed mountain range, rising beautifully and mysteriously before our eyes.

We were driven straight from the plane to the large, main mess hall for lunch. It was packed with men. There were no women's facilities on the base and women were considered an impossible sight to see. But no one turned his head or blinked an eye when Allie walked past with her tray of food. It was not because they objected to her being there, the men later told me, it was just the surprise of seeing one of their half-forgotten opposite sex appearing suddenly among them.

We got an invitation to go and live at the Hudson's Bay Company post that was only a few miles further down the bay, and not long after that we left the base. The young fur trader, Wulferd Tolboom, a Dutchman, and his wife offered us their other bedroom in the small house, putting their Newfoundland clerk, Ernie Decker, on the sofa.

We started right away to make arrangements for our journey across Baffin Island. We contacted Lake Harbour (Kingmerok) on the HBC radio transmitter and asked them to send a dog team, as there seemed to be no suitable team around Frobisher. In the meantime, we set about having some items of warm clothing made.

We saw very little of the Inuit who had originally been among the sixteen families trading into Frobisher Bay before and during the war. These families, fewer than two hundred persons, had now gathered together, living off to one side of the military in an area they called Iqaluit – fishes – because of the abundant char runs in the Sylvia Grinnel River. We learned that those people had become disenchanted, and no wonder, with the comings and goings of so many military strangers who by that time scarcely gave a glance or paid any attention to the local inhabitants. The land, meanwhile, had turned into a huge military depot. Countless thousands of barrels of aviation gas and diesel fuel lay in immense football-field-sized reserves. They were not worth transporting south, but would never be used. The air was full of rumors that with the war over the whole operation was about to be closed down and forgotten like so many other military bases everywhere.

We watched the two teams, numbering eighteen dogs, as they arrived, moving slowly across the width of the frozen bay. We were more than curious to meet, to shake hands, and to get to know Siutiapik and Utai, the two drivers, for we expected to spend a month of travel with them. I was secretly worried about putting my new wife to such a test.

After all the waiting, we were eager to be on our way. On a bright, stinging cold morning, with a smart wind blowing and the temperature hovering at minus thirty degrees Fahrenheit (about minus twenty degrees Celsius), we took off across the ice of Frobisher Bay toward the ominous, blue-shadowed mountains that lay beyond.

18

Dog Teams on the Trail

After you learn enough to jump off a moving sled, run beside it, then hop back on again without it getting away from you, it quickly becomes fascinating to watch the competitive workings of a dog team and, even better, the competition between two dog teams. The Inuit use a fan hitch, which has lines of varying length, one line for each dog. The dogs may fan out and pull, or close the fan and run almost in a straight line close together in front of the sled. This method of using sled dogs is completely different from the Nome or tandem hitch used by western Arctic drivers.

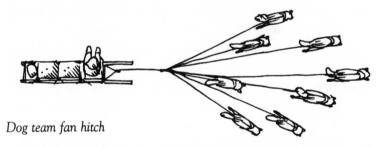

Dog team fan hitch

Both hitches have been developed not just by choice but by local conditions. In wooded country, a fan hitch would quickly get you tangled in the trees. There the single or tandem hitch is essential. But in the eastern Arctic where traveling is done over open tundra, on the land, and more often on the sea ice, the fan hitch is superior. Dogs pulling a working sled through rough, tidal ice that has been broken and stacked into jagged piles must have the liberty to find their own separate footing and pull. Dogs that must pull a sled over wide cracks in the ice may go into the water, but if they are attached by individual lines, they can usually swim across and pull themselves out on the other side.

Dog-team travel in the eastern Arctic is an ancient method of transportation. But that is not to say that it is simple or primitive.

We whites understood so little about it that in the 1940s, during the war, the Americans introduced the Nansen sled, a clumsy affair unsuitable for this country. A basket attached to its top made it difficult to overturn if you wanted to halt the dogs. Being bolted together it had no give or pliability in rough ice, which meant it would stop or break. In a country desperate for hardwood these Nansen sleds were soon scattered around Frobisher Bay, discarded as useless by their second owners, realistic Inuit sled-drivers.

Dogs in teams are by their nature enormously competitive. They hate to fall behind, so it is wise on a big trip to split into two teams. It cuts down on the fighting and the tangling of the dog traces and the journey goes more quickly. On a still, beautiful day in the strong, spring sun, traveling with a well-fed dog team can seem like a dream come true. But when the wind rises and the weather goes down and you know you've got twelve hours of running, sitting, shivering, then running again to keep warm, you feel it's an accomplishment to have made it through the day.

Conversation is usually the surest way to use up time, along with observing nature very closely, especially that ever-fascinating piece of live theater provided by the individual dogs acting out their parts in the two teams. Traveling day after day for a long period of time with them will make you admire some and despise others as you observe their social, sometimes tyrannical, and often loving team life or sexual life, so that you view them on different days in different ways.

When you travel by dog team with Inuit, it is smart to leave the decisions entirely up to them because they know all about what they are doing in this strange harsh world of theirs, and you do not. A day's travel, which may start at 6:00 a.m. in early spring, may go on until 7:00 or 8:00 p.m., with only a brief break for noonday tea and a hardtack biscuit while untangling snarled dog lines. Once we get them hitched up and under way the dogs act somewhat predictably. On the trail they do their jobs, but all too often they tangle their traces while they hop over to visit or fight with various other characters holding strong opinions in the team.

But you might suddenly notice another dog team track converging onto the trail you have been following. The teams stop to sniff it, yellow it, grow excited and alert. Then another track cuts in. You feel that you are traveling on a highway. Even though it might be the end of a long day, the dogs raise their heads, curl their tails. When you thought they hadn't any kind of spunk left in them, they run on, as lively as a gang of kids on their way to a party. Then you cross another track. The highway broadens. The teams are listening. Then far away you hear faint howling. Our teams answer, then strain forward, straightening out their tails, which means they're really pulling. Now there can be no more running alongside the sleds for us. The dogs are moving much too fast.

If you feel yourself somewhat of an old hand at staying aboard a lurching *kamotik,* you slowly rise up on your knees or even stand like a circus performer to get a better view. Yes, there it is. You see a person running. You hear him calling to someone. Suddenly, there are others coming out of nowhere. No, not nowhere. They're coming out of igloos or snow-walled tents that cannot at first be seen. It's the camp, all right. There's nothing else for fifty miles each side of this small group of four families, this warm, wild clutch of human life.

You jump off to guide or run behind the sled when it reaches the barrier ice that has been piled up against the shore in front of the camp. Because of the speed at which the heavy sled is moving, it's dangerous. Loaded sleds may turn over onto an inexperienced person's ribs or arms or legs and break them against such upheavals of ice.

Always when we were through the barrier, an immense dog fight would break out. Our dogs seemed delighted to do battle and the camp dogs were always more than eager to defend their turf. Hunters on both sides would wade in to save their dogs from getting seriously hurt. There were a lot of well-aimed kicks from soft, skin boots, and whip handles went whacking down here and there until our teams, other visiting teams, and excited camp dogs were finally separated to snarl and yelp insults back and forth at each other and proudly lick their wounds. Soon you could not believe how intimately they were getting on together.

Dogs are sometimes given as a gift, which is a questionable sort of blessing, since a new dog must fight every other strong dog in the team to see where he's going to be allowed to fit in to the team's pecking order.

Inuit dogs have been bred and raised as work dogs, not by careful breeding control, but simply by the frequent exchange of dogs while traveling and visiting other camps. The nomadic movement of teams through various parts of the country left dogs free to roam together for a few days, which always led to better breeding.

19

The Crossing

In the mountains where the going was tough, the dogs felt the strain as much as we did, and they showed it. Finally, after an almost unbelievably long day, we halted the teams and unhitched them. Then we went about the task of building our first igloo on this journey. Siutiapik, using the traditional snow knife, and Utai, using a worn out Swedish hand saw, pitched into the building of this house which was to be of the faster-built, most uncomplicated variety. First cutting out and flipping away a wedge shape, they began cutting the blocks wide as a hand span, an arm's length long, and knee-to-ankle deep. The cut went straight down, for they were excavating the basement where we would eventually sleep.

When the circle of blocks had been removed of exactly the size we would require for four persons, Siutiapik stepped inside. He took the role of master builder, putting the blocks in place. He roughed up the hard snow surface to make the blocks stick as he wriggled one against the other. When he had completed the circle, he went back and with his long-bladed snow knife he cut the blocks away until they formed a rising curve. This caused a pressure tension as he placed more blocks of the second ring on top of them, the kind of pressure he needed to form a strong dome.

Together with Utai, we knelt to chink the igloo blocks with snow. For Southerners used to making snowballs from wet snow that sounds easy. But it was impossible for anyone to pick up scoops of snow that had been driven and packed by winds so that if you brought your skin-booted heel down hard, you made absolutely no impression on the snow. I got a meat knife from the grub box on the sled and we began cutting out chunks of snow and chopping them fine. It takes practice, but after days at it, you start to get the hang of packing the dry, sandlike material into cracks between blocks and holding it there for a moment until, acting like cement, it sticks. If you don't do that, the dry snow will run out like sand through an hourglass.

These mortaring efforts kept us warm and as darkness fell, we stood back to admire our work. Siutiapik, who was still inside, dropped the pie-shaped, key block piece flat into place. Utai had no hesitation in climbing up and laying his full weight against the dome to pack and smooth the outside against the violence of a possible blizzard.

Siutiapik cut a low entranceway and we passed in the sealskins and caribou skins which would form our bed, then the sleeping bags and other equipment we would need, along with anything else a dog could possibly eat. Our rifles in their canvas covers we laid on top of the igloo dome. Allie crawled inside to get out of the rising wind and lit the Primus stove.

Siutiapik crawled out to help Utai who had already begun to feed the dogs. What an uproar! What a savage, shouldering, scrambling fight for the chunks of fist-sized, frozen walrus meat. It was over in an incredible few minutes, and the dogs started to lick their chops and minor wounds as they circled around like any other dogs, then dropped into their chosen place to sleep beside the igloo. There's no need to tether them. Dogs won't run away. They need the hands that feed them as much as the travelers need the dogs.

The building of the igloo and the feeding of the dogs had taken about an hour. When we three men crawled inside and drew the block to close the entrance, Siutiapik lit two short, fat, emergency candles and affixed them with melted wax to the handles of his snow knife and a meat knife, both of which he stuck at shoulder height into the wall.

Candle attached to igloo wall

Siutiapik showed Allie how to place chunks of snow inside the kettle to be placed carefully on the Primus. He politely took out half of the snow because it will not melt immediately, as ice will, and may allow the Primus's hot flame to burn out the kettle. That lesson learned and with the kettle about to boil, we all started to do a good deal of scraping and thumping with Utai's wooden snow beater, to drive most of the fine snow out of our boots and pants and parka. This is a serious task if you wish to keep these dandruff-like snow bits from forming into ice in the relative warmth inside the igloo. I say relative, because we would not wish to raise the temperature above the freezing point for fear of causing fog and even rain inside the igloo.

The four of us comfortably stretched our tired legs on the sleeping skins and lay on our backs against the still-rolled sleeping bags and sighed. What a hell of an awful, wonderful day it had been! We wiggled our toes and fingers. Yes, circulation was starting to come back again. The coffee boiling in the kettle was letting off a delicious smell. Allie poured it into our chipped, enamel mugs and we each dumped in sugar from its canvas sack. Nothing ever tasted so grand.

None of us could stand upright in our traveling igloo. Because heat rises and we wanted it to stay down with us, we had made the ceiling deliberately low. We lay back, staring up at the snow-domed ceiling just above our heads, sparkling with a million frozen crystals that flashed and glowed in the candlelight. So small was our house that our breath, our body heat, and the kettle steam were helping to raise the temperature.

"I never thought I'd live to see this," Allie said. "It's like a shining dream. When I was small, I heard of Eskimos from a man who had sailed north and seen them. He told us at school that Eskimo children loved to eat little bits of bacon rind and right now, so would I."

I tried to translate that to Utai as he put meat in the pot to thaw and boil, and we tried to cut a pie-shaped piece of bannock. It was frozen solid and we had to hack it into four. There was no such thing as waiting. We made it sodden in our coffee, then ate like wolves.

After the meat was finished and we were feeling newlywed and shy, we left the other two and went outside. Hell, we were still civilized folk, weren't we? This was going to be a long and good, or not so good, or maybe even a hard, adventure. We didn't even try to imagine how it would turn out. We crawled back in and beat ourselves free of snow again. I had buttoned – for the zippered sleeping bag had not yet been invented – our two sleeping bags into one large pouch. That turned out to be one of the best ideas I ever had.

"Good night," we called to our two fellow travelers only inches away, who politely seemed to be already sound asleep.

20

The Waterfall

In the morning, we drank tea, brewed until it was almost black, probably a practice learned from the Scottish whalers. I mention this because there were so many differences, both large and small, between these hunting people and us, differences well worth considering. Certainly, these two hunters had a close-up view of a *kallunait* woman sleeping in their igloo.

Not too many young wives, I feel, would have cheerfully undertaken such an adventure. But from the very beginning, Allie had good feelings about Inuit and living in that country. No matter how hard it got, she had enough bounce to go on. She liked the Inuit and they liked her. To this day, that has never ceased.

Before we left, we cut out the side of the igloo. That was almost always done with abandoned igloos, to allow them to fill with snow. I cannot think of any practical reason for doing so, but perhaps there is some magical one.

We suffered bad weather in the mountains and new deep drifts, making us wish that we had chosen a different route. And then we hit the frozen waterfall. We had been traveling up a river course that led through the mountains when we reached the bottom of the waterfall, where we stopped and built our second igloo. We arose early the following morning and began our task, one of the worst that I have ever faced, before or since. The frozen waterfall before us was rough and sleek and taller than a barn. On both sides of the frozen waterfall were steep tumbles of broken granite blown clear by violent downdrafts, quite unthinkable to climb with dogs and sleds and a half-ton of dog food and supplies. We would have to go straight up the ice formed by the waterfall.

"Is there no other way?" I asked.

"Ayii, yes," Siutiapik nodded. "Around by the coast, five, maybe six more sleeps. That way no people. And bad ice at the mouth of the rivers."

When I didn't answer, Siutiapik took up our long-handled ice chisel and started probing, searching for the best way up this unthinkable hazard. I got the hand ax, Utai the chisel end of his seal harpoon, and we started laboriously chopping small hand- and foot-holes, working slowly up the nearly vertical ice. It was noon before the climbing notches were completed and although the mean wind and frigid temperature had not changed, we were bathed in sweat. To make matters worse, we had only smooth-bottomed sealskin boots, which made climbing on ice a toe-clutching nightmare.

When Siutiapik reached the top of the frozen falls, he secured a sealskin line around a boulder, and dangled its end down to me. "Kingmik atauasitwak," he shouted. "Dogs one at a time."

Utai and I caught the lead bitch and tied the rope securely, tightening her harness.

"*Atai!*" we shouted.

Siutiapik started to haul her upwards. We pushed at her rear end and she tried to scramble in her own fashion. Eventually, he got her on top.

Siutiapik yelled down, telling me to tie the next dog's mouth closed. I was glad to do it, but feared he would bite me in the process. He weighed almost twice as much as the bitch, and as we shoved him up my arms ached and trembled. But we got him to the top of the falls.

Securing each of the other sixteen dogs, some with their mouths tied shut if their temperament demanded, we hauled and pulled, managing somehow to get them to the top one by one. We lay gasping on the snow, wet with quickly chilling sweat. But our technique was improving. Utai took the heavy grub box up with Siutiapik pulling from the top and me pushing up on Utai's rear end while trying to stay in the ice-chopped steps.

I changed places with Siutiapik. Up on top, it seemed easier at first to pull than to climb the steps on the face of the falls, but the icy wind was stronger now, causing a ground drift to moan along the frozen river, and the sweat seemed to freeze on my back. I looked down at Allie who was trying to organize the bundles of skins and sleeping bags that must be lifted. The sight of her made me wish that she and I were anywhere else on earth. She stayed down at the foot of the falls by our old snowhouse and with the Swedish Primus she made tea for all of us.

We climbed down sometime after noon and crouched exhausted on the sleds, grateful to have meat and bannock, tea and American military cigarettes, at that time costing four-and-a-half cents for a pack of twenty. Then we got the two 14-foot *kamotiks* and pushed and hauled again until they reached the top. Next we had the problem of bringing up the other two grub boxes, containing our food, dog food, sacks of frozen walrus meat, and then the lighter sleeping bags, rolled sleeping skins, rifles, harpoons, everything.

When Siutiapik pushed the last load up over the edge of the falls with Utai and me and Allie pulling, we collapsed. Lying on the load like children, we rested for a little while, letting the rising evening wind rip over our exhausted, overheated bodies. When we started to grow cold, we forced ourselves to start building the snowhouse. Small, this one was, as small as we could make it and still pack the four of us inside. But Siutiapik built it strong enough to withstand the rising wind that might tear it apart. In such a wind it would be impossible to build another.

We fed the dogs by opening a sack and running, scattering frozen chunks of walrus meat across the snow. Then we watched the two teams fight for it, snarling, snapping, bolting down the fist-sized pieces, a savage sight to see. We went in and aimed a few kicks at some of the big male dogs who, still hungry, were trying to make a smaller bitch throw up her frozen meal. Like wolves, these dogs still have the habit of carrying food in their stomachs so they can then regurgitate it to feed their young.

Working together, we finished this house in forty minutes. The drivers buried the remaining walrus meat beneath the snow inside our igloo, for our only way to guard it was to sleep on it. Inside we spread out the soft caribou skins, lighting a single candle, then the little Primus stove, thawing the meat and bannock enough to bite into it. Allie made coffee, but not too strong. Inuit hate strong coffee. Probably they developed the tradition of stretching coffee so thin from trading with the frugal American whalers in earlier years.

Allie arranged the thick skins as a mattress for the double sleeping bag. I rolled my fur pants tight to be a pillow and collapsed into an exhausted sleep as the first feelings of warmth began to circulate in the bag.

21

A Long Way to Cape Dorset

Siutiapik shook me awake and I sat up, hearing a sound that I had never heard before. It was a low, weird moaning, a groaning coming from the throats of all our dogs around the igloo.

"*Shoonukiak?* What is it?" I asked.

"*Kauyimangilunga*, I don't know," he answered.

As he pulled on his parka, he jerked the snow knife out of the wall, cut the snow block from the entrance, and crawled outside. Our rifles in their cases were on the roof of the igloo, the metal so cold you dared not touch it with your bare hand.

When Siutiapik was outside, he called, "*Tuavi laureet! Tuavi! Takoaluk!* Hurry! Take a look!"

I hauled on clothing and crawled out behind Utai. Looking up, I was so struck with what I saw that I forgot to rise.

Northern lights, aurora borealis, far stronger than any I'd ever seen before, were thrusting downwards like the strong airport lights you see today, cutting their way toward earth in the star-filled dome of sky.

"What is it?" Allie called to me. "Is it a bear?"

"No. Come out and look."

She came out, still pulling on her parka, then laid back against the curve of the igloo looking up. None of us spoke. We'd never dreamed we'd see an overwhelming sight like that!

"What time is it?" Allie asked.

"I don't know. I've let my wristwatch stop. It doesn't matter about the time. The big thing is that the wind is down."

"*Coppitilaurit*," Siutiapik said to Allie and nodded toward the entrance.

She understood we should have coffee. That meant we were going to stay up and get going. We didn't know where dawn was and we didn't care. It helps to be young when you're dog-team traveling and using igloos. I know. I tried it again not so long ago at Igloolik and I must admit that it had lost some of its charm for me.

Inuit are masters of the fast take-off in the mornings. We left that little snowhouse, which was in easy sight of the one before, and we were off again. The huskies had not worked at all the day before and they were eager to pull.

There would be no Inuit camps until Kingmerok, our first destination. We arrived there on the fifth day of our journey. It looked like a postcard of a small Danish trading post in Greenland. Winter or summer, it was protected by a bowl of wind-worn, snow-laced cliffs that dropped steeply into a frozen fiord. Three neat, red-roofed Hudson's Bay Company buildings were at its head, a small Anglican mission on one side, and a mounted police detachment on the other, set safely apart on either side of the harbor.

Geordie Anderson, the post manager, and the few others there came out to greet us. Geordie was an old Arctic hand who had done Company service in Pangnirtung and had witnessed Inuit taking one of the last great bowhead whales for food using an old-fashioned hand-held whaling gun. The Andersons invited us to stay with them, to relax and straighten our kit before we started west again.

When a traveler first comes off the trail, where even in the snowhouse at night you're living constantly below freezing, the glare of lights and blast of heat inside a house seem intolerable. You can't wait to tear off your long, woolen underwear and heavy socks, strip off everything and just sit gasping. But no. You must sit down properly at a table, eat very carefully, and act exactly as though nothing is in any way unusual. Don't forget the Hudson's Bay Company is a very British company, with a three-hundred-year tradition in their part of the world. They know what it is to travel hard and they don't suffer fools. They expect you first to tell them any outside news of the world they may have missed. Then in return they'll tell you the much more immediate news from inside which will prove vastly more interesting and perhaps useful in the days that lie ahead.

At that time, the Inuit had little understanding of what was going on outside. They did not yet have an understanding of money, for they had had no use for it. Arctic traders had always practiced direct trade. "Give me a skin and I'll trade you for it." That was their method. *Pro pelle cutem*, that was their motto. Using brass tokens, they would lay out what the Company considered the worth of half a dozen white foxes that the hunter had brought in to trade. For example, one white fox for one box of cartridges, or four white foxes for enough canvas to make a tent, three white foxes and a skin bag full of walrus tusks for a small rifle.

A hunter returning to Kingmerok after a visit by dog team to the military air base at Frobisher Bay once told me proudly of the valuable piece of *kenouyutsat*, paper money with the face on it, that he had received in exchange for two elaborate ivory carvings he had made. Fishing into his parka hood, he produced a worthless Quaker Oats coupon.

Next day, he took this coupon to the Hudson's Bay post and I went with him, for I have always had an endless curiosity about swift-changing facial expressions and the local methods of trading.

When the hunter grandly laid the Quaker-faced coupon on the counter, Geordie Anderson examined this imagined piece of currency with rising dismay. He flashed it at me, saying in his flinty, Scottish accent, "Wouldn't ye love to wrap yer finger bones around the windpipe of the son-of-a-bitch who passed this piece of paper off on him?"

Then, without comment to the hunter, Geordie laid five brass tokens on the counter and traded the useless bit of paper as though it had been a genuine five-dollar bill. I suppose he was trying to save face for all of us foreigners against the scoundrels among us who have pulled off deals taking advantage of the ancient habit of trust which honest people still possess in many of the far-flung corners of the world.

With some of the other hunters inland in search of caribou and the missionary off in a camp somewhere, Anawakaluk, a tall, distinguished-looking hunter, had come in to trade, and offered to take us out to stay with him. Since his camp was off the trail that we intended to travel, we went out with him, planning to stay there for a while, then return to Kingmerok to restart our journey west. Anawakaluk's wife, Pitsulala, was the first Inuit woman that Allie truly had a chance to know, and later Pitsulala said that she had not known any *kallunait* woman so well. They enjoyed each other immensely in spite of the fact that they had only a few words between them. But Allie was keeping a diary and making her own word list. We also learned that when eating meat, raw or boiled, one is never supposed to take up the bone and gnaw at it with your teeth as we barbarians in the South sometimes do with a chicken leg. If we tried this approach, our hosts politely turned their heads away. In Inuit society, it's good manners to hold the bone upright, then strip the meat with a knife or with your fingers and place it in your mouth. Anawakaluk's half-tent, half-igloo, with its low, red wooden door was a reflection of the old whaler's style. We were sorry to leave, to return to Kingmerok, ready to resume our journey west.

I still believe that the Lake Harbour carvings we saw at that time stood in strong contrast to the work of carvers living further to the West. Why were they so different and so uninteresting? I think it was because Lake Harbour had long suffered from nineteenth-century whalers' tastes and ideas of style based on Victorian tastes from Dundee, Scotland, and New London, Connecticut. It took Inuit carvers there seventy years to throw off that old dead weight, but finally, by the 1960s, they were free.

The moment of departure is an exciting event in any country. This dog-team journey we were about to take seemed especially so to us. We were leaving from the very corner of the Company storage shed and had lashed onto the sleds our dog food in sacks, our rolled sleeping skins, sleeping bags, and new full food boxes, for, if possible, it is best not to have to hunt for food during a long journey but to press on to your destination.

With our sixteen dogs harnessed and in an uproar, eager to go and fighting with excitement, we started saying goodbye to Inuit, Geordie, and other friends who had gathered to see us off. In the excitement, Siutiapik and I, who were responsible for the load, both made the mistake of thinking that the emergency food box was on the other sled. So we took off with many Inuit running beside us, helping our teams get through the barrier ice on to the flatter ice beyond. Our box remained among other boxes on the storage ramp.

I will not burden you with much of that long, cold journey. We built new igloos every night unless we slept in Inuit camps, which we did often, for we stopped at virtually every one along the Baffin coast. In my role of finding carvings and an outlet for Inuit art, we were visiting all of the communities to try to understand the carving possibilities in each place, and to find out what importance carvings bought from these people and sold in galleries outside might have for them. In the camps, I found that there was very little walrus ivory, and stone was scarcely used except for making seal-oil lamps. Antlers, which caribou shed annually, seemed a good material, and I heard tales of great piles of whalebone from the kills of the American and Scottish whalers who had hunted off these coasts a century earlier.

In our first camp on our journey west, we visited a plump and friendly man named Kipernik and the three families who lived there and traded into Lake Harbour. We considered Kipernik the best Baffin carver we had seen so far.

We were three sleeps west of Kingmerok when we discovered that the forgotten box was not a part of the load on either sled. Returning for it, then getting back to this point, would have taken us six days. Nobody thought that a good idea. The emptiness of a meat cache that we had been counting on before we reached the next camp at Amadjuak now caused us much concern. As it turned out, we had been overgenerous in sharing food, as was the Inuit custom, in the camps on the journey so far. This meant that we were now seriously in need of the emergency box of food that we had left in Kingmerok. We felt sure that Simioni, a well-known hunter at Amadjuak, would have food for us and our dogs.

When we did meet Simioni at Amadjuak, however, we discovered that everyone there was short of human food and dog food. The rest of the journey began to look bleak. Because we had a shortage of dog food and Siutiapik and Utai would have to get back to Kingmerok with the two teams, we agreed that Simioni and his son, Eisiak, would borrow some additional dogs and Allie and I would continue to Kingait with them, while Siutiapik and Utai returned home, with a share of the last of the dog food.

On the next day out, we finished the tea we had left. What we had in the kettle (and had boiled several times) were leaves turned pale as sand. I went out of the igloo, disgusted with myself for leaving our emergency box behind, and I flung the old, used tea leaves on the snow. Camp children who had followed me leapt on the tea leaves and ate them. Later at night when we were really hungry, I wished that I had eaten them myself, or in the Inuit fashion shared them with Allie and our new friends in that night's igloo.

We both liked Simioni and his son, Eisiak, immediately. Simioni was an older man, short, broad-shouldered, wise and thoughtful. One thing we found odd was that he and his son did not share in our remaining food, implying that they had some food of their own.

There was no use stopping to try and hunt seal, for a huge windstorm, coupled with a high tide, had broken the outer ice into pieces too small to drive a dog team over, yet too large to force a canoe or kayak through. The south wind held this mess of broken ice against the edge of the thick shore ice on which we were traveling.

On the second night, we couldn't really feed the dogs and we ourselves were tired and hungry.

"Why not build the igloo here out on the ice?" I suggested to Simioni.

He stopped to consider that, then said, "No. We should go in to shore to build. Pootoogook's camp . . . we'll reach it soon. He'll have food for us and lots of dog food, certainly."

We built our igloo on the shore. A huge spring blizzard came to us sometime that night and pinned us down for two whole days. When we went outside in the morning, the weather had cleared and the waters of Hudson Strait sparkled blue quite close to us.

"Oh, my God!" I said to Allie. "What if we had built out on the ice as I had wanted to do? We'd be adrift and miles from here."

"The dogs are dead," said Allie. "Look, they're covered with snow."

I gave the nearest one a light kick and it scrambled to its feet. "Dogs purposely let themselves get snowed in during a blizzard – that's how they stay warm."

We went more slowly on this day. The drifts were whipped high across the sea ice like the top of your mother's meringue pie. The dogs were dispirited and so were we. We spent a night at Akiaktolaolavik. I didn't like the sound of that name, for it means "the place we last had something good to eat." So it was with us.

One more sleep and we arrived at Pootoogook's place, the long-sought isthmus, Ikeraksak.

"We'll be all right now," I told Allie. "I've heard he built a little house out of salvage from the HBC ship, *Nascopi*, when she wrecked on a shoal near Cape Dorset in 1947. It was the ship's cabin, with brass portholes."

"There's the house," Allie said. "Why aren't the dogs excited? Why haven't the people come out?"

We drove the teams up through the barrier ice and halted. Silence was all around us.

"*Pootoogookut nowtima?* Pootoogook's family, where are they?"

"*Achooli*, I don't know," said Simioni.

I called out, then cautiously went and pushed open the door – no one. The place was empty. The dogs and sleds were gone.

"Why did they leave?"

"I don't know," said Simioni, looking grave.

We turned the sleds around, which was easy to do now that we had lost so much of our load and were both used to harder, heavier work. We rarely rode the sleds now, but walked or pushed beside them. I was feeling guilty. *One helluva wonderful honeymoon I've thought up to start out life with this new wife.* Allie didn't complain, but still you could tell that she was feeling the strain. Once she told me, "I hate that big brute of a dog. Did you see him bite the good-looking gray one? That was rotten of him." When you hear someone seriously analyzing the characters of individual dogs in the team, you know they're really becoming a part of the whole game.

We gasped with relief when we finally saw the camp at Itiliakjuk after crossing the huge Andrew Gordon Bay. It used to be the custom to stop a sled before arriving at a camp and tidy up, take off your old working parka cover, and put on a clean one, take off your wind pants, if it was not blowing, brush back your hair, and go into camp looking neat and hardy. But there was none of that any more. We just wanted to get there. As we approached, the dogs were livelier, and everyone was out to greet us. Saggiak was the camp boss but he had apparently agreed that Osuitok would shake hands with us first and ask us to stay with him, which we did. It was the start of an everlasting friendship.

Everyone was worried about dog food. Most had none left and were hoping desperately that the wind would change and allow them to go out and hunt, which was their best hope of getting any food. It had been a hard, late winter with the wind blowing from the south, pressing loose ice from Hudson Strait against the coast, making seal hunting impossible.

Osuitok had traveled to the post at Cape Dorset to trade three foxes ten days earlier and said the hunting had been bad everywhere because of broken ice. He had traded, receiving cartridges, flour, sugar, and tea. His wife, Nipisa, seeing we were hungry, made us an unleavened bannock in her frying pan, using the last of the seal fat as lard. Normally that's a taste that takes you some time to appreciate, but Allie took to it right away and so, by God, did I!

Finally, with hot mugs of tea in our hands, we were able to lie back on the bed with them and admire the interior of their house. Osuitok and his wife had the neatest, most impressive tent igloo I had ever seen. It had canvas pinned to a light, wooden, inner frame that was protected by outer snow blocks. It was evenly warmed by a well-tended seal-oil lamp. Animal and bird drawings from the pages of ornithologist Dewey Soper's books had been carefully removed and pasted to the low ceiling so that one could lie in Osuitok's wide, family bed and look up and carefully study them. The warm hospitality of this compact dwelling included the small Tukakikaluk, who would escape his mother's hood and crawl naked and laughing across your chest in early morning. Allie and I were so impressed with them that I asked Osuitok if he would come and see me later after the hunting improved, and he agreed to do that.

We left Itiliakjuk to make our way slowly toward Kingait, or Cape Dorset. Some days when dog-team traveling, you could develop a kind of Arctic gloom that would keep you feeling low all day. On one such day late in our journey, I had never felt so cold in all my life. The air was still and the horizon shimmered, distorted through the mauve-gray fog that hung just above the sea ice. I sat on the sled mumbling to myself, looking at Allie on the other sled, and kicking my right skin boot against my left. Both feet had lost all feeling. Heaving myself off the sled, I walked and trotted in a half-hearted attempt to warm them.

Feeling the weight change behind him, Eisiak leapt off the grub box and, without looking back, rattled the trap chain, yelling threats at the dogs. None of us was in a good mood that day. We had worked too long and hard together and we were hungry. The extreme cold had taken hold of all of us, running its icy fingers through our layers of clothing.

If I suggested that Eisiak stop, I knew he would do so some time, but if I told him I thought my foot was frozen, he would stop instantly. We'd stopped before to check for frostbite, seen others do it, but in our case it had always been just a case of blue feet that would come back to life and turn pink again if exercised.

I tried to flex my toes as I hobbled along beside the sled, but my left foot had lost all feeling. I closed my eyes and imagined myself waking in a clean, white hospital room and looking down the bed and seeing the flat covers where my left foot should have been and calling to a nurse hysterically, "Where have the doctors put my foot?"

When we finally had gone as far as we could go that night, we made a snowhouse and got inside. I unrolled our sleeping bag. Both Allie and I pulled off our boots and examined our feet. Hell, my left foot wasn't white, it was only blue. In fifteen minutes, our four feet felt as if we had laid them in a fire to roast. That meant they were going to be fine. Sitting huddled too long on a sled, that gets you every time.

We calculated our rate of travel. With luck, we estimated, it would take us only one more sleep before we would arrive in Kingait.

The next day, as the weather cleared, we could see Kingait Mountain standing like a white-glazed loaf of bread in magnificent isolation. We knew that the fiord that protected the Hudson's Bay post at Cape Dorset lay just in front. But the weather played one last trick on us and pinned us down for an extra day. In the next camp, the people had nothing but were glad to offer us shelter, and we discovered a lot about the carving possibilities.

We set out once more with Simioni and his son, heading slowly for Kiaktok, the camp nearest to Cape Dorset. There we met a man we came to know as Pitseolak. (Years later, when the government began insisting that everyone have two names, we heard him called Peter Pitseolak. He, like many others, added his missionary-given name to his proper Inuit name to comply with the government rule.) Pitseolak welcomed our slow, bedraggled arrival with his usual warmth and took us in to visit him. He had flour and he supervised his wife, Agio, as she made two thick, pan-sized pancakes. The smell was so good it was unbearable. With a thin trickle of precious black molasses over each one the pancakes seemed like food fallen down from heaven. But there was nothing for the dogs.

I remember that Markosi, the five-year-old son of Pitseolak, did a wonderfully clever dance for us. He was the apple of his father's eye. Twenty-two years later, I hired Markosi for a film. By then he was a powerful figure of a young married man and he very success-fully played the wrestler in *The White Dawn*.

In the morning, we remustered our forces, pitiful as they were, and started west again on the last leg of our journey, walking by the nearly empty sleds instead of riding. Even the energy to do that, Allie and I agreed, came from the pancakes Pitseolak and his family had given to us.

When we turned into Kingait Bay and could see the distant red roofs of the post, I said, "Now the dogs will get food."

"No," Simioni said. "Look."

We could see a lone man walking, still far away from us.

"Who's that?" I asked.

"*Nivirti*, the trader," he answered, not using the usual name *angiukuk*, the boss. "He's coming to shake hands."

"Good," I said.

"Not good," Simioni said. "His dogs? Where are they? These dogs pulling our sled will be dead soon."

I shut up until we drew together. Allie and I and the drivers shook hands with Bob Griffith, the post manager at Kingait.

"Have you food for these dogs?" was my first question.

"You can turn them loose to lick the walls of our walrus shed," he told me. "It's empty. But I can give you and these two men with you some food."

I turned and looked at Simioni, but he said nothing.

We were taken into the post. The longest, hardest trip of our lives was over.

The post really did not have much food. We cooked a lot of dried spaghetti and split the contents of a large tin of bully beef, a food that had been haunting my mind for more than a week. We didn't have to sit up and eat politely. We had gone too far for that.

After eating, we walked down to the old Baffin Trading Company where our sleeping bags and packs had been tossed at our request. We slept, it seems to me, for about twenty-four hours, waking up only to step outdoors every once in a while, or to dip a pilot biscuit into coffee, before falling back into our downy sack.

We were awakened at one point by Eisiak. He said the wind had changed the ice and there was now open water off to the south side of Kingait Island. He asked if he could borrow my rifle and some cartridges because he wanted to go sealing with other hunters. Thinking of the miserable state of the dogs, I gladly lent them to him and went back to sleep. About six hours later, we heard a lot of screaming from the women and children. We went outside. Coming into the fiord, we could see two dog teams moving slowly.

"*Opinani*, no wonder," I said to a woman. "They're starving."

"No. Look at their bellies. Look at their heads all red with blood. Those dogs are going slowly because they've eaten too much. The men must have got all the seals that we've been hungry for."

That's how the long journey had come to an end. We each got on the Hudson's Bay Company fur bale scales and carefully adjusted the round weights. We weighed each other. In those days we had been lean to start with but still we had each lost more than ten kilograms, about twenty-two pounds, a lot no matter how you calculate it. And after the long sleep and much more food, we both felt better than we had before we left.

Allie had changed enormously on the trip. She had laughed sometimes and cried a little, but she had kept up. We had both sworn to each other during the last part of the trip that we would never, ever make another dog-team journey. But its hard parts started to fade in our minds. One day, an older woman named Ekilashusi, the wife of Parr, came and gave Allie two large red-bellied Arctic char, a fish that looks like a salmon but is *Sylvilanus alpinus*, a species of trout. When we were eating these and gasping over the delicious taste of the bright pink flesh, Allie said, "She brought these from Tessiuakjuak. It's the fish lake, just a day's dog-team traveling from here, I think."

I laughed and reminded her that she had said she was never going anywhere on a team again.

"Well, women have the right to change their minds." Allie smiled.

It was not long before we were running beside the puppies again. It all seemed totally different in the glorious glare of late spring sunshine.

22

The Ghost of Felix Conrad

The Baffin Trading Company, financed by Baring Brothers bank, had been boldly set up by James Cantley, a breakaway Scot who had been Special Assistant to the Fur Trade Commissioner of the Hudson's Bay Company. His new company lasted about ten poor fox years.

In Cape Dorset, both companies' small, rival trading posts stood five minutes' walk apart, with no other buildings for more than four hundred kilometers in any direction except an unused Oblate mission built in a valley hidden from the posts. The Oblates, having made no converts there, had departed.

Felix Conrad helped to build this little Baffin Trading Company house and store in one lowslung building, twenty-eight feet long and sixteen feet wide. It had one door and four windows, and was painted a shabby shade of green. Cold-weather insulation in the South was beginning to be used in those days, but it was almost non-existent in the Arctic. Felix stuffed the hollow space between his walls with tundra moss. It made a lovely nesting place for lemmings. I heard them scampering about at night when I lived there from time to time during the fifties. He also built into one wall a bottle of gin, which he forgot. We found it later when the house was taken down.

Felix Conrad was a man I never knew alive. He died violently at Cape Dorset during the winter of 1948, three years before I arrived there after our never-to-be-forgotten dog-team journey across Baffin Island. Conrad had been one of those restless, wandering, Arctic men whose life became impossibly entwined with Inuit living near him. For the most part the closeness between them was a good thing in the beginning, but it turned bad in the end.

When he died at Dorset, Felix Conrad was not buried in the ordinary place near local Inuit graves, but was set apart on a hill, not far from the narrow path that weaves its way into the next valley and then around the east side of Kingait Mountain. It was along that path that the other trader and local Inuit decided to put the stones on him.

Arctic grave

You cannot dig a grave on Kingait island. It's solid stone beneath the occasional layer of tundra moss. Burying people over ground is the only answer. Inuit construct a grave by piling heavy stones around and on top of the body. The stones keep animals away, and also "hold" the body down; it is believed that a well-weighted body usually cannot rise and walk around moaning, terrifying humans and dogs.

It was in autumn that Felix Conrad's final troubles came to him. Earlier that autumn, Conrad had made some wine of sugar, raisins, dried apricots, prunes, and local lingon berries, which he had had Inuit children gather. Such wines grow potent when aged beside a lantern with careful temperature control.

Felix Conrad also had in his store some tins of methyl hydrate. The tins had scarlet skulls and crossbones on the labels, and warnings in several languages against drinking the contents. The pungent alcohol, which is used to start Primus stoves, sends its ice-cold warning to your fingertips when you touch the can, but locals said that Felix Conrad ignored the deadly warning and used it to spike the wine. They say he died a noisy, thrashing death, lying halfway in and halfway out his door, a significant position in Inuit eyes.

Conrad's body was fearfully carried up the hill and the heavy stones were put upon him. Inuit have no special fear of the dead after they are properly weighted down. But Felix Conrad continued to make his presence felt for at least thirty years. Long after his death, many still doubted he had gone. Some said they could hear him screaming in that doorway on the darkest autumn nights.

When I lived in that little abandoned trading post, I could not seem to keep his door closed. Coming home at night or just at dawn, I'd find it standing ajar, the way it was, they say, the night he died. Inuit did not like to pass that door at night. I've often seen them make a wide detour around it. Other times, even when I did not see them, I'd observe the way their tracks in new, light snow looped out in wide arcs to avoid the house.

Inuit say that they have seen small lights moving inside the house when it was vacant and heard muffled grunts and groans and foreign words. I never experienced anything like that, but twice I found the tin of methyl hydrate that I used to prime my Primus stove tipped over on its side, empty, in the morning. This worried me, for I was always fearful of fire in that sagging, wooden house.

My Inuit neighbors admitted that they were afraid to enter that house unless they knew that I was there. Because I worried about the methyl hydrate overturning, I kept it outside, tightly capped and hidden beneath a stone. But I, myself, saw neither hide nor hair of Felix Conrad.

23
Hunting at the Floe Edge

We had one walrus floating and three seals lying in a row near the edge of the ice. By Inuit rules, all this meat must be cut up and cached or loaded on their sleds before going home. Hell, that would take forever! These hunters rarely rushed such work. They were hardier than white men, so easily given to trembling in the damp, night cold. Inuit prefer to proceed in a leisurely fashion, with good conversation and much resharpening of their homemade double–bladed knives.

Meat knife

I kicked my numb feet together. What a grand sight we were going to make much later, I forced myself to think, with our dog team red-headed and our meat piled on the sleds, moving heavy-laden along the frozen bay, with joyful women and children and dogs all watching us.

Revived by this image of success that I held in my mind's eye, I decided to leave the meat cutters and make the long walk into Kingait by myself. As I started away, Pingwarktok held up my heavy rifle and called, "Your rifle? Don't you want to take it?"

"*Ohomaitualuk*, too heavy," I answered.

Silence. I continued.

"*Nanook kapiashuk ungilatit?*" he shouted. "Bear, afraid of, you are not?"

"*Nanook!* Bear!" That word grabbed me. "Ooops!" I wheeled around, ran back and took the heavy rifle that Pingwarktok held out to me. *You're damned right,* I thought. *I am afraid of polar bears that aren't inside of zoos!*

A friend of mine told me an old story he had heard about a hunter who saw two sets of bear tracks in the snow and followed them until he came to an igloo of a different shape. The tracks led inside and the hunter could hear human sounds. Fearing to go in among such creatures, he cautiously climbed onto the igloo's outer wall and with his snowknife cut a small hole. Placing his eye to this hole, he could see not two, but six naked persons seated comfortably together on the sleeping bench.

How could this be? Then looking around the inside of the igloo, he saw six large, white, fur coats very neatly folded. That is how the hunter discovered that bears, and most of the other animals, can pull off their parkas just like humans.

When this man called out to these bears, they were so startled that they bumped into each other while they pulled on their clothes and chased him away.

24
Sharing

Sharing is one of the most basic words in Inuktitut. We like to use that word, but it seems to me that we rarely practice it to the extent that Inuit do.

When a boy kills his first bird or seal or caribou, his mother will carefully count the number of persons living in his camp, including, of course, the oldest widow and the newest infant. With help from a grandparent – if he still has one – the meat will be cut into exactly the appropriate number of pieces. He will not, however, be allowed to take a piece for himself.

This is a major celebration in the boy's life. The person he appoints – grandparent, father, or mother – will call out loudly until everyone in the camp has assembled. Then, announcing the purpose, that person will fling the pieces of meat high into the air. These witnesses who scramble for their rightful share will remember the message: *This boy has become a hunter among us. He has come of age. See, he takes not one bite for himself. He gladly shares his food with us.*

This may sound to you like some ancient, ritualistic celebration. It is not. Sharing fairly is one of the most important aspects of an Arctic hunting family's life.

I was in a boat when Lukta, then a young man just starting to be a carver, was the first to see a large polar bear running on the beach. Lukta shot it. This was his first bear taken and the men he was with numbered half a dozen. They had almost consumed the bear meat by the time their sea hunt ended and they returned to camp, so fairly distributing the meat was not an option. Lukta's mother, with her sharp, moon-shaped knife, helped her son divide the bear's hide into approximately three dozen square pieces. I could scarcely believe my eyes as this large, prime white skin that he could have traded to the Company for articles worth many dollars was instead divided equally among all those in his hunting camp. Useless? No, not quite. You could stand or kneel on this scrap of bearskin while waiting at a seal or fish hole. That made it a warm and useful gift.

The desire to be generous and share fairly with your neighbors is deeply ingrained in Inuit. How long will it take us to alter that, with polar bear skins selling now for five thousand dollars or more? My son, John, who lives around Inuit much more than I do these days, says that the reason so few will accept the concept of having and using a personal art agent in the South is not because they don't know that such an arrangement might bring them a good deal more money for their carvings or their prints. He thinks it is because of the traditional, close-fitting relationships between their neighbors and themselves. John feels that doing something entirely on your own is still considered unfitting behavior for an Inuit. If one from the camp succeeds, all should succeed, as with the all-important sharing of meat.

One good man we know is said to have a private bank account of a few thousand dollars in the South. John says that he and perhaps his neighbors still feel that hoarding money for yourself is doing something wrong.

The wonder of the Arctic is not in its physical vastness, but rather in its smallness, its intimacy. Persons, families living days' travel between each other, still consider themselves intimate, a part of an extended family willing to share everything with those almost distant, yet near neighbors.

I am not for a moment suggesting that these Inuit are superior people. I am only saying that I believe the situation that they have so long known has given them a greater compassion for each other and for all of us, and a ready willingness to share all they have in the name of survival. I felt myself so fortunate to have lived with Inuit when life and death were still perceived in such a fearless, open-minded way, open to all mankind and to the animals as well. What other people will ever even consider a life so closely bound with nature?

25

Arctic Inventions

I trust Inuit will be eager to study engineering, architecture, marine design, geographical survey. These are all subjects that have keenly interested them – something that was noted in the nineteenth century – and for which they seem to have a natural bent.

You may have heard of them carving various outboard engine parts in bone to replace a broken part, or making a set of teeth out of walrus ivory for themselves after their dental plate had broken, or shoeing the bottom of a peg leg with the handspan-sized boss of a muskox horn so the narrow leg would not drop them through spring snow. Old files in their hands become the best of knives. Our worn-out hand saws are shaped with hacksaws into a number of blades. It would take pages to describe their major innovations in housing and in clothing, but except for the parka and the kayak, which we ourselves have adopted, we continue to ignore Inuit inventive skills.

On many occasions, a man, through trade, would be able to buy a new rifle at the HBC. This was an important day in the life of a hunter who fed his family with his rifle. The first person I was aware of who did that was Kiaksuk. He was old and wise, and I wondered if his sight were failing. To test his new tool, he suggested I walk with some other hunters to the beach. In the Canadian army, I had taught a course in the latter part of World War II called "Shoot to Live" and Inuit soon realized that I had a lively interest in their shooting skills.

Kiaksuk pointed to a round, black baseball-shaped rock about two stone throws from shore. He opened his new box, twenty rounds of .300-caliber ammunition, and put one in the chamber. Looking back to make sure I was watching, he raised the rifle and fired. The bullet landed at the right range, but splashed into the water about fourteen inches to the left.

"Try again," I called to him.

"Why?" he asked. "I now know where it shoots. I'm not wanting to use up any more of this ammunition shooting at rocks."

"Yes," another hunter agreed, "that new rifle shoots just where that bullet landed."

"If you're sure," I said, "come up with me and I'll fix it for you. I'll move the front sight over so you'll hit the stone."

"I can hit the stone," he said, and reluctantly he put another precious bullet in the rifle. He aimed and fired. No splash this time. The bullet ricocheted off the rock and into the air.

"Good," I said, "but still I'll fix it for you."

"No need for that," he said. "I know where it shoots."

Kiaksuk got as much food with that rifle as any other hunter around there, but he never changed that sight. He just calculated the distance it was off and fired. No wasteful zeroing-in for him.

Inuit thought of rifles as tools, not for war or defense, but for the provision of family food. Hunters were always eager to examine any unfamiliar rifle I had. They usually found some virtue in these guns, but they also disapproved of some aspects.

"What?" I would ask them.

"Look at the size and roundness of this rear sight." They'd get you to agree it was like looking through a pile of rocks.

"Here," they'd volunteer, "if you've got a file, we'll flatten the sight off for you."

"Leave a little center nick," I'd say.

"Why? You don't need it. We don't use it. Just judge halfway along the flat. Then we'll flatten the top of that front sight for you and you can shoot over it."

"Why cut everything back here flat and make the front sight so narrow?"

"So you can see," they said. "If your lumpy back sight doesn't hide a seal head in the water, then your front sight will. Bring us a rifle."

The embarrassing part was that I tried their system a thousand times, and it worked marvelously.

Look at their craft of hunting, then and now. When I was first learning the art of offhand shooting from a boat, usually bobbing in the water, I was convinced that the object was to kill the seal. When I first was invited to shoot at a big one, a bearded seal at a considerable distance, my friends seemed glad that I had narrowly missed, scaring the seal, and congratulated me on my good shooting. The same round of congratulations ensued when I shot and missed the next time, prompting the seal to dive below the surface fast. The next shot, when I hit it in the head and killed it, I was overwhelmed with myself, but to my surprise my always cheerful hunting companions looked glum. We went over to the place where I had hit my seal. There was a patch of a little blood and grease in the water, but the seal was gone, sunk dead into water too deep for its retrieval.

Later, when another big seal's head appeared some way off, Pudlat approached me in the bow and put his hand on my rifle. "*Watciau*, later," he said. "*Takovitluk*." He pointed with his rifle barrel at the seal, then moved the barrel a finger's width in front of the seal. He fired. The bullet struck a hand span in front of the seal's nose. It ducked down under in fright.

"*Ajurnarmat*, it can't be helped," I said.

They started the small engine and hurried toward the spot where we had last seen the animal. A bearded seal is a powerful swimmer and can stay down for up to twenty minutes. But this seal that had purposely been given a fright had ducked under without having time to fill its lungs with air.

"Look all around," they told me. "He'll be up soon. Be careful not to hit him."

When the seal appeared again, I waited and saw another small-caliber bullet splash not far from its head. The seal quickly ducked again and we moved in closer to it.

Now it was coming over me. This was a complicated business. In the early part of this endeavor, the worst thing you could do was actually hit the seal, which I had done.

When the animal appeared again, its back was floating high. It needed air. But nobody fired. We used the time to move in as close as possible. The seal rolled and Pudlat, who had taken up a heavy-caliber rifle, shot the seal behind the lungs. It wasn't down too long before it reappeared. This time we could see that it was in no hurry to go down. The harpooner took up his harpoon and sealskin float. Driving the harpoon head into the animal, he flung in the float that would mark its last underwater journey. When it next appeared, someone quickly shot it in the head. Now the dead air rushed out of its lungs and it sank. But we were able to drag it up from the depths. By butchering it skillfully in the water, we were able to haul all of it, piece by piece, into the boat. It weighed as much as a good-sized buffalo, its body was that size. And we used it all – hide, fat, and meat.

How many other age-old methods could I learn from these

people? Take mirages, for example. You've seen them shimmering in the summer heat above a highway. You might not have tried to read them. Inuit would look at them like a map. Look closely. A heat mirage above the road will probably show you the next highway cut-off. Inuit have learned how to see the path that will guide them through packed ice when all that seems visible is an impenetrable barrier of ice.

By way of contrast, some of our inventions have not been a roaring success in the North. For example, one of the Hudson's Bay Company's twentieth-century inventions was a boot softener, an English chewing device they had designed to masticate and soften Inuit skin boots. This mechanical chewer was cleverly built of the finest Sheffield steel. It was meant to free hunters' wives from the age-old task of chewing the boots. The invention, in the manner of da Vinci, proved, however, to have one slight drawback. When the crank handle was turned and iron teeth came together, instead of softening the soles, they actually ate the boots and spat them out in little pieces.

26
Inuit Myths and Legends

Inuit myths and legends are usually short, dramatic forms dealing with the wonders of the islands of the sea, the sky, or of birth, love, old age, hunting and sharing of food, polygamy, rape, murder, incest, infanticide, death, and the dreamlike mysteries of an afterlife. Even in recent times, Inuit storytellers will sometimes remodel old myths and update legends to accommodate trade goods, rifles, radio signals, airplanes, and satellite TV, still subtly disguising the true identities of the neighboring family members once involved.

Inuit myths are rarely simple, and usually lacking the details we would need in order to understand them. Inuit have long believed that they have a close, mystical relationship with all of nature, and that the animals have the power to hear and understand the words of humans. For this reason, hunters in their camps, when singing or speaking of walrus or seal, speak softly and may carefully refer to them as maggots or lice, or call caribou lemmings, thus soothing the animals that are the object of the hunt, those essential for Inuit survival.

Until modern times, Inuit agreed that there were other worlds beneath the sea, inside the earth, and in the sky where a gifted *angakuk* (a shaman, either male or female) had the power to journey in trances and in dreams, visiting places that ordinary mortals would only experience in an afterlife.

Dreams have always played an important part in their lives, and are interpreted with care. Dreams of white bears are said to have sexual overtones. Dreams of weasels suggest troubles. Bird dreams forewarn of blizzards, and on and on.

Some Inuit myths are thought-provoking in any language. One says that all white men are descended from dog children and only through that litter are they related to Inuit.

A story may take three nights to tell, since relaxed time is not measured and rushed by them. Among the most famous of the vast array of myths is the one that concerns the sea goddess who has various names – Sedna, Nuliayuk, Taluliyuk. The heart of this story tells of the father, with other hunters, going in an *umiak* and taking his daughter with them: On their way back to their summer hunting bay, a huge storm rose and the boatmen feared that the overloaded boat would be swamped and sunk by waves. They decided they had to lighten the load to save their lives. They threw overboard first their whole catch of meat and then the daughter. When she tried to climb back into the boat, her father cut off her fingers. These became all the seals in the sea. She tried to grab the boat again and he cut off her hands, and they turned into all the walrus. She made one last attempt to save herself and he cut off her forearms, which became the whales of all the oceans. After that, she sank into the depths and became the famous goddess – that half woman, half seal – who tends her lamp beneath the sea. It is she who controls all the creatures that live in the sea. Many songs are sung to this powerful goddess.

Traditionally, as each new season begins, a piece of liver of the first killed sea mammal would be returned to her in the water, in the hope that Sedna would release her creatures to the hunters so that they might feed their families.

Many societies, like the Inuit, wish to preserve their history through myths and legends. Sometimes these are small, tight-knit societies where everybody knows his neighbors well and is often related to them. This closeness means that to repeat the true tale of a wife-stealing or a murder within a nomadic group would not only fail to be acceptable, it would be downright dangerous. But by transforming one's enemies into frightful, mythical beasts, and family members into much more likeable creatures, even unknown humans, the storyteller and his story might thus travel safely into folklore.

Carvings, lamps, and pots may be lost and frozen in the permafrost for countless centuries. But the ancient stories, songs, and dances of the Inuit become extinct the moment the last person who could remember them dies.

27
Pootoogook

Pootoogook, who became the unofficial leader of the *Sikusalingmiut* – the people who live near the ripped opening in the ice – was a man of great distinction. I believe he was fortunate to have been born in the eastern Arctic, for if he had appeared further to the south, in his time he would probably have been little more than the head of one of North America's larger business corporations. As it was, his was much more the role of some ancient king.

Pootoogook, propped up on one elbow on a sheaf of coffee-colored caribou hides, resting in his large summer tent with the golden light spread across its smoothly curried gravel floor, looked like some great khan, a ruler out of China's western deserts. His face was deeply tanned from the spring and summer sun reflected off the ice, his cheekbones wide and round as goose eggs, his face all powerful. His dark eyes were drawn and hooded, with a fatty fold that protected them. His nose was small, his mouth expressive. With the slightest twitch, it could express disapproval or affection. Those near him always paid attention, stayed alert. They were always watchful, careful of his moods.

His parents had been born in the Ungava region of Arctic Quebec and had migrated around the coast to Sugluk, now called Salluit, before they crossed the strait at the turn of the century. Pootoogook's elders had chosen to travel that way, taking nearly a year, it is said, so they could encourage their strongest man to challenge in a wrestling match the most powerful man at Sugluk. These influential families who had traveled so far from their Ungava home admit their man lost.

The crossing itself had occurred when Pootoogook was a young man. They island-hopped across the ice-strewn strait. Several older persons whom I knew had been born on Tugjuk, Nottingham Island, in the course of their dangerous crossing. The women rowed an *umiak* flotilla of perhaps half a dozen women's boats, filled with old people, children, and dogs, and surrounded by hunters in their kayaks. Pootoogook's people, immigrants to west Baffin Island, soon mixed and married with the *Sikusalingmiut*, the people who live near *polynyas*, lakelike tidal holes ripped and kept open in the winter ice. These days they are called *Kingaimiut*, the people living near the mountain. Pootoogook's Ungava people were particularly clever at catching white foxes, an art that the Baffin Islanders scarcely knew, for in their lives a fox pelt had been considered largely useless.

When he was a young man, Pootoogook fell on an ice-slick deck and was plunged into frigid water. Until that very moment, Pootoogook said, he had believed in the practices of shamanism, in spite of the fact that he had met Canon Shepherd, a missionary from Britain who had occasionally visited west Baffin Island by dog team from Lake Harbour in the late 1920s. While he was struggling underwater and feared that he would lose his life, Pootoogook swore that if he lived, he would become a Christian. When he rose to the surface, he was hauled from the freezing water by his hunting companions. Pootoogook says he went forward with his promise and was baptized by Canon Shepherd during his next visit to the nomadic camps along that coast.

West Baffin did not have a Protestant missionary until the mid-1950s. Pootoogook felt that this was because there was no church. So, after a good lemming year followed by a great fox year, he undertook to order the materials, then organized and paid for the building of the church himself. The building was erected by Inuit under his close supervision during my time there.

I remember going out on the autumn walrus hunt on Pootoogook's boat, *Ivik*, with Paulassi and Pudlat, two of his sons, and their crew of three. The other brothers and our friends were up on the church roof, finishing the framing. We were away for approximately eight days during which time an autumn storm swept over us. When we returned with a full load of walrus, I remember the ground was white with snow and to our horror, the church had totally disappeared!

"What happened?" we asked when a canoe came out to meet us.

"*Anowayaluk!* A big wind came and tore it to pieces!" they said.

But Pootoogook had everyone out that day gathering the precious lumber that lay scattered across the hills and washed ashore on Malik Island. Using rocks as anvils, they straightened every nail and rebuilt the church.

Pootoogook was a man of enormous determination. In times of hunger, he used his walrus caches to feed other, less successful neighboring camps or sent his dog teams out with meat to share with distant people. He was, in the best sense, the government on west Baffin Island. He ran his own relief program. Pootoogook was a powerful man in spite of the fact that he had never used or understood money.

Pootoogook had three extremely interesting brothers and together they have fathered a large, extended family that has followed after them. Pootoogook's eldest son, Salomonie Inukjuakjuk, adopted me, Saomik, the Left-Handed, and my wife, Allie, Arnakotak, the Long Woman, as his brother and sister, an act which we considered a tremendous honor.

28

A Traveling Show

In mid-August, 1951, the government icebreaker, the C.D. Howe, arrived on its annual Eastern Arctic Patrol. Allie and I packed up, leaped eagerly aboard, signed on as crew under Captain Chouinard – no ordinary passengers allowed – and headed off to other Baffin Island posts.

Our first stop was Kingmerok, where we showed off a small display of the better carvings and crafts. We had gathered together a variety of carvings from different eastern Arctic regions, including some Ungava-type baskets and some sewn skin appliqués. We carefully arranged these on a piece of sailcloth on the counter of the Hudson's Bay Store. During the course of the day, we would observe that every Inuit, young and old, who had gathered for ship-time, came in to see this unheard-of exhibition of Canadian Inuit arts and crafts – not once, but often twice!

We had learned that purchasing untanned sealskins or feathered items presented real problems. Ivory, anyone could see, would soon become as unacceptable as selling elephant tusks or rhino horns. We showed examples of some flat, incised stone blocks and of scraped sealskin appliqués, which I now see as the original indication that printmaking would be the logical next step to follow, though I did not recognize it at that time.

These remarkable unschooled artists had the hunter's ability to observe the animals and humans around them and to capture the essence of their movements. Human beings have been doing this for countless thousands of years, but in the last half of this century the Inuit are clearly the masters of the art.

Pangnirtung, before Iqaluit grew out of Frobisher Bay in more recent times, used to be the largest settlement in the eastern or central Arctic because it was a famous old center for the Scottish whalers and, later, because it had a small hospital and the only doctor in that vast territory. When the C.D. Howe anchored there, all of us aboard were impressed by its handsome setting among the snow-laced blue mountains in the wide, deep Pangnirtung Fiord.

Summer tent

We once again displayed our carvings and there was great interest shown by Inuit viewing them. Unfortunately, Pangnirtung, even in ancient times, used to import its stone for lamps by trading with their Inuit neighbors living to the north. But we especially noted to the Guild that the women of Pangnirtung were skillful at designing and sewing decorations on their clothing.

Clyde River, our next stop, had relatively few families living there. They did have good stone, but there was little evidence of carving, although they examined every item in our small display with interest. I remember watching a skin kayak coming out to greet the ship, its paddler fully dressed in handsome sealskin. Many people photographed this traditional arrival, but were surprised to see when he came aboard that the man in sealskin was Gabriel Gely, a Parisien, a sometimes painter, and more often a chef at the Department of Transport weather station there. Gabriel was, and still is, a person with a passion for the Arctic. I will tell you something very un-French, and especially un-Parisien, about him later.

Pond Inlet is on Lancaster Sound and offers the true entrance to the long-sought Northwest Passage. There you have a perfect view of Bylot Island because of the clear air and flattening effect near the top of the world which makes this mountainous, snow-clad beauty forty kilometers, or about twenty-five miles, away appear so close you feel that you could reach out and touch it.

At Arctic Bay the local Inuit paid great attention to our exhibition of stone pieces, as did the HBC man, our friend Irving Gardner, who had been posted there. We heard that near Arctic Bay there was good lamp stone, *ukusiiksuk*, easily available, but we did not get many carvings in the first few years, although Arctic Bay later proved to have some important sculptors.

Having done our best to spread the idea of trading carvings, we started the long voyage south down the Labrador coast into the sweet perfume of pine trees along the St. Lawrence River to Montreal. There we pitched in to help arrange a wonderful exhibition held in the Guild's gallery. On opening night, before anyone came in, there was a long queue down Peel Street that curled around the block.

29
Chimo '52

When we returned from a different kind of winter visit to Mexico in the spring of 1952, we flew straight back into the Arctic, this time through Montreal into Fort Chimo, now called Kuujjuaq, near the river's mouth that flows north into Ungava Bay. We stayed at the old Anglican mission house off by itself about a twenty-minute walk along the riverbank.

It had been suggested by the Guild that I might try purchasing both Inuit and Nascopi Indian arts or crafts there, since the two groups, though separated, used the same store to trade fur. We did purchase some Inuit carvings there, but we were overwhelmed by the eagerness the Nascopi showed in creating and trading the various uniquely different articles they made. Caribou skin drums, rattles, berry boxes, wooden ladles, paddles – all of these they usually painted with their traditional double-curved motifs and dot designs, as well as with images of birds, fish, animals, and humans. In total, it represented a lively folk art from these inland hunting people who had depended entirely on caribou, fish, and birds, then finally the fur trade, until the inland posts were closed and the people came out to live on the coast near Chimo or south to Schefferville.

Nascopi wooden ladle

An event that I shall never forget occurred in Chimo on the wide Koksoak River one cold spring day when the river ice had just broken and was flowing north in great chunks to spread out over Ungava Bay. An Inuk woman I knew shouted to me, pointing out to mid-river, where I could see an upturned canoe and two heads bobbing in the water.

"They just went over! I saw them go," she screamed.

I ran for help. We organized a local boat with an outboard engine and it put out fast, weaving through the drifting pans of soggy ice.

"They were at the old base picking up some lumber that the military had thrown away. They tried to bring too big a load. I saw the ice upset them," she told me as we anxiously watched one man struggling desperately to climb on top of the canoe. I could only see the other person's head as he clung to the stern.

Our rescue boat reached them, and I watched the survivors being hauled inboard and the canoe uprighted and taken in tow. Both boats came weaving through the ice to where we waited on the eastern shore of the river.

A very old man was sitting hunched in the boat with someone's parka wrapped around him, shuddering violently, gray in the face from cold and shock. His name was Natawapio. I did not recognize his boatmate, a young Nascopi in his twenties; he was sodden wet, with silverish frost gathered on his hair and clothing, but he seemed cheerful and alert. As the boat grounded on the river's edge, the young man hopped out of the boat into knee-deep water, took several paces toward us, then collapsed face down.

Two of us rushed in and hauled him in to shore. I knelt astride him and started pumping on his rib cage, using a method I'd seen illustrated in a first-aid book. The nurse ran from the nursing station, but said she'd never done resuscitation and felt she wasn't strong enough. She asked me to go on with it. For forty minutes I tried desperately to get him breathing, and I felt heartsick when my efforts failed. We rolled him over and checked him every way we could. The nurse determined that he was dead.

Natawapio, by that time, was swathed in several blankets and had a mug of tea. He refused to be taken back to his tent until he heard the condition of his nephew who, by the old man's account, had urged Natawapio to climb up and lie on top of the overturned vessel, while the young Nascopi had continued to hang down in the freezing water, steadying the canoe.

We wrapped the body in a blanket and his friends bore him away to his family tent where we could hear his female relatives start their mournful screaming.

To warm his heart, Allie gave the old man two long gulps of the cognac she had taken from our medical box, the first having been intended for him and the other for his now departed relative. It was a belief of the Nascopi that a shade of the dead, especially if death occurred by drowning, would linger near the campsite for some days and nights before going only slowly, perhaps reluctantly, into the other world.

We were both surprised to see old Natawapio coming slowly toward us along the river path next day. He waved a newly carved print rocker at me that he wanted to trade.

Print Rocker

When I had written out his payment slip to be traded at the Hudson's Bay post, he told me through another young relative who had come to support him that he still felt cold and not quite right, but that he thought he could take two more shots of cognac – one for himself and one for the shade of his nephew. He said that should put both of them in good order again.

An Inuit song goes:

> Ayii, ayii.
> Cold and mosquitoes,
> Mosquitoes and cold.
> Thankful are we
> That these two plagues
> Come never together!
> Ayii, ayii.

I believe with all my heart that I shall never again encounter mosquitoes in such determined hordes as those at Fort Chimo! Mosquitoes in the far north on a still evening are more serious than ones in southern Canada or New England. It is not just their size that most travelers like to talk about, the difference is in their suicidal determination. Arctic and sub-Arctic mosquitoes don't try to evade your hand when in a single sweep you kill hundreds off your parka. They are willing to die for just one sip of you!

We departed from Fort Chimo on our way north again in mid-July. The government had arranged a Norseman charter to fly us north to Payne Bay on the west coast of Ungava near Akpatok Island. We flew over Leif Bay, not so far away, where Rachel Carson first predicted, from Washington D.C., the highest tide in the world, over fifty-five feet or about seventeen meters. Then the Dominion hydrographers actually recorded it.

At Payne Bay at that time the tide was wrong for a landing in the river, so the pilot had to leave us on an island not far from the post. Like most other Arctic pilots, he didn't trust the weather; he was in one helluva hurry to go south again. We sat with our gear on the island and watched the Norseman dip down and noisily circle the post to signal our arrival. There, we thought, that will wake them up. They'll come and get us now.

Nothing happened.

The mosquitoes were bad, but not quite as bad as Chimo, if you kept waving a bandanna in front of your face, the only exposed area of your body, and even that deeply buried in your parka's fur-trimmed hood. Every now and then we'd give each other a direct and powerful burst of DDT spray straight into the face from a handy can we'd purchased for this purpose. "There," we'd say, "that ought to teach the little bastards a lesson!" That was the standard way of thinking in mosquito country. People did not have the negative attitude toward a direct application of DDT spray up the nose that they do today.

It was a clear, summer night that had no intention of getting dark. But for a long time, there was no sign of life at all around the post. Finally, we saw a canoe put out from the cove, paddling vigorously toward the two of us. Before it landed on the island, we realized that it was powered by four Inuit women, paddling strongly against the rising tide that was entering the river. We didn't have much gear, but what we did have they encouraged us to cache on the highest rocks. We climbed into the canoe and went zinging back to the post on the tide. Inuit women are strong paddlers and used to boats, and they often tended nets, but in those days they never worked an outboard motor.

All the men from Payne Bay, including Sam Ford, the Labradorian HBC manager there, were off on their annual walrus hunt on a rock near Akpatok Island. We moved into the post until the hunters returned a few days later. Checking the local carving situation, I found that there was little carving in stone, and I wasn't interested in new, green walrus ivory.

We heard on the Company radio that the government advised us to try and find transport to connect with our old friend, the icebreaker *C.D. Howe*. The message said they would be prepared to pick us up near a place called Cape Hope's Advance, a name given to that point in the sixteenth century by explorers in their long search for a Northwest Passage to the Orient.

The Peterhead we were able to hire from somewhere along the coast was the dirtiest boat that I had ever been near. It had come off a walrus hunt, with no time for scrubbing down its deck or hold. The smell aboard was overpowering, but we had no other choice. We said goodbye to Ford and the Inuit gathered there, and headed north, holding our breath.

The eligible-looking girl traveling with us to her family camp shared the small fo'c's'le on our way to Cape Hope's Advance. She certainly seemed to pay for her trip that night, poor dear, being required to go out on deck and back again I don't know how many times. In early morning, I crawled out of the reeking fo'c's'le and breathed deeply. It was a clear blue, summer morning and there before us, not a kilometer away, was the government icebreaker, huge and clean, reflecting its image in the icy stillness of the waters. Our friend, the captain, let out a welcome *hoot-hoot* on the ship's horn.

It felt good to climb the swaying ladder and sign on again as crew. We showered thoroughly and changed our clothes before we had breakfast at a table surrounded by friends.

When we arrived at Kingait, we had the feeling of coming home. From the moment we stepped off the icebreaker, we were with Inuit again: the old people, the hunters and their wives, the teenagers, the children and the infants in their mothers' hoods. They crowded around us, making us feel welcome. We were soon wildly busy making sure our few treasured possessions got safely ashore, most especially the material for our double-walled tent, which I hoped would work for us in a nomadic way during our journeys to the camps in the coming winter.

30
A Family Divided

In the morning, there was a dusting of new snow on Kingait's sheltering granite shoulders, and the waters of the fiord lay still as ice. The tide was out and on the wide, dark, tidal beach a little knot of

Inuit – a man, a woman, and some children – had gathered. The woman wore her best white *amautik* cover. I walked toward them, wondering why they waited there.

Saggiak, a fifty-year-old hunter, turned to look at me. He was almost the only outsider who, in recent times, had come from across the strait at Sugluk with the Baffin Trading Company. I could hardly understand his words. He was pale and red-eyed, for he had been crying. "She's going," he said, reaching out and touching his wife, Liisii, on the shoulder. "They say she's got to leave on the ship and die outside in the hospital. I'll never see her again."

His wife's face was helpless as she clutched her two young children to her. Her son, who was twelve, looked out to sea so I would not see that he was crying.

"She'll be all right. Your mother will be back," I answered awkwardly. "She'll get better."

"Do you know that?" Saggiak, her husband, asked me.

"No," I admitted.

They were silent.

"Without her," he said, "how can I take care of our children?"

"Other women will help with them," I said, but I could not bring myself to look at the very small girl who clutched her mother's hand.

"My wife says she wants to stay and die here in her own country with me . . . and our own children."

"She can't," I told him. "She may make them sick . . . and you as well, and maybe others." I had to turn my head away so he wouldn't see my face.

Saggiak stepped closer to me and whispered, "Saomik, can you give me some cigarettes for her?"

I took a whole new package out of my pocket and gave them to him. He didn't take one, but put the package into his wife's hand. She had never had a whole package of cigarettes in her life. She started crying. She tore the package open, shaking them out like long, white bullets, trying to give her husband half of them and some back to me. But he pressed them to her. It was the only thing he had to give her.

Saggiak looked at me as though he were going to be sick. Then he took her bravely by the shoulder and started walking her toward the barge that was collecting the other *Sikusalingmiut* whose chest X-rays had shown a problem. *Oh, God,* I thought, *there she goes, frightened and alone, to a land jammed full of cigarettes.*

On the barge, Saggiak's wife stood among a knot of seamen, her long-tailed, white parka cover standing out against their drab hip boots and work clothes. The flat, iron barge began to move. Behind it two long, silver ripples spread out in a perfect V as it headed toward the ship, leaving the cold, glassy waters to think of nothing but becoming ice.

I looked away, finding it unbearable to watch her leaving, staring back at us as Saggiak picked up their little girl, who was starting to cry. *God, help her to find her way back here to him,* I thought, *and to their two children.*

We waited together among the tide-blackened rocks until we heard the loud squealing of the ship's crane cables lifting the barge on board. Then I went to help organize the freight.

Quite a long time later, I looked down the beach. Saggiak and the two children were still standing at the tide's edge, staring at the place where the once-a-year icebreaker had taken the greatest thing in his life and disappeared.

Liisii was away in hospital for several years but finally she came back, cured, to that same beach. Inuit did not believe in any of our expansive emotional public displays. The husband and wife formally shook hands, then Liisii placed her arm on the shoulder of her daughter, Eva, who had grown much taller. They walked slowly back to the tent where they would live until they all returned to Itiliakjuk, Saggiak's winter camp, their home.

31
A Journey to Hell

Pingwarktok related his experience of being taken out to hospital. His story told of his first ship's journey, and his first big car ride, which was in a station wagon with a woman driver. He said he had no idea how to get in or to use the back seat. He knelt on the floor. He spoke of his terror of the complications of being admitted to hospital. He told me of the horror on that first, rainy night when he saw strange car lights racing in through the slatted window blinds, and apparently hanging beside his bed. He remembered his awful start when a bright electric light above him flashed on and there stood someone with a pale, sad face, dressed in long, black, flowing robes with a while cowl around the face. Pingwarktok hid his face, he says, fearful that he had died and was entering another world. And in a way, he was.

That was back in the terrible days when it seemed that tuberculosis might wipe out the country's entire Inuit population. Sanitariums were being built around the world when suddenly the new wonder drug was discovered and they fell empty. Tuberculosis almost disappeared, though some say that affliction is reappearing in the South today.

Pingwarktok was one of the lucky ones, like Liisii. He was hospitalized and survived to return to Kingait, to tell the tale.

32
Clouds

Nuvujuak, a name meaning giant clouds, was the most northern area inhabited by the *Sikusalingmiut* during the fifties. I was doubly anxious to go up there because I had recently seen a few splendid stone carvings that had come down from the camp at Nuuata and I was always on the lookout for any hint of new carving stone deposits. The trip north, if I hoped to find and transport stone, would have to occur by boat in summer. But the heavy drift ice was incredibly slow in clearing from Foxe Basin and did not really do so until the end of August.

I made arrangements to go north in Pootoogook's Peterhead, *Ivik*, with Osuchiak as his pilot, and his sons, Pudlat, and Paulassi, with Munamee as crew. Allie was eager to join us. I supplied two drums of gasoline, but Pootoogook, a frugal man, had instructed his crew to save it and use sail whenever possible. It was not a hunting expedition, except to take a few seals for family consumption.

At the end of our first day out, we ran in and anchored in a place Inuit called Schooner Harbour, although it was unusual for them to use a foreign word. On shore, we could see the ruins of a stone house, long, low, and fairly well built, though one end was already frost-heaved and beginning to tumble down. Inside the house, there was nothing. Originally, this low building, which looked like an old Scottish croft, must have had ship's timber roof-beams, probably covered with seal hides or with sail canvas, held down and weather-proofed with sods of tundra moss. Wood being of incredible rarity in that country, every speck of it would have been removed to make harpoon shafts, sleds, kayak and tent frames, snow beaters, sun goggles, even wound pins used to keep blood in animals. An oceanographer once told me that because of the drift and slowly rotating mass of polar ice, the incredibly small amount of driftwood that occasionally reached the Baffin coast came not from our South, but from Russian rivers draining into their side of the Arctic Ocean.

Snow beater

This whaler's house was built, Pudlat told me, because some American hunters pulled into the harbor to hunt caribou and take fresh water. During their brief stay, a hard freeze caught their schooner and froze it into the ice, forcing them to remain in that harbor over the winter. During that late autumn, they worked hard, according to an Inuit story handed down, and built the house. The Americans explained to Inuit hunters that they felt sure that the moving ice in spring would crush their vessel. Their fears were groundless. The hunters assured them that the harbor ice would rot out slowly during summer and safely free the schooner – which is exactly what it did.

Early the following morning, we hauled up anchor and left the stone house, wondering if it would fall down soon or, like the ancient Viking church at Hvalsey on west Greenland, look the same in a thousand years. Allie said she felt sure it would last forever.

That evening, we anchored in the lee of a point of land called Inuksuksalik, the place of human likenesses. There are a couple of stories about this place and why such a large concentration of these *inuksuk*, stone figures, exist in that place. Both legends may possibly be correct. One has it that these figures mark the nearest point on Baffin Island from which to depart on a sea crossing of 125 kilometers, about eighty miles, to Seahorse Point on Southampton Island, a famous walrus hunting place. This ancient crossing was made in sealskin *umiaks* and kayaks in summer, whole families running the risk of being caught in ice and carried south into central Hudson Bay where they would have had only the slimmest chance of survival.

Another guess is that this group of fairly modest-sized stone figures, arranged like objects in a sculpture garden, was erected as a way to kill time or as an artistic competition, or a feat of strength, among hunters and their sons. While waiting for favorable wind and ice conditions, they could range out to select and carry in suitable stones to build the humanlike statues.

What is certain is that it is a famous spot in the North, a sort of Stonehenge. Charles Gimpel, Director of Gimpel Fils in London, made an art pilgrimage there with Terry Ryan in the mid-sixties when snowmobiles had started to appear in the country. I know that when we encountered the figures in the silent immensity of an Arctic summer sunset, it was a sight I shall never forget.

Our journey north was uneventful except that we ate herring gulls that the hunters shot out of the air with .22-caliber rifles. You learn all sorts of tricks when you travel with Inuit. Pudlat was quick to point out that one mustn't shoot the white- and gray-feathered adult birds, but only the younger, brown ones born that spring. They were nearly as large as their parents, but more tender. I found them just as tasty as chicken. I think southern folks from places like Toronto, New York, Vancouver should know these things. There's no telling when this so-called civilized life may run out on us, and you might desperately need a similar trick or two. I should also mention that I learned from Inuit that a neck artery cut in a freshly killed seal will fill a pot with rich blood. Allie agreed one didn't need to fool around with onions or any other seasoning. Blood heated to a boil turns into a rich brown gravy. I swear it is as good as any soup I've ever tasted, even in France's three-star restaurants.

We anchored near the camp at Nuvujuak and were greeted by a short, dynamic man named Sarki. He, his fellow hunters, and their families lived in that camp, the most remote one trading into Dorset. We were shown the stone deposit at Nuuata, and left it there for that camp's use. From that stone these northerners traditionally made their seal-oil lamps and pots, and small figures to accompany them.

It is said that a stone lamp or pot has no soul to help it endure rough sled travel, and so the carver of the lamp should make a small figure of some animal, bird, fish, or human to give the lamp both soul and strength. This small stone figure is then tossed away, for it has done its job. There is another strange thing said about amulets, the shamanistic charms many people wear. It is believed that if you lose them somewhere, no matter how far away, they will keep on working for you just as readily as if you had them strung around your neck.

Some of the Nuuata family tents were shaped with an extended entrance passage. This was to make the living and storage space larger and to keep out winds. It was a bright, useful place for women to sit and sew without being attacked by the mosquitoes, and for small children to play under the watchful eye of their mothers and older sisters. All of their dogs were usually put out on an island for the summer, a time when they were not needed and only occasionally fed. They were expected to fish for themselves to find something to eat in the tidal shallows. The teams grew lean on this diet, but they could be built up after the autumn walrus hunt, before the serious blizzards began and dog-team traveling was once more vital to the families' survival.

A wind came up, blowing the whole sky clear, chasing in freezing air before it died in the evening light. We anchored in the lee of Wild Bird Island, never dreaming then that not far north of us lay an immense, uncharted island, perhaps the last major island to be discovered in this world. Pilots had probably flown over it during World War II, but in the winter it had been hidden from them by snow. Later, Bill Baldwin, a Canadian geographer and an old regimental friend of mine, came up and stayed with us, then took off with Inuit in their old twenty-two-foot trap boat and successfully reached the island by weaving through the moving ice. They found evidence in the form of ancient stone tent rings that Inuit families had lived there long before. My suggestion at the time of the royal wedding was that Prince Charles and Diana, Princess of Wales might find plenty of excitement on this large, almost unknown island that was named Prince Charles Island in his honor. Later, when I saw the summer ice amassed in the Foxe Basin surrounding that forbidden place, I felt it was fortunate they had not taken up that invitation.

Next morning, when we heard a long creaking sound that ended with an explosion as loud as a heavy rifle, I thrust my head out of the Peterhead's fo'c's'le and saw new ice spread smoothly all around us, reaching out toward the western horizon as far as the eye could see, while on the other side the ice clung tightly to shore.

Pudlat climbed out of the engine housing and down over the side. Then, holding on to the boat's side, he skated on his smooth skin boots all around the Peterhead. He stamped hard with both feet. The ice was thick. The morning was clear, windless and stinging cold. It brought up an image of that American whaler's topsail schooner long ago trapped in its harbor for the winter. Could this be final? Could our boat be trapped here for the winter? No dogs, no sled, no meat caches. No radio – receiver or transmitter – nothing.

*Peterhead boat
with canoe*

The three Inuit aboard looked at the ice and grimaced. Allie pumped up our small Primus stove and made tea. We shared some sea biscuits with seal meat while we stared at the endless gray expanse of ice that was beginning to glow and soften along the late morning's bleary path of sunlight.

I climbed down onto the ice, this time with Pudlat, as he began to chop at the ice edge near the hull with a long-handled chisel. The ice had softened somewhat and began to break more easily. He pointed at the sun. "Later, it will get us out of here."

We were delighted when we started the engine and began chopping down hard from the bow with our two chisels. Soon the ice was softening, breaking – whole, huge sheets of it sliding up on top of one another like playing cards as we forced our passage southward. Finally, we were free of it and started toward home.

The more frightening things appear to be, the greater your exhilaration once you've escaped and you are free. I'm not sure that it's bad to live a part of your life on the dangerous side. It makes you realize how absolutely worthwhile a more sensible life can be.

33
The Costume Contest

During my nine years in Cape Dorset, I had only two upsets, both with the same man. Those were with Pitseolak (later Peter Pitseolak, when the Government decided that everyone had to have at least two names. Allie and I had first met him when he fed us on our long trip to Cape Dorset). He was a wonderful person in so many ways, but he could sometimes be absolutely unreasonable, for he had a flaring temper. Pitseolak was, I think, west Baffin Island's foremost historian. He knew about everything – the scandals, the myths, the legends, and the songs. He had, even in those days, become a heavy man, which was, as in China, a mark of grandeur and distinction. He was still a wonderfully graceful dancer.

Almost the first project given me by the old Federal Department of Mines and Resources, who governed the Northwest Territories from Ottawa, was to see what could be done with sealskins. The market prices for Atlantic hair sealskins had plummeted drastically by 1950. They were out of style in the world of fashion and the Company was paying only twenty-five cents apiece for them. The skins made splendidly handsome, weatherproof, Arctic clothing, but sealskins had also fallen somewhat out of style among the Inuit; as parka covers they were being swiftly replaced by canvas sailcloth that wives made impressive with multicolored trim.

The government had suggested that I hold a contest and give several prizes, for the best sealskin pants, parka, mitts, and boots. For centuries, this had been the traditional Inuit eastern Arctic garb. To our surprise, only the family of Peter Pitseolak and his son and another almost unknown and very humble family took part in the contest.

We gathered on the given day in the newly built, one-room, federal day school, which was about the size of a double garage. Pitseolak and his handsome son, Asevak, appeared sensationally dressed in new, knee-high sealskin boots, pants, and parka that his wife, Agio, had made for both of them. Their costumes had inset stripes that followed the form in light skin, beautifully married against darker skins. The other family who had taken part had done a very simple, untrimmed parka that could not compete against Agio's costumes in any way.

We gave first prize to Agio, feeling that her work was a masterpiece of skillful sinew sewing.

As soon as Pitseolak realized what had been done, he went into a rage and shortly after had Agio, who was in tears, bring the prize straight back to me. "It should have gone to my *uvinga*, husband," she said. "He's mad at you, Saomik, and at Arnakotak, and at me."

It took some time for things to settle down. On reflection, if he really designed the winning costume and Agio executed his design, he may have had a case. The art world is quite familiar with problems of this sort.

When we were outside (in the North you always talk about going "outside") in 1954 for the birth of John, Peter Pitseolak was sent south to the Ottawa Hospital and had his gallbladder removed. During part of his recuperation, he came to stay with us. John was less than a month old. I remember Pitseolak holding him and making long speeches to him in Inuktitut which he declared John understood.

We had an enjoyable time together. I took Pitseolak to the National Museum, which he loved, and to the National Gallery, at that time showing an exhibition of non-objective art, which he laughed at and disliked. We went to see one of Kirosawa's famous Japanese films, *The Gates of Hell*. Like me, Pitseolak was overwhelmed by that film, and at one point in the picture, he leapt to his feet and angrily shouted, "*Unaaluk!* Big you!" at the bad guy on the screen. It was the first colored film he had ever seen.

Pitseolak mistrusted street-crossing signals. I assured him that car drivers always stopped on red, but Pitseolak worried that he couldn't see their eyes and therefore could not judge what they would do.

34
Ikeraksak

Ikeraksak, an arm of land projecting outward to the Hudson Strait, was the winter site for Pootoogook's nomadic camp. Its name means "isthmus." This place had been made famous by Pootoogook and his regal style. There he had his family's walrus caches stored like vintage wine.

We left Cape Dorset and accompanied that family eastward in their boat in the autumn of 1952. It was our idea to remain in Ikeraksak until the following summer, living in our double-walled, octagonal winter tent that I had so confidently designed. I planned during that period to survey and encourage carving. The central location would allow me to visit other camps that winter and to hunt with the Pootoogookut from Ikeraksak.

Allie started to conduct an itinerant school, one that could move like a nomad camp. It would be the first to do so, we believed, in the Canadian Arctic. The Department's idea, and ours, was that we would take the classroom to Inuit children. This system avoided the endless difficulties and changes in lifestyle that these families would have to undergo to depart from their traditional hunting grounds or, worse, to leave their children to stay with some other family in order to attend settlement schools, which was against all local tradition. Pootoogook and his wife, Ningiukaluk, were eager to help us with this new school experiment, and they did. However, I believe in hindsight that neither a school in Dorset nor our itinerant school would have provided a satisfactory answer to education in the eastern Arctic in those years. But we were more than anxious to give it a try and get a closer taste of Inuit life.

What a grand time we had – before the trouble came!

35
Lost

I was a slow learner, especially about the weather.

One morning in mid-November, I was lying in our sleeping bag, thinking. It was dark inside my far-from-perfect, Arctic tent and I could see my breath rising toward the roof. I was thinking about my years in the army when everyone had been forced to rise at 6:00 a.m. At first, I had thought that situation ghastly. But when the Toronto Scottish, my regiment, had soldiered with the Saskatoon Light Infantry, another heavy machine-gun regiment, I came into quarters late one night – or should I call it early in the morning – it was 5:00 a.m., and I saw a lot of those prairie lads already up, shaved, and fully dressed. They were sitting on the sides of their beds, swinging their legs with boots all shined, waiting for reveille to sound so that they could leap into the breakfast line.

I lay there, putting together different time conceptions, when suddenly I heard a whir of wings pass over the tent. I leapt up, flung on my heaviest shirt, stamped into my sealskin boots, and, wearing my long winter underwear, went outside. It was nippy. There, on the side of the near low hill, I saw two to three dozen ptarmigan. They were pullet-sized, snow-white birds with a few neat black wing and tail feathers. If ptarmigan stop, they become almost invisible. But these were on the move.

I ducked back inside the tent, believing the birds would not go far. I dressed quickly, pulling on a thin but very natty-looking pair of riding britches that I favored and jerking on a woolen sweater, which I covered with a Greenland type of anorak. It had a hood, but it was really just a canvas windbreaker. But there was no need to get warmly dressed. I intended to do my hunting quickly that morning and within sight of the tent. I pulled on a balaclava, one heavy mitten, and one light shooting glove, put a box of .22 ammunition in my pocket, hurried outside and grabbed my rifle.

Our food had not been all that exciting lately, although we had been given our fair share of all the camp's meat. What a chance, I thought, to knock over a dozen or so of these plump birds, keeping some for ourselves, then sending some kids to go distribute the rest of my catch to the other families.

Ptarmigan are not a difficult bird to hunt if you do it Inuit style, since a .22-caliber rifle makes very little noise. When the bullet lands in or near the flock, it will not usually cause them to fly. The important thing is to get yourself quietly into position and not to move during the firing. I had gathered this knowledge, of course, from real Inuit hunters and I was eager to see if I could do it right. I moved toward the flock, but they saw me, stopped pecking at the seeds in the windswept tundra, and ran together into a small valley. I followed them, looking at the same time for a rock where I could position myself for firing. They were still moving eastward. The palest light of dawn was beginning to spread. I trotted after them, hoping they would settle down.

I slipped and fell, for after the driving wind storm of the week before, the snow had become polished hard and was slick enough to shine like water in moonlight. The clumsy action of my falling frightened the flock and they rose again and flew. I didn't see them, but I heard the whirring of their wings stop further along the valley. I felt nicely warm from the exercise and had no intention of allowing these plump white dinners to get away from me. I pressed on until I saw them again.

They had split into two flocks this time. But they were still close together and in range. I knelt down, racked a shell into the chamber, aimed and fired. They should have stayed put, but they didn't. The whole lot of them rose and flew further down the valley. I saw one falter and fall. I went forward, picked it up, and hurried after the rest. They had turned north and were feeding again. The light was improving. When I got near them in the protection of rocks, the snow was deeper. I leaned against a boulder and managed to shoot three more before both flocks rose and flew again. I left the four birds piled on a boulder where they would be easily seen when I came back to pick them up.

I went on and shot another, then another. I followed them again and missed several times, but managed to shoot another four in all. This time, the separated flock joined together in the air and in a flash of white wings against the dark rocks, they flew much further inland.

That's enough, I thought, not wanting to get too far away. I squatted on the snow, took off my mitt and glove to cool myself, and pulled at the neck of my sweater to let out my body heat. It took no time at all to cool down. Looking around, I saw the sky had darkened with clouds. The light of dawn had disappeared and the whole world around showed no direction. I put my rifle over my shoulder and followed my own trail back to find the birds. I easily picked up three of them. But ptarmigan, in their white phase, and in the stillness of death, can be all but impossible to see against the snow. I traipsed slowly around for some time, searching for the fourth bird without success. I was getting cold. *Awh, hell, leave it,* I thought, *bring out some kids to look for it. They'll find it later, they can find anything.*

I followed my trail further and then saw that it turned and doubled back. My God, where was I? Which direction should I take to find the tent? The gray wall of sky around me looked exactly the same. There was no sign to show me east or north, south or west. I didn't know which way to turn. I was lost!

The wool sweater that had made me too hot now seemed thin and inadequate. I shuddered. What kind of fool had I been to go wandering off on a dark Arctic morning dressed like some city sport out for an autumn stroll?

I was in trouble, but at first there seemed no reason to panic. I raised my head, not wishing to be misled by my deceptive zigzag tracks. I cupped my mitt around my mouth and let out a primeval shout. I listened, head cocked like an owl, but I heard nothing except the slight whispering of the rising wind that was sharpening the drifts. I yelled again, this time with a feeling of real terror. I had never been in a place so gray and cold, so lonely, a situation where, it seemed to me, no human belonged. Firing off a rifle three times, which is the traditional signal of distress, meant nothing here. Firing off my .22-caliber in a wind would make only the slightest pop.

I turned and ran along my trail, burning with fear and excitement. The trail turned, then disappeared on the hard-packed snow. I looked for the dent where I had fallen, but it wasn't there.

The wind was increasing. It was growing colder. My clothing felt like army summer drills. Everything was wrong. I felt my crotch. It was numb. No feeling. I had a Zippo lighter – but nothing to light, no trees, nothing. My God! Which way would I turn? I yelled again so loud it hurt my throat. No answer. Nothing. I was terrified. I squatted, trembling by a rock, then leaned against it, watching as new snow began to drift in. *So it ends like this*, I thought, *nothing heroic, just a damned fool in summer dress found frozen to death, lost not far from his camp.*

I stripped the skin and feathers off one ptarmigan's breast and took a bite. The dark meat was neither warm nor cold. Eating it did nothing to help me change my state of mind. I stood up, shuddering with cold, deciding that since I knew no direction, I would walk with the wind behind me.

I had not taken a dozen steps when I heard the high, sweet howling of a Husky far away. I whirled around and ran with fresh strength arrow-straight toward the sound, with new snow blowing in my face, desperate to keep the direction from which the wind had carried that one long, lonely howl.

Suddenly, there on a granite rock before me, I saw my first four birds piled and I gasped with delight, for I knew then that I was on the right path. Hurrying on, I passed two of Pootoogook's walrus caches piled like human graves with stones. Then I saw a dog team lying scattered about near Munamee's igloo.

Could I pick out the dog that had called to me? I wondered. The one to which, perhaps, I owed my life?

36
Camp Life

New salt ice was forming in the fiords around Ikeraksak and I was glad to go out with the hunters whenever possible, to leave our tent for Allie to conduct her itinerant school. The trouble with seal hunting on new autumn ice is that as the cold increases it extends outward each day, meaning that it is always thin where the hunting is best. You can sometimes watch seals punch their dark heads up through this thin ice to make their breathing holes. Of course, that thickness of ice will not hold a man.

At first, I was very cavalier about walking on thin ice with the hunters, until Pudlat, frustrated by my foolishness, insisted that I walk directly behind him and watch his feet. To my horror I saw the thin salt sea ice let his weight go down almost as though he and the others were walking on a rubber trampoline. When he stopped he plunged down his ice chisel on the end of his harpoon. It easily broke through, causing the water to spill up over the ice.

When I veered from following in the hunters' footsteps next day, I plunged through up to my armpits. Believe me, the shock of that water gives a person a huge incentive to heave himself out of such a fix. Once I was out and on my feet again, my hunting companions urged me to return to the thicker snow-covered ice, calling, "Roll in the snow! Lie on your back! Kick your legs in the air! Loosen your boots! Let the water drain out! Now run back to camp fast before your clothing freezes stiff."

I was warm when I got back to our bedroom classroom tent but still very wet and embarrassed. Those children didn't laugh. They offered to bring their mothers over to take my clothes and dry them out while I jumped naked into the sleeping bag.

In spite of this and several other mishaps, Allie and I were starting to get the hang of winter life in camp. One morning, I found our tent entrance drifted in. I started probing around in the snow for the wooden shovel Pootoogook had lent me.

Snow Shovel

When he saw what I was looking for, Pootoogook gave me some good old-fashioned advice. "Always stand a shovel upright in the snow. If you don't, it will get away from you."

Older Inuit had told him that a snow shovel hates to be left lying flat. A dropped shovel will grow angry, and leap up and run away to hide from you. Oh, yes, you may find that shovel when summer comes and the snow has disappeared. But will you need it then?

I felt that out in Ikeraksak we were learning one thing after another every single day. The hunters appeared with better and better carvings and they shared their meat with us as we shared our food with them, all of us experiencing something strange and exotic.

37
Trouble

Allie sat up in the cold of our winter tent, her breath steaming. She groaned, then got up, ran to the door, and threw up outside.

"I've got an awful pain in my stomach, down here on the right side."

"Is it a cramp?" I asked her. "Did you eat something bad?"

"I don't know," she answered, "but it hurts."

"Have you felt it before?"

"A little bit, but nothing like this."

"Would you like to get up, put your parka on? We'll walk around inside the tent, maybe outside, until it goes away."

We tried that, but it only seemed to make the pain worse. I felt her head. It was hot even though my unsuccessful winter tent design was shudderingly cold inside. I looked in my medical fish-bait box, but I didn't know what to give her. I tried two Aspirin, then pumped up our pressure lantern, which gave better light than the candle flame. I began to study my small St. John Ambulance book. Finally, I turned to "appendix," a word all northerners dread when they are far from medical help. I read the entry to myself: most common in persons under thirty-five, characterized by a sudden onset of nausea, vomiting, and pain in the lower right abdomen – requires immediate surgical treatment.

We were both truly worried, but hoped that it was something far less serious than appendicitis and that the pain would go away. When the camp children came that morning to attend Allie's itin-erant school, I told them that Arnakotak was sick. They hurried away and in a moment all their mothers were in the tent, leaning over Allie, feeling her head, holding her hands, and making com-forting sounds.

"Yes, she's sick," they told me. And in their honest way, they said, "Women here have had this, too. Something in her belly has gone wrong. *Ajurnarmat*, it can't be helped. No one here knows how to fix it."

Ningiukaluk gave me a worried glance as she ducked out our low tent door. In no time, Pootogook, her husband, came in and stood beside me, looking down at Allie's face. It was ashen pale and gleaming with sweat. "My wife says Arnakotak is very sick."

"She's strong," I told him, trying to buck up my own courage and Allie's, too, for she had heard his words. "If she's not better by tonight, I'll be thinking of how to take her into Kingait tomorrow morning."

"I'll have my team ready," he said. "I've told my sons of the best way around the bay and overland. It will be difficult. Most of the sea ice now is not thick enough to carry a loaded sled, and trying to go over the land before the heavy snows is *peungitoaluk*, very bad. So many hard bumps." He looked sympathetically at Allie.

Not long after he left, Allie threw up again. She couldn't eat and when she drank she groaned in pain. That night I didn't sleep a wink. I was up and dressed long before dawn, arranging and rearranging what I thought we should take, wishing to God I had a radio transmitter. Except for military people no one traveled with fancy gear like that.

In the morning, still before dawn, I heard a *kamotik*'s runners squealing as it was hand-hauled up in front of our tent entrance. When I went outside, Pudlat and Pauloosi, Pootoogook's two eldest sons, were there with their father's longest walrus sled. By Inuit standards, it was the equivalent of a stretch Cadillac, a limousine. Behind the grub box, where the drivers could sit when they were not running or pushing, were a number of boxes of equal size, open to receive our two packs and my sleeping bag, our Primus stove, medical kit, and so on.

Long sled

A small crowd had gathered and they helped me stuff our kit inside. Then on top of the level boxes they spread several thick winter caribou skins. To top that off, a white bearskin, hair up, was laid down to form a bed. Halfway toward the back of this sled's length, to mark the importance of the occasion, they had lashed down a large Union Jack. I don't think anyone down South would have approved of the flag of Empire being used in that way, but I didn't interfere. I was busy worrying about Allie, not the flag.

The women wrapped her in the sleeping bag and helped me carry her out very gently, placing her head forward on the sled. The drivers tied her tightly into position.

"*Atai, audlukvit tugvaosi.* Now, go you. Goodbye to all of you," Pootoogook called.

We started off from Ikeraksak with everyone pushing the sled and calling *"Tugvaosi,* goodbye!" to us as they stood up to watch us go.

Pauloosi and Pudlat did not go down through the rough barrier ice and onto the sea ice, which was the usual route. Until they felt it was safe to go out onto the thicker shore ice, which was solidly formed, they headed westward, overland, which meant going around the upper curve of Andrew Gordon Bay.

We soon discovered that traveling overland was extremely rough and hard to do. The snow was not yet deep enough to cover most of the rocks, and wind storms had opened large stretches of tundra around which we had to navigate. We were traveling on iron-shod sled runners instead of the preferred mud coating frozen into icy forms like two long, flat, bicycle tires. Pootoogook had known that the mud pack would not stay on the runners through the sled's heavy thumping over the rocks. It must have been a nightmare for Allie.

Before we could get down off the land and through another hard barrier of tidal ice we would have to run the gauntlet of tipped barrier ice, which could stand more than one story high. We were rarely free of worry that the heavy sled would tip or roll over, a thing that it is well known to do in barrier ice. So we had to get Allie off the *kamotik,* for who could face the image of that happening with Allie lashed on top unable to leap free! Trying to prevent an accident gave me nervous strength until I could feel the sweat trickling down my back, leaving little snail-like trails that later seemed to turn to ice. I would walk her through the icy hazard, and then Pauloosi and Pudlat would tie her back onto the sled.

Finally, we were halfway round and heading south toward Etiliakjuk, an Inuit camp we hoped to reach by nightfall. When we were once again on flat sea ice, we stopped to rest the dogs and catch our breaths, then settle Allie on the sled. Pudlat, Pauloosi, and I drank beef tea and ate chunks of meat with bannock made from seal fat. Snow clouds were gathering out over the Hudson Strait, which was normal enough for late November. I prayed that we would find the camp before dark. In all probability, Etiliakjuk would show no light that we could see. My hopes faded when darkness closed in around us about four o'clock.

Our dogs found the camp. They went scrambling off into the blackness and soon we heard other sled dogs howling and saw the silhouette of a man and boy running toward us like shadows against the snow. We had found Etiliakjuk. Osuitok's family was there, Saggiak's family was there, and Pingwarktok's, too. It was decided that we should stay with Pingwarktok's family. We got Allie into the place they made for us in the very center of their low, wide bed.

We were lent fresh dogs and left the weaker ones to rest. Then we started overland again, next morning. It was better for a while. Then came stretches covered with so many glacial boulders that it looked like a gigantic egg crate packed with skull-shaped rocks. There were far too many to find our way around them. There was no choice except to go straight across, which we did, the sled thumping and bumping like a farm wagon without springs.

Sometimes Allie lay there crying and sometimes she sang. Pauloosi and Pudlat looked sick because they knew there was nothing any of us could do to ease the jolting. We ran on until five o'clock, well after dark, then stopped and untied Allie for the second time that day. I asked her if she'd like us to build an igloo where all of us could get some rest. Pudlat was making tea when I asked her the question.

She said, "What do all of you think is best?"

"*Isumungitok*, it's up to you. I think we should keep going, if you can," said Pauloosi. "A storm now could hold us here for days."

We all agreed to continue. Tying Allie down again, we went forward in the darkness over tilted tundra flats and into the punishing fields of rock again. This time they were almost impossible to see. If we were lucky, we'd find a long, beachlike drift of snow; and later we did find one and traveled on it gratefully for an hour or so before it ran out on us. Then it was back to the dreaded jarring and bouncing in the blackness, with sparks flashing off the steel runners as they ground against the rocks. I looked at Allie's face, then arranged her hood almost completely closed for warmth. We passed near no Inuit camps where we might have paused to rest and change the dogs. Our course continued overland well behind the coastal camps, in an area where in this season no hunter would consider traveling.

At midnight, we stopped again, exhausted, and let Allie off the sled while we made tea. We had used ourselves hard for two days. I would have given anything just to lie down somewhere, anywhere! I forced that thought out of my head as we tied her down again and started out. It was three in the morning before we found the best way through a new upheaval of tidal ice. Now, gratefully, we were on the flat, frozen sea again.

I had been longing to reach that smooth, wide highway of snow-covered ice, but even the sight of it set me worrying. How would we cross Kingait Bay? Pudlat had guessed it would probably still be open, or the new-formed ice too thin. That would bar our best course into Dorset.

Our lives were almost totally in the hands of Pauloosi and Pudlat who were both hoarse from endless yelling, urging the tired dogs forward while the three of us pushed hard and sometimes, when the ice was smooth, leaned on the sled and did an exhausted dogtrot beside Allie.

The brothers discussed various possibilities, deciding to keep away from the unknown bay ice and to cross at Telik. That route would take longer but the ice, they knew, would be stronger at Telik. If we could make that crossing, I knew we would then go almost straight into Kingait. When we turned again toward the fiord, we could see that its entrance was still black with open water. We had to bypass that, then slowly, painfully, kept moving forward along the edge of Malik Island before we finally started across.

There was not a single light in Dorset. The half dozen buildings and sheds looked dead and deserted until the dogs there caught our scent and sent up a howling. Our tired team somehow found the strength to pull as we joined with the tracks of other sleds that narrowed toward the best path through the barrier ice.

"We're back!" I shook Allie. "We've made it. Hear their dogs? We've reached Kingait!"

We ran the kamotik straight to the small teacherage beside the one-room school where we had stayed when we were last in Dorset.

No one was awake at that early hour. We untied Allie from the white bearskin on the flag-draped sled and helped her inside the freezing house and quickly into a bed. Pudlat lit the oil stove while I went over to get Ruth Horky, the new nurse. She had come in at shiptime and we scarcely knew her, having been away so much. But, my God, I felt a sense of relief when I knocked and heard her moving around inside the abandoned Baffin trading post that had been repainted and referred to as a one-bed nursing station. The nurse lit a lamp, then opened the door. When she heard what had happened, Ruth pulled on her boots and parka and came back with me. Pauloosi was feeding the dogs when we passed him. I wanted to say "Arnakotak will be fine now," but I couldn't.

The nurse and I left Allie and went up to the Company for the eight o'clock radio sked. She sent a message to the Department of Northern Health Services, I sent a message to the Chief, Arctic Division: both describing the situation. The departments answered us on that night's sked, advising me to check carefully and inform them of the exact thickness of the ice, and the greatest length of aircraft runway possible, with no high hills involved. Northern Health directed the nurse to be prepared to evacuate the patient on short notice.

Next morning, I walked out with Tukiasuk and Freddie Knight, the HBC man, to what appeared to be the center of the longest, strongest stretch of ice on Kingait Fiord. We cut a fist-sized hole down through it with an ice chisel. I had brought a wooden yardstick, hoping the ice would be at least an arm's length thick. It was less than that by half. We cut two more holes in different places, while I prayed that the first had somehow been over some freakish, thin spot, but it wasn't. We didn't have the ice for them to land the heavier aircraft that would be required to reach us.

That night, I reported the ice thickness on the evening sked and Ottawa relayed a message back to me next day, saying that they could not risk landing the Search and Rescue plane until I could report twenty-four inches, or sixty centimeters, of solid ice. If I could find a place with ninety centimeters, they said that would be greatly preferred.

Allie's real condition remained unknown, but Ruth, the nurse, did all she could for her. I questioned old Parr and his son, Kovinatiliak, who lived north near the fish lakes. They told us that the first salt ice formed earlier near them and they believed it should be thicker there. Kovinatiliak and Parr went up with us next day and cut new holes. The ice there averaged about twenty-two inches, or fifty-four centimeters. Oh, God, I wanted to tell them we had enough, but, of course, I couldn't do that. The risks that Search and Rescue were about to take would be great enough without thin ice.

That night it was cold. You could hear the pressure cracks in the ice make long ripping sounds like some giant pulling up his zipper. I sent them another message with my new ice report and new location, describing the large bay in front of Tessiuakjuak with measurements of its runway space. It was long east and west but a whole lot shorter north and south. I have forgotten now the length of runway required for landing larger, specially equipped Search and Rescue planes, but it seemed to me one helluva lot. Not at all like the Otters that came later with ski wheels and amazingly short landing and takeoff abilities.

A summer earlier, Allie and I had traveled north from Dorset on the government icebreaker with Dr. Hermann, a surgeon. We both had liked him very much. Now we were informed by the Department that Dr. Hermann had offered to jump by parachute into Dorset and operate on the spot if that would prove the best solution.

Allie, in the meantime, was holding up and it was judged that her appendix had not yet burst. But she was no better, either. That's what was worrying everyone.

The next day was cold and clear. Tomi Tigugligak and I went back to the place we had selected as the landing site, two hours' travel from Dorset. This time, to our delight, the ice was twenty-eight inches, seventy centimeters, thick, enough to meet Search and Rescue's landing requirements. We were back in time to make the sked that night and were able to report that the thickness of ice was right. The clear weather pattern seemed to be holding. The reply came back that Search and Rescue had already sent their plane from Greenwood, Nova Scotia, north to Goose Bay, Labrador, and that if we could give them favorable weather conditions at 8:00 a.m. the following morning, they would take off for a direct flight to the ice strip we had described.

Osuitok and I had carefully paced out and marked this emergency strip with some empty coal sacks we had found behind the Baffin Trading shed because they were simple to carry and, showing black against the snow, would be easily seen from the air; at the same time, if an aircraft hit and ran over one, it would do the plane no harm.

To attract the plane, Kovinatiliak had brought a rusted fuel drum from his camp nearby. He had almost filled it with dried tundra and soaked it, as we had been asked, with seal oil. We added used diesel oil.

When I got back to Allie on the sled, she said, "I'm going to be fine as soon as I get into a hospital. I hope you'll stay here and keep buying carvings until I get back."

"I think I should come out with you."

"No," she said. "If you do that, they might not let us come back here. But if you're here, they'll let me come back in."

I agreed with that, for we were both eager to know more of the west Baffin people and dreaded the sound of the message we had recently gotten from the Guild telling me to reduce the purchasing of carvings. We both knew that the carvings were definitely getting better and we were getting more of them. Together, we agreed that I would stay and keep things going and wait for her to return.

We had a stretcher now and there were lots of hands to carry Allie down through the rough ice and once more tie her to our sled. This time with the nurse beside her, we left in the middle of a caravan of dog teams. Pitseolak, our on-again-off-again friend, had come in to Kingait and he led the procession.

When we reached the marked-out strip, I checked my watch. The pilot had estimated the time the plane would arrive, which would be soon, trying for the best of light for that season of the year. We went and lit the barrel of oil-soaked tundra. It burned fast, sending up a long plume of black smoke that drifted out over the hills, driven by the rising west wind. We hoped this would tell the pilot exactly where we had laid out the strip, and also indicate the wind direction.

"*Kungatasho, kungatasho,* airplane!" I heard sharp-eyed children calling, pointing to a black dot almost too small to see. That's how we first knew that the plane was in sight. From that point on everything worked just right. Twin-engined ski-wheel planes of the kind Search and Rescue was using at that time were extremely rare. The fact that it had arrived right on time was critical, for we were fast losing daylight. The aircraft lowered its flaps and circled the airstrip, then came in, landing smoothly between the coal sacks. The Dakota turned and taxied to the place where we were waiting. They had an air force nurse aboard with them and another stretcher.

We quickly helped get Allie aboard. The pilot shouted to me, "Hey, friend, jump now or stay. We're taking off!"

I let go of Allie's hand and jumped. The freight door of the Dakota slammed shut behind me. The aircraft was moving.

Oh, God, there she goes, I thought. *I should have stayed with her.*

At nine o'clock that night, we listened to a pre-arranged late sked with Kingait. It read: "RCAF Search and Rescue plane has landed at Goose Bay Air Base, Labrador. Surgery on Mrs. Houston has been performed. Will contact you at 8:00 a.m. tomorrow morning."

I had endless visitors. Pitseolak said he'd seen me crying on the dog sled coming home, but he added that he didn't blame me for being worried, that lots of Inuit wives had died from just such belly pains.

I didn't sleep at all that night and was drinking coffee with Ralph and Freddie Knight beside the Company radio transmitter long before sked time. At 8:00 a.m. the word came through that Allie's appendix had been removed, that the operation had been successful, and that she was recovering in the Goose Bay military hospital. They would keep me informed.

I went floating across the snow as though a tremendous weight had been lifted from me. I fell into bed and slept for about twelve hours.

I received a radio message two days later: "Feeling much better. Stop. Be back as soon as doctors allow. Stop. Love, Allie."

Even more exciting carvings were being brought to me. I knew we absolutely could not give up buying them. But not long after Allie's trip out, I received another message from the Guild saying that Allie had arrived in Montreal to recuperate there and that she would not return to the Arctic until the annual resupply at shiptime.

Shiptime! That seemed like a hundred years away. I counted. It was actually about eight months away.

Not long after that I had another message saying that I should come out whenever possible. That a single-engine Norseman air-craft was planning to come into Frobisher on skis and might be available for partial charter if it was operating near Kingait. And further, that I should be ready to board it on short notice and start south.

I carefully packed up all the best carvings in two wooden crates. Inuit carvers who had heard that I was going kept coming in with still better carvings, until that rare winter happening occurred – Frobisher and Kingait both reported clear weather. The pilot took off immediately, but had to return to base when the weather in the middle turned bad on him – there were no navigational aids in Dorset or the other remote Arctic posts at that time. But finally the Norseman's determined pilot made it.

What a lot of friends to have to leave at Kingait! But it meant that I would be seeing Allie. I told the Kingaimiut I would be back.

When we met at the Montreal airport, Allie looked especially lean to me, but she assured me she was on the mend. We went to see all our friends at the Guild next day. They showed us the storeroom full of unpacked carving boxes and said they had not had much success in selling them. I knew there were good carv-ings inside those boxes and that the prices were reasonable, thanks to the fact that the Guild was a non-profit organization, as it remains today.

"What are we going to do?" I asked at a meeting. "In the Arctic, everything's going fine, better than I dared to hope it would. The carvers are now creating their art in half a dozen places. They've got to have the chance to go on."

"Jim, that's our problem," Jack Molson said. "They're coming in much faster than we can manage to finance or sell them."

Allie and I went down with them to look at the carvings on the sales floor. There were only a few laid out, the least expensive, and, we thought, not well-displayed.

"We've got to do something," I told them. "We've got to find a stronger market. We're going to visit a friend of mine to see if he can help."

38
A Financial Fix

We left Montreal in the early spring of 1953 more than a little discouraged. Carrying our own large, square, leather traveling case carefully packed with many of the best Inuit carvings, we flew to New York and then Chicago, where we had been asked to talk about the perils of an appendix attack in the North. When that was done, I telephoned my friend, Eugene B. Power, who had visited me in Grand'Mère, Quebec. He lived in Ann Arbor, Michigan, and was then president of University Microfilms, involved in microfilming the world's great libraries and documents in order to preserve them and make them more accessible to students everywhere. He asked us to come and stay with him. Power's actions were about to change the course of Canadian Inuit art and our lives, both for the better.

I had told Power on the phone from Chicago that we were bringing some important Arctic art objects with us. He in turn invited some art professors including Dr. Robert Hatt, director of the Cranbrook Museum and Dr. Bruce Inverarity, a famous art anthropologist (who has recently given to the British Museum his remarkable collection of contemporary Inuit art, which he began that evening).

At the right moment, in good light on top of a grand piano, Allie and I displayed the carvings, explaining, as we did, something about the Inuit sculptors who had carved them. The guests were enthralled by the carvings and considered the prices low. They all asked us how they could acquire some. And what was more significant, they asked us to help them arrange an exhibition at the art gallery at the University of Michigan and join in the preparation of a catalogue.

After several exciting days of talk on this subject, Power suggested that we form a board of knowledgeable persons and create Eskimo Art, Inc. He started phoning people right away. And having parted with those wonderful carvings (all in prestigious museums now), we returned to Montreal and started to prepare for another Canadian exhibition at the Guild.

This exhibition, like every other that presented Inuit art, was an outstanding success. Dr. Alan Jarvis, the Director of the National Gallery of Canada, Dr. Evan Turner, Director of the Montreal Museum of Fine Arts, and Dr. Ted Heinrich, Director of the Royal Ontario Museum, all came to dinner, then to the Guild to see those carvings and to give their enthusiastic, unqualified support just when the Guild had drastically reduced my purchasing power to buy Inuit arts and crafts. What boosted the Guild's flagging morale was the fact that Eskimo Art, Inc. called them from Ann Arbor and announced that they wished to purchase the Guild's entire inventory of Inuit carvings and also all those to be received from the Arctic in the following year!

This news prompted the Guild to hold a meeting, which Allie and I attended. They wondered what the Guild should do about this surprising new offer. They decided that they could not allow all these marvelous Canadian carvings to go down and disappear into the United States. So they refused Mr. Power's larger offer, but did agree to ship him carvings from a substantial number of cases that had not yet been opened. Thank God! The Canadian Inuit and their carvings were back in action! New funds to purchase carvings had appeared.

But another big change had occurred. In the beginning, the Guild had the exclusive right to handle carvings, as agreed by the Hudson's Bay Company who arranged and developed the local purchasing details and the shipping arrangements south. But on December 10, 1952, the day that the Guild radioed me declaring they were no longer prepared to finance and sell the number of Inuit carvings they were receiving, the Hudson's Bay Company immediately, and quite rightly, announced that they themselves were in the business of buying carvings, to distribute as they saw fit. The HBC could see that something new and exciting was happening in the Arctic and that contemporary Inuit art might generate a whole new kind of income.

Of course, income from art is not normally a substitute for another type of income. In those days, no one really thought that possible, certainly not me. I was quoted internationally in the February 22, 1960 issue of Time magazine saying that all I could hope was that Inuit art might act as an economic bridge that would help until some new Inuit economy could be established. Even that task then seemed to demand too much of the artists. But, frankly, there was nothing else in sight in those days, and they were more than eager to earn their own way – as thirty-five years later, they still are.

The greatest feat that Eskimo Art, Inc. accomplished in the United States was to have contemporary Canadian Inuit art declared an art form and the carvings recognized as art objects by U.S. Customs so that they would qualify as duty-free even if an individual item were small and cost only a few dollars. I doubt that such a development would ever have been possible in those crucial times without the determination of Eugene B. Power. Eskimo Art, Inc. also helped arrange a sizeable traveling exhibition of Canadian Inuit art through the Smithsonian Institute in Washington. That exhibit was seen throughout the U.S. and in many countries and had a great effect on the credibility and enthusiasm for contemporary Inuit art. Sales shops in museums began vying for small Inuit carvings. Early exhibitions were held at the Field Museum in Chicago and at the Museum of Natural History in New York. Canadian galleries

suddenly became aware of the existence of this new art phenomenon born in Arctic Canada, and of the remarkable individual
quality of the sculptures. Collectors began to know the names of the
sculptors, and in time Inuit art appeared on postal stamps.

39

New Shamen

The Church of England missionary, one of the old-fashioned types,
who was traveling north again after his furlough in Great Britain,
gave an after-dinner lecture in the icebreaker's dining room. He
became furious because some joker had secretly mixed up his Arctic
slides, interspersing them with wildly uninhibited shots of naked
West African girls of unbelievably grand proportions. Pandemon-
ium broke loose whenever one of these gorgeous girls appeared
between the church ruins of southern England and his Arctic
dwelling, leaving the missionary nervous, afraid to go on, yet afraid
to halt his slide show and admit defeat.

After a dozen of his proper slides had appeared in his own carefully prearranged order, he got his nerve back and said, "Here is the
dear old Eskimo lady who keeps my mission house for me."

He pressed the button and *voilà*, another gorgeous Venus flashed
upon the screen. The missionary was livid and the ship's surgeon
laughed so hard that his friend and cohort in the crime, the dentist,
had to pound him on the back. The missionary's somber wife was
not nearly so amused!

It would be hard to say that I admired most of the missionaries
I've known from my Arctic days, largely because they demonstrated
so little kindness or charity toward each other, especially those
priests of opposing faiths. They allowed their historical animosities
to stand in the way of their whole relationship with a remote
society of people who already believed they had a satisfactory religion of their own.

In the end, the missionary factions battled so desperately hard against each other to win converts that they have all but managed to run each other out of the Arctic, and have reopened that vast, almost virgin land to the uncertain future brought by evangelicals and other new religious groups. They, in turn, come tumbling into the country with their guitars and cowboy hats to try and win the high ground from each other. Inuit say that at this time, shamanism is growing again.

Shamanism of the Arctic breed had to be a strong religion to have withstood the ages so long on its own. Imagine a religion with no related priesthood, no written word, no head of church, no collection plates, no church! A religion that is based on one person, male or female, teaching one apprentice in their area at any one time. A religion that is expected through that apprenticeship to rebuild itself and continue to survive during all the changing generations and to cling on and remain meaningful. Shamanism has managed to endure since Paleolithic times when early man left his prolific shamanistic drawings in the caves of central France and northern Spain.

Shamanism can and does co-exist with Christianity in Inuit thinking. Why should it not? What kind of weak religion would shamanism be if after 16,000 years of its known existence it could be knocked down dead by a handful of new, squabbling missionaries who wandered into the vastness of the Arctic world less than a century ago?

40

Journey to Ellesmere

When the ice began to open in the summer of '53, we journeyed to Inukjuak on the east coast of Hudson Bay, where I had spent parts of the past three years. We were greeted there by many old friends. Because I had married since my last visit, they gathered on the icebreaker's deck and made a gift to Allie of a pair of elaborately designed, knee-high sealskin boots.

The truly memorable event that occurred in Inukjuak at that time was the beginning of a long Inuit journey gladly undertaken by hunters, their wives, grandparents, and children. Whole families came aboard the icebreaker with their tents, kayaks, canoes, sleds, and nearly a hundred dogs. These people certainly appeared happy and excited and seemed to be looking forward to this adventurous voyage to the most northern island of Canada's Arctic Archipelago where they were going to settle.

We went west to Churchill to await supplies. Ice reports showed remarkably favorable ice conditions in the high Arctic. On the way north, we again visited Pangnirtung, that famous rendezvous for Scottish and American whalers in their tall ships in the old days. There was not much stone available at Pangnirtung, but we saw splendid sewing and designs, and displayed our small exhibition, which every Inuit came to see.

At that time, I recall seeing Inuit canoes and kayaks herding white whales into a bay by using bottles full of gunpowder, their oil-soaked fuses lit and quickly thrown. These were not intended to hurt the whales, but to frighten and corral them, a technique invented by the earlier bowhead or right whalers who had hunted them almost to extinction.

One or two of these last enormous Arctic bowheads have recently been seen near Pangnirtung. In my opinion the bowhead was saved by, of all people, John D. Rockefeller, when he financed the development of rock oil in 1865. Petroleum quickly ruined the already fading whaling trade as animal fat rendered into oil fell out of fashion. Whaling had been the largest industry in North America, with twenty thousand American seamen out in a single year whale-hunting from the ports of New Bedford, Massachusetts, New London, Connecticut, and other lesser ports. Its departure hurt New England for a time, and must have had a considerable, yet unrecorded, effect on those Inuit families who had worked so closely with the whalemen.

At Pond Inlet, our icebreaker picked up two Royal Canadian

Mounted Police officers, Constable Sargent and Constable Barr, and two local Inuit families. The man I best remember was Kayak, a truly outstanding person who had spent his life in the high Arctic. He knew the seasons and understood the hunting and fishing patterns and many other invaluable, far northern characteristics that were unknown to the Inukjuak hunting families, who had spent their lives in Arctic Quebec, and were now coming north to settle on Ellesmere Island.

We left them at Craig Harbour on a beautifully clear, summer night where the sun beamed down endlessly. But this, of course, would soon change into a long winter's night.

Akeeaktesuk and his family were among those who went north to live on Ellesmere Island, moving to the new settlement site at Grise Fiord. He died out on the ice during a walrus hunt, and the world lost a marvelous carver.

41
Awh, the Food!

It was sometime in the night that the icebreaker moved into the narrower part of the Gulf of St. Lawrence. When we went out on deck in the morning, the rich smell of trees, of pines, carried out over the warm saltwater, was almost overwhelming. The distant shores of the river in autumn looked like an endless array of farms and evergreen forests and distant bouquets of yellow, red, and gold. It continued like that throughout the day. The icebreaker docked at 6:00 a.m. on another beautiful morning beneath the very French-looking fortress of Quebec City, whose stone ramparts face the river.

Hôpital Parc Savard had sent an ambulance and some station wagons for the Inuit TB patients and we shook hands with them sadly as each one departed. We ourselves signed off as ship's crew, said goodbye to all our other shipmates, and brimming with the thousand expectations one has when first returning south, we flung our kit into a cab and sped uptown.

Checking into the Château Frontenac, that splendid, old hotel that looks like a castle, we lay stretched, flopped down on our wide double bed, then bathed in a huge tub. We telephoned our friends, marveling at the fact that we could talk once more with absolutely anyone anywhere, except the Arctic. We laughed. Imagine, lunch in a place like this after three months at sea, a lunch where every morsel would be fresh.

Old friends were downstairs to meet us. We two sat like wide-eyed children staring at the enormous, six-page menu. "Oh, yes, the *pâté de foie gras.*"

"*Oui,* oysters on the half shell. *Certainement.*"

"Yes, lobster."

"Certainly *crême brulé,* espresso and cognac. Yes, indeed!"

Imagine anything tasting so grand. We went upstairs and lay down, groaning to the point of nausea, trying to adjust ourselves to the fact that we had reached the great outside again.

The Baffin coastline was fading like a dream until we woke and went to *Hôpital* Parc Savard next day and saw our Inuit friends. They reported that the hospital was not so bad, but the food was strange and sickening. They asked whether we could ask the doctor to find them some plain *netsivinik,* seal meat.

"Don't cook it," they said. "Just give us a sharp knife or two."

"Just have him ask our people, they'll be glad to share real meat with us. And *ikaluvinik,* fish, meat, yes, don't forget the fish!"

A few days later, we had adjusted to southern food again. To me, our regular diet of country meat, gull eggs long past their prime, and even fish that might cause you to catch your breath, was much easier to digest than that first exciting plunge into a really good restaurant loaded with gourmet food.

We returned a number of times to *Hôpital* Parc Savard in Quebec City and to the Hamilton Sanatorium. Young Joanasie Salomonie was a patient there like his father, Inukjuakjuk, who had adopted us. When he died we wept together that day, my seven-year-old new nephew and I.

42

Arctic Fever

A Frenchman caught and ensnared by the Arctic magic, Gabriel Gely first worked as a cook for the Department of Transport at Clyde River on east Baffin Island. It was at Clyde River that he made such an impression when he paddled out to meet us in his skin kayak, dressed in sealskin, from head to foot. Always a hopeful artist, Gabriel painted while he learned Inuktitut.

I ran into him in an Ottawa hotel when we were both freshly out of the country and he was on his way home to France. I was on my way back to Cape Dorset. I thought, *How wonderful to meet a chef and painter returning home to his native France, the place that all Frenchmen understandably care so much about.* Gabriel seemed very excited.

Several days later, to my surprise, I met him in the lobby of the same hotel.

"I thought you were going home to France!"

"I went, James, but, you see, I'm back."

"How long did you stay?" I asked.

"One day, one night," he answered. "That was enough for me. Paris is not to my taste these days. I'm going back up north tomorrow."

And he did. I lost track of Gabriel for a few years. He got married and was in and out of the country after that. I met him again cooking at the Department of Transport station at Ennadai Lake in the Keewatin. It was inland caribou country, no HBC, no school, no mission, no nothing. He said he was cooking for the crew of four, but that he was really there for the painting, which he would soon begin, he said. I knew he was a clever, compassionate, restless man, always on the move.

Most French citizens cannot bear to leave France. There are so few Parisien expatriates, they say, because the French believe they are already living in the best country and the best city in the world. For the same reasons, few Inuit could bear to leave the Arctic for any length of time.

Gabriel phoned me recently and said, "James, you seem to be contented living outside the Arctic now. What's wrong with me? I miss it so."

That's what I call endless Arctic fever. It takes some travelers only an instant to catch it and a whole lifetime later, they're not truly rid of it. Believe me, I know.

43
Serious Service

During my early roving days around Inukjuak, I met an officer from the Department of Mines and Resources, Stanley Bailey, who was passing through on an Arctic survey. We stood on the beach discussing Eskimo art. Following the conversation, Bailey suggested to me that I go with the government. They would start to pay me a salary for my work and my problems of transportation could be more easily solved. He told me that he would have someone get in touch with me.

The result was that J. G. Wright, Chief, Mines and Resources, invited me to come to Ottawa and meet everyone involved in their Arctic Division. They offered me a newly created job entitled "Crafts Officer." I was the first in the country to hold such a position. It gave me a greater opportunity to travel and live in the country and to deal directly with the art of the people there, which had long entranced me. Great stress was placed on the word "crafts" in Canada at that time, for it seemed unthinkable to most that anything called art could exist among Canada's contemporary native peoples.

I helped to make a little booklet in Inuktitut, *Shanungwak*, illustrating simple crafts with even simpler drawings of the kind that suited Guild and government concepts. This childish pamphlet fortunately had little or no effect. But the Queen's Printer's publication, *Canadian Eskimo Art*, 1954, that I designed and wrote with R. A. J. Phillips, used notable Inuit carvings photographed by Bert Beaver and the National Film Board. It had a very great effect. That booklet was distributed to every Inuit family in Canada and was widely sold in museums and bookstores. It went into ten printings over a twenty-five-year period and, like other art catalogues, it was absorbed by artists and art dealers everywhere. It is now a collector's item.

In 1955, I was commissioned Northern Service Officer, the first for west Baffin Island, which required me while in the Arctic to expand my interest to matters other than art – to care for the welfare of Inuit, to become Game and Fisheries Officer, Explosives Officer, Mineral Claims Officer, Fur Officer, Dog Officer. That last grand title made me nervous, for during winter gatherings there would be hundreds and hundreds of unchained sled dogs roving loose, and Inuit children everywhere.

I did a greatly increased amount of Arctic travel, but never straight east to west because no planes flew that way. I always had to go south, then west, then north into the Arctic again. One way or another, I believe I visited every Arctic settlement except Old Crow and Perry River, both of which I missed because of bad weather. It gave me a wonderful picture of Inuit and Indian art and varying conditions of life. It made for a busy, exciting, fractured life at times, but it did offer the chance to roam much more of the Arctic than most people are privileged to see. I met many now-famous Inuit who came to hold important positions in the North and helped decide the course the government has taken.

Traveling in and out of the Arctic allowed me to help with Inuit exhibitions in Canada and the U.S. and to give the odd lecture. For example, I was involved when a selection of Inuit carvings was made for an exhibition at the Phillips Gallery in Washington, D.C. The Phillips Gallery is small, but one of the most prestigious in North America. They arranged a splendid display of the carvings.

This exhibition was photographed by *Life* magazine, in May

1954, and as a result the finest carvings in that exhibition were seen worldwide. Make no mistake about it – widely respected publicity at an art museum level is exactly what I have always sought for Canadian Inuit art. The government had hired me with the written understanding that I was to try to improve the economy of its Arctic people, and I came to see that was exactly what their art could do for them.

I was always interested in showing Inuit people and Inuit art in the most favorable light possible. I believe the opening of Canada's Arctic was as exciting in the 1950s and 1960s as the opening of the North American West a century earlier. I was not one to deromanticize life in the North as I tried to help build Inuit art. In the early years, 96 per cent of all Canadians would say to me, "Well, I hear you've been to Alaska." "No," I would say, "I've been to the Canadian eastern (or central or western) Arctic, a land straight north of here that is many times the size of Alaska and is part of your own country."

Canada's Prime Minister Louis St. Laurent said when he came into office, "We have looked after our vast Northwest Territories in a state of absentmindedness. From now on, this will change." And, by God, it did!

44
Trading a Carving in the Early Days

In the winter of 1953–54, I flew to Cape Dorset to make sure that everything was back on track on west Baffin Island. As first Crafts Officer for the Department of Mines and Resources, I visited the camps, returning south at the beginning of summer for the birth of our first son, John.

Hitchhiking by dog team was a common event around Kingait, the Inuit name for Cape Dorset. I had heard strange, shamanistic tales of the camp at Akiaktolaolavik, meaning "the place we last had something to eat," and of the conjuring tricks of a man named Alariak. I wanted to go there to spend some time with them.

When I arrived, the driver of the team helped build a small igloo for me because I wanted to be free to come and go as I wished. I already had two good carvings from a man there named Shoovagar and I wanted to know if they had a stone deposit near the camp and whether the other hunters there, who included a man named Oshaweetok A (as the Hudson's Bay Company used to list him), could be carvers. The dog team driver who had left me there said that they would return that way in four days to give me a lift back to Kingait.

Sometime early in the middle of that fourth day, I was awakened by the sound of coughing outside the igloo. Inuit believe that sleep is very close to death, and those sleeping should not be disturbed. I coughed to show I was awake and Oshaweetok A came in, closely followed by his wife.

I was surprised at this very early visit. There was only a small candle flame inside the igloo and it was cold. I sat up and pumped my Primus stove and put the kettle on without getting out of my sleeping bag, a skill that I had by now perfected. I offered both of them a seat on the other part of the sleeping skins that I did not occupy. I had watched Oshaweetok A, a tall, handsome, muscular man, double over so neatly when coming through my entrance that he had cleverly avoided rubbing any snow on his back. I had a lot to learn before I could pull off an acrobatic stunt like that!

I discovered as we three were awkwardly having tea that Oshaweetok A was one of the shyest persons I had ever met. His wife had probably forced him to come and see me, and if necessary she was ready to do the talking for him. We sat in silence.

"Saomik, *senunwak okasiksait, pieumavit*. Left-handed, a lamp-stone carving, do you want?" she finally asked.

"Yes," I said.

She looked at her husband, who studied the scars on his hands and said nothing.

"Have you got a carving?" I asked.

No answer.

"Do you make carvings?"

No answer. There was another long pause.

"Yes, he's made a carving," she whispered.

"*Piungituk*, it's bad," he gasped. "Piece broken off the foot. Rough stone, no good!"

"*Nowtima*, where is it?" I asked.

"Lost in the snow," he said.

His wife jumped up. "I'll go and try to find it."

She hurried out of the igloo and returned a moment later with a caribou skin wrapped into a protective ball.

"Here, you show him," she said, handing it carefully to her husband.

Reluctantly, he revealed a mother and child, larger than most, and one of the very best Inuit sculptures that I have ever seen. Oshaweetok A was quick to point out to me the chip off the carving's toe and how crude his work was.

"*Piiumavunga*, I want it," I told him, holding up the carving in the candlelight.

"*Tunivoapik*, take it, a little gift," he shrugged. "I'm not clever, like some, at making such things."

Now I knew about this same man's problem, having been made aware of it two days earlier. He owned a cheap, foreign import rifle, a .35-caliber bolt action, if I remember correctly. It had a cartridge jammed in it that he could not extract. I had tried, as others had, but none of us could get it out. (There had been a similar situation several years before where an Inuit hunter, in desperation, had tried to unjam his rifle by borrowing the gun of another man and placing both rifle muzzles together. He had fired the other rifle into the barrel of his jammed rifle and split the barrel wide open. Luckily, no one was hurt.) Still, this hunter without a firearm was desperate. I wondered what I should pay him for such a carving that would go toward his buying another rifle. I guessed this was the reason this family was so eager to trade before I had the chance to leave. Probably he had just finished this wonderful carving, which his wife had undoubtedly smoothed.

Suddenly, it came to me. I asked his wife to bring inside the canvas case that I had stashed in its usual place on top of the igloo's dome. I owned two rifles and thought of this one as my hard-knocks rifle. The other one in Kingait was fancier, but it was no better than the sturdy Winchester rifle I had brought with me. I preferred this one on rough *kamotik* trips, knowing that it was certain to receive harsh treatment.

When his wife handed me the rifle and I pulled it out of its case, Oshaweetok A's eyes lit up.

"*Tusunaami*, you're fortunate, *kukutipaluk*, beautiful rifle," he said, admiring its every detail.

"*Peungitualuk!*" I said. "It's bad. See that scratch on the butt? Probably I've knocked the barrel crooked on this trip. It won't shoot straight. Take it if you want, it's a little gift to you." I handed him the canvas case and both boxes of cartridges.

Staring at me, his eyes wide, he heaved himself to his feet, eager to leave, fearful perhaps that I would suddenly return to my senses and try to get it back.

"The carving?" I asked.

"Keep it, it's yours," he said, then clutching the rifle he bent nearly double, and led his wife out of the snowhouse.

Next day, when the sled arrived, I placed the carefully wrapped carving in the safest place that I could find inside the grub box that was lashed on the sled. The driver had a rifle, so I would have no need of one on our way back to Kingait. I was glad I had been able to give a carver something that he needed exactly when he needed it. That same carving by Oshaweetok A, which appeared in *Canadian Eskimo Art*, today is in the collection of the Metropolitan Museum of Art in New York, along with a number of other important Inuit prints and carvings.

I had hoped that my immediate trade with that shy carver would perhaps inspire him to go on and become a famous sculptor. But no, that did not happen. Like a number of other hunters, he made one or two more successful carvings, then gave up art entirely. Art critics who wish to label Inuit art commercial should think about this fact.

Carvers like Oshaweetok A wanted to do original carvings, and unless they felt moved to carve, they stopped. The truly surprising thing about the carvers and the printmakers who did continue so enthusiastically was that they went on being truly original, creative artists. That has become increasingly rare in our world of art today.

In 1971, in a book published by University of Toronto Press, entitled *Sculpture/Inuit*, I wrote:

> The Metropolitan Museum of Art in New York in a recent exhibition, *Masterpieces of Fifty Centuries*, showed three contemporary Canadian Eskimo sculptures. They were displayed along with the great works of Egyptian tomb builders and Greek temple makers, Leonardo da Vinci and Rembrandt, Hokusai and Picasso. It was a heart-warming sight to view these three stone carvings of the Arctic, a sea goddess, a seated woman with child [Oshaweetok A's same carving], and a wild green bear, all resting in timeless harmony with so many other works of genius.

45
Baby Trouble

It was a soggy, gray midday in late November. We were living in a small camp along the coast near an opening in the ice, hoping to take some seals. But when the southeast wind blew in off the water, the hunting was usually bad. The temperature had grown warm, the salt ice rubbery, and the snowhouses turned gray and soggy with an icy fog forming inside the igloos. It was the kind of near thaw that sometimes happens to families just after they have abandoned their tents and built their first winter snowhouses. The babies cried and the old people coughed endlessly.

I burrowed into my kit and found my last unread pocket book, *Life in the Amazon Basin*. I adjusted my candle and hunkered down in my sleeping bag to read until my eyelids drooped. I fell asleep, then woke and ate some caribou meat, lit the emergency candle again, and read some more. *What the hell,* I thought. *Take a day off, a week off. What does the federal government know or care? I'm just wintering here until someone comes to get me. That'll be months and months away.* The book kept falling on my chest. I drifted back to sleep again.

When I awoke and crawled outside, it was still dark. The hunters were busy cutting the tops off igloos and spreading tent canvas over them, for when a soggy snowhouse dome collapses, it can break children's bones.

Okalik's little boy came in with wet snowflakes clinging to his hair, and said to me in his high-pitched voice, "*Kaigeelaureet,* come, please. My *annanasiak,* grandmother, says come, you."

There was something in the way he asked that worried me. I went inside, unrolled my parka, which had been my pillow, and pulled it over my head, then hurried after the small boy, following him down inside his family's igloo. I was bent double in the entrance passage, easing myself past two frozen walrus seals, when I heard the first scream, a sound so full of pain and terror that it stopped me. The boy disappeared into the dome-shaped room of the igloo. I got up my nerve and followed him. Both seal-oil lamps were burning brightly and in the center was a female cousin of the family, an older woman, and a young woman, kneeling, legs spread on the bed. The young boy ran outside.

"The baby won't come out," said the woman who was behind her. She pressed her arms around the kneeling girl's stomach. The girl's teeth were clenched, her face drawn and covered with sweat. Her eyes were so wild with pain that I wondered if she even saw me.

"The baby won't come out," the woman cried, and pressed again on the girl's stomach, which made her scream again. "The water broke a long time ago. Can you get it out? We tried, it won't come out."

The girl remained kneeling, her elbows now on the bed, and when I came near her, she flopped herself back and I saw the swelling beneath her under her parka. Some smart observer I was. Like the others, she was usually so bulkily dressed in winter with her long, apron-fronted *amautik*, parka, that I hadn't even known she was going to have a baby. Oh, Lord, what was I going to do? I had a vision of myself bravely bundling her into a Montreal or Toronto taxi and telling the driver to rush to the nearest hospital. I called the boy and sent him running back for the fishing tackle medical box that held my first-aid kit and the St. John Ambulance book, and I asked him to bring two, no, four candles. The boy and his older brother returned with the green metal box and the candles.

Seeing that I was doing nothing, the grandmother pressed the girl's stomach hard and she cried out. It was the usual way I later heard, but I asked her to stop. Examine the mother, St. John Ambulance said. So I got those around us to hold the four candles and I looked. She was open and distended, and I felt inside, trying to see if it was breached. I felt the baby's head a little to one side and I just pushed sideways with the heel of my left hand and suddenly I could feel the head coming toward me, coming quick. I held out both hands, almost trying to hold it back. But I couldn't, and in no time there was the whole baby lying between her legs and all the cord. Oh, God, I felt frightened and mixed up. The infant lay against my hands, all steaming hot and kind of gray and wet and shuddering and I thought, *Oh, God, help us, it's my fault*, and I wanted to jump up and run outside.

The older woman let go of the girl and sprang at the baby, lifting it out of the shallow depression in the bed lined with soft caribou fawn skin that they had so carefully prepared for its arrival. The other woman was all business now, shaking the baby, neatly biting off the umbilical cord, wiping the infant clean, and calling out orders to the children, who ran to pass out the news to tell her husband who was away on purpose, fishing or hunting somewhere, they said, near the lake.

I bent double and squeezed out of the low entrance to the snow-house. After glancing around to see that no one was watching me, I wiped my wet hands on the wall of the snowhouse, the fronts and backs and sides of them very carefully until they felt totally numb. I wanted to pull up my parka and stuff my hands in the pockets the woman had made especially for me inside my caribou pants, but they weren't dry enough for that. I just stood there in the darkness, holding them pulled a bit into my parka sleeves and staring up at the sky.

The whole land was hidden in a rising fog. But up above, the sky was velvet black and each star shone with a bright intensity that I had never noticed before. A new life had arrived here tonight. I had touched it, felt it moving, hot and wet in my hands. I looked for some sign in the sky, something that might help me with a new way of seeing things, of understanding, but I saw nothing strange.

My hands seemed to be swelling and they felt jabbed with pins and needles the way wet hands do in cold. My little fingers and the tips of all the others were numb. So I turned, still holding them away from me, and made my way back down through the passage and inside the house.

The older woman, the midwife in charge, looked at me, then rummaged around in her gray canvas sack before pulling out a bright purplish calico skirt that I could remember her wearing over her caribou pants and knee-high skin boots. She leaned forward and handed her skirt to me. Then when I didn't accept it, not wishing to use her skirt, she went ahead herself and wiped my hands for me. When that was finished, I watched her throw the skirt away, which may have been usual after a birthing.

I thought, *Some wonderful amateur first-aid hero you are – you didn't even have a handkerchief or toilet paper to wipe your hands. And did you wash before you touched that girl or her new baby? No. Some no-good first-aid expert you turned out to be.* I took my tin medicine box and went back to my place and slept.

46
X Marks the Spot

When I was acquiring carvings in the camps, I didn't believe that all the ones I came across were of the highest quality. That same comment could be made today, but perhaps for quite different reasons. In the old days, some Inuit carvings were truly rough, crude expressions of life – of mother and child, a hunter, a seal, a bear, a caribou, a fish, a dog. In the early 1950s, these were unchanged from those collected by Knud Rasmussen and sea captains whaling in Hudson Bay in the 1890s. It was said by Inuit that some of these had been made by the carvers of stone lamps or pots to provide an *inua*, a soul, for the lamps and pots, thus giving them the strength to prevent breaking. The shape of the *inua* was determined by holding a small piece of the pot stone, *okushiksak*, and singing a song to it, then deciding on the image that was hiding in the stone and releasing it.

In those days, I was excited by almost every carving I received and delighted to be in such close contact with the carvers. I literally traded for each one of them, paying more, of course, for some than others. I believed that the important point was not to make harsh judgments that would cause these grandfathers, their sons or grandsons (women did not admit to carving in those days) to lose face by having their work rejected.

The now famous carver, Kiawak, son of that remarkable printmaker, the widow Pitseolak, was at that time only nine years old, but he was carving and even then showing remarkable promise. I gladly acquired all of his work for the Guild to display and sell in their Montreal showrooms. I am delighted that Kiawak was encouraged to keep on carving, for he is now recognized as one of Canada's best living sculptors.

Sometimes I used to wake up in the dark, mid-winter mornings wondering how I was going to justify all those carvings I had traded from boys and older hunters, lesser works that I did not plan to send south to face the sterner gaze of art critics and buyers. I wanted to exhibit only the better sculptures so that they would help build the good reputation that Inuit carvings were so quickly gaining.

One night when I could bear my carving fears no longer, I rose, pulled on my skin boots, wind pants, and warmest parka, took my flashlight, and went outside. The world was pitch dark and starless under heavy snow clouds. I made my way to our carving storage tent and ran my weakening light beam over the four boxes where I had hidden away the most questionable carvings. I skidded these heavy boxes out and wrestled them onto the short sled we had built to haul blocks of ice from the freshwater lake above us. This sled worked just as well for stone carvings.

When I first tried to pull the sled, it seemed impossibly heavy. A kick at its closest, upcurved runner broke the icy bond between the hard-packed snow and the flat, iron runner. The trail was downhill to the broken tidal area where the ice between sea and land had been upheaved and broken. The snow on top was windswept into long, hard drifts. Hitching myself doglike to the sled, I started weaving through the broken ice. When that was done, I stuck the long, fading flashlight inside my waistband underneath my parka, trying to warm its weakened batteries.

Almost a mile away across the fiord, I knew there was a raised pressure ridge in the sea ice. I marched steadily toward it. The tide was out, and I knew this long white upheaval would have opened and drawn apart. When I arrived at the crack, I took out the flashlight and ran its beam along its black snakelike length. It was not a dangerous place, for the mid-winter ice was very thick and the crack too narrow for a man to fall through.

I unharnessed myself, unlashed the boxes on the sled, and pried off their tops. Then with the light, I examined each carving again before I sadly dropped them one by one down through the crack. *Is this right?* I thought. *Should I be doing this?* I put the sixth, seventh, then the eighth carving back into the boxes. Who the hell was I, out here alone, to be making such lordly decisions?

Soon all but the eight carvings I'd held back were gone. I cast the fading light on those again and studied them, then snatching up the worst four, I dropped them quickly through the crack. I stored the lid slat back inside the boxes, for wood in the Arctic was almost as precious as good carving stone.

Feeling very unsure of what I'd done, I turned and started back. All was darkness on the shore. The dark silhouettes of winter tents and six or seven buildings were half buried in the night's gray snow. I could scarcely see the visitors' igloos. I climbed up through the ice barrier again and unhitched myself beside the carving tent, took out the rescued carvings, and stacked the empty boxes back inside, hoping that no one would notice, knowing all the while that Inuit hunters and carvers notice everything. I hurried back to my sleeping place feeling good again with none of the sense of shame that I had worried about. I'd mark up the price of better carvings to offset the loss.

I had only thrown the very crudest carvings away, but during other years in Dorset, I never got my courage up to put other carvings through the ice.

My son, John Houston, during his career as a filmmaker, took a course in the Bahama Islands learning to dive with an aqua lung so he could direct underwater shots for a film that he was helping to produce. Sometime in his youth, John had heard my scandalous confession about making those early carvings disappear. When he came out to the Queen Charlotte Islands to fly-fish with me, we studied a maritime chart of the west Baffin Island coast. He asked me to tell him the story again. When I did, he said, "Dad, would you mind making an X over the exact spot where you think you dropped those carvings, the ones that you judged to be not good enough?"

I looked at John and thought, *Wait a minute, what if I was wrong? What if something down there looks like a Henry Moore, a Brancusi? I'm not too old, am I? Shouldn't I be the one to dive down and retrieve those early carvings?*

But later I remembered seeing a boisterous team of rosy-cheeked, young scientific divers in their double wetsuits flip backwards into a steaming hole, then flap their flippers as they stroked gracefully downward into the gray-green darkness underneath the Arctic ice. They came up six minutes later, their faces pale blue and puckered like prune-faced old men.

As it turned out, John had to put off his long-awaited dive for those stone and ivory treasures. That may be just as well for me!

47
Moon Man

An overwhelming number of the important spirits in the Inuit world are female. The sun goddess is a woman named Saranik. The goddess of the air is a woman named Sila. The wind goddess is Aunra. The earth goddess is Nuna, and on and on it goes.

Almost the only strong and important male god is Tukik, the moon. There are various stories concerning him. Here is one that I came across.

A strong-minded woman whom I knew pointed out to her husband that the walls of their igloo had grown thin, icy, and sooty with lamp smoke, and she told him that she wanted him to build a new igloo for their family before the moon grew full again. She got her brother over from a nearby igloo to help him, and the new house began to rise in the cold, still morning, less than a snowball's throw away from their old igloo. The main dome of the house was finished not long after midday and a good-sized meat porch and a short windbreak tunnel were soon added.

The husband went with his wife's brother to the fish lake where they dug out from beneath the snow a smooth, clear piece of fresh-water ice that they had cut and stored when the ice was new and unclouded and just about the thickness of his wrist. This they put on the hand sled and dragged back to the new house. He could see that his wife was already packing up the old house, so eager was she to move into the new one. He laid the ice window in its tradition-al position above the igloo's one and only entrance, which faced the frozen sea. He pierced down four times, through the top, bottom, and both sides, then cut away the square, angling the cut in so that it would hold the window snugly. The brother-in-law climbed up on top of the meat porch, which was now strong enough to hold his weight, and glued the window edges tight with fine-cut snow which he firmly packed in place. He cleared the ice pane with his mitten until they could see a pale shaft of moonlight illuminating the center of the wide, snow sleeping platform.

In no time at all, the wife was busy inside, chopping their bed soft with her *ulu*, laying out their dance clothing that she had safely sewn inside soft pillows at the back curve of the sleeping platform, then driving wooden sticks into the igloo walls beside her traditional sleeping place on the left-hand side of the bed so they would support her drying rack.

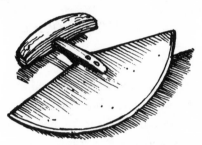

Ulu

She and her daughter spread four old sealskins, hair down, over the chopped-up snow, and these she covered with two yellowing bearskins, also hair down. Then four thick, winter caribou skins, hair up. Then an assortment of woolen trade blankets, old army blankets, and caribou skins were put on top.

The long stone lamp, which had been protectively carried from the old house to the new, still lighted, had new seal fat laid in it, which would melt and keep on feeding the flame that would light and heat the house. The *kunukai*, nose, a small air vent, was in place above the ice window, and the wife was contentedly settling in again.

Next day, I was with the men when we went hunting at the floe edge, and we took two bearded seals and two ringed seals, which was considered a good haul. The moon that night had risen close and full, a golden miracle running its path across the white sea.

"Tukik, the moon, is big tonight," Tukiaksuk, the oldest Inuk, said. "He's on the move hunting for ice windows to look through."

"Why windows?" I asked.

"The women say that if they're sitting sewing in their place by the lamp when Tukik comes and shines down through the window at them, he can make them pregnant."

"Pregnant?" I said. "Do women tell you that the moon can make them pregnant?"

"Yes," the younger hunters answered. "That's what the women say. We're never there when it happens. But it must be so." And they lay back and drank their tea, contented with the powers of the moon.

48
A Hunting Society

An Inuit camp in the early fifties averaged about thirty to thirty-five persons. In most ways, they did not think of themselves as individuals, but as families in a camp of people joined together by human relationships and the constant need to gather and share their food.

There has never been any sense of land ownership among them. Thus, they have never needed to stay in an undesirable situation simply because they owned it and needed to defend their property. If they became offended by their neighbors' actions in a camp, they simply packed up their few possessions and with their dogs and sled moved on to another camp. There was no arguing! The whole land belonged to everyone.

A man was eager to name a friend as his hunting companion. Like a good insurance policy, it would give him peace of mind to know that if he died, his friend would take care of his wife and children, bringing her into his family to protect her as his second wife and help to feed the younger children. There was no warfare (Inuit do not even have a word for war) and in the eastern Arctic, at least, even family feuds were rare.

It was thought to be immensely rude to come in from hunting and say, "I got two seals." That raised the question, "How many seals did each of the other hunters get?" Hunters, like everyone else, have good hunting days and bad. It was decided best not to mention their share of the catch. It was believed that a man did not simply take an animal because he was skillful with a hunting tool, but because he and others in the camp had obeyed the rules of life. For that reason alone, a certain animal had decided to give its body to the camp, thus releasing its soul to seek another form of life.

In most countries, humans have a warm sun, and wood or clay with which to build houses, and wood for fires to smoke and preserve meat and bake grain. In the far North, everything was different. Inuit were blessed with wind and hard snow to shape and build their houses in a treeless land, and cold to freeze their food for much of the year, and good, fresh water in abundance everywhere, in itself a rare benefit today. The whole complex Arctic hunting society was, I believe, meticulously formed by trial and error over many thousands of years.

49
Perfume and Tissue: The Ladies' Trap

The gathering, wearing, and trading of furs has been a Native American prerogative from long before first contact with Europeans. We simply encouraged them to excesses to further our profits and to warm our men and beautify our women, before that became one of the great no-nos of the contemporary environmental age.

On Baffin Island in a good year, in the days before carving and printmaking overtook fur-gathering as a way of making a living, women were usually nearly as successful as their husbands in the all-important art of trapping white fox. Nomadic Inuit hunting camps at that time used to number on average four or five families. White fox ran near those camps and Inuit women set out short trap lines that they could walk each day.

A wolverine, would sometimes become their worst nightmare, for that aggressive, bearlike but beaver-sized creature will often stay near a trap line, repeatedly devouring the catch. Wolverines are usually too cunning to be trapped and too wary to be shot.

A woman's answer to that problem was to chew a piece of meat into the size of a small hamburger while with a knife she split a long thin bone splinter from the shin bone of a caribou. Sharpening each end of the splinter into a double arrow, she then coiled the bone like a watch spring and imbedded it in the meat she had taken from her mouth. She would hold this meat tightly in her mittened hand for a few minutes until it would freeze. Then she threw it near her trap.

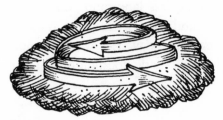

Coiled-spring bone in meat

This meat, gulped down whole by the wolverine, would warm inside its stomach. Then the coiled arrows would spring open!

When a woman found a wolverine that she had killed in this way, she would turn its pelt into wonderful parka trim for someone in her family. Wolverine is the only kind of trim which when breathed on in the cold will not rime up with frost.

Even thirty years ago, modern elements had been added to the trappers' tools. The No. 7 Victor trap was standard, but foxes are smart enough to avoid the trap if they can see it. To overcome this, for perhaps a century Arctic trappers have concealed the snapping jaws by carefully carving out a pie-sized crust of snow, setting a trap inside the hole, then carefully replacing the deceptive cover. However, if the weather warms by a fraction, this snow lid collapses in midday, then refreezes at night, rendering the trap useless.

To offset this problem, Inuit women invented a new trick by taking a thick, white, old-fashioned Kleenex, licking its edges, and stretching it like a drumhead over the round jaws of the trap. This paper tissue was amazingly efficient. It concealed the trap, yet was unaffected by any change in temperature.

The traditional bait for a trap was a ptarmigan's head, but when these are frozen, they do not give off much odor. The women, as they walked their trap lines, had time to allow their thoughts to dwell on this problem, which caused them to think of the over-whelming smell of the lilac perfume sold by their local trader. One bold girl tried it, dousing the bait with this perfume, with great success. The trail of a fox would swerve when it caught the passionate scent of that perfume. Soon it was part of everyone's trapping technique.

I, for one, am not sorry that the desperate need for Arctic fur-gathering has now greatly diminished, pushed toward extinction by Inuit carving and printmaking. But I am saddened by the fact that the nomadic way of life of these families who once moved with the animals and understood them so well seems to be fading fast. With the decline of serious hunting and trapping, their age-old skills required for living in the North began to fall away. They were left with little except a new world from a TV satellite dish.

50

Pups

It was not an Inuit practice to consider sled dogs as pets. We had a businesslike relationship with our dogs, about the same, I believe, as a farmer had with his work horses. As the horseless carriage changed everything for him, so the snowmobile came along and changed travel by dog team.

In early days when the teams still flourished, Inuit children occasionally brought small pups into the igloo to play with; soon enough, that would lead their father to make a small sled. Then the mother would cut and sew some harnesses and the children would hitch the pups and play, watched over by some older child or adult because of the uncertainty of sled dogs, which can be unpredictable around small children. The children were not urged to just play as our children are. Instead, they were encouraged to understand the smartest and the strongest and the weakest of the pups in their small team. Soon, they would place them in their proper places, shortening the lines of the weaker ones and lengthening the lines on the stronger, and especially on the smartest young dog or bitch that would most readily answer their commands.

Eventually, the father would ask the children about their growing pups and would be told, perhaps, that a particular bitch is not so strong, but she is much the quickest to respond to orders: go left, go right, stop, go. The fathers pay close attention to their children's early opinions of the pups, for they are usually proven right. That advances the whole process of developing a team and I think the children gained a lot of knowledge and appreciated being a part of the family's work.

51

The Little Sweet Harmonica

When the sea ice was strong enough for traveling, a young hunter journeyed with two others on the long dog-team trip to Iqaluit to ask a father for his daughter. This marriage plan had been made by the parents at least ten years earlier. But the girl's parents said she was still too young and he should wait another year. He returned home in the spring, sorry that he would have to wait.

To ease his disappointment, his own people decided to welcome him back by holding a dance. The young man forgot his troubles and while others were trying to regain their breath he took a harmonica from his pocket. It was of a much smaller size than anyone there had ever seen. This mouth organ had a sliding device that changed the musical sounds in wondrous ways that enchanted everyone. Some say he must have practiced playing it all the way across Baffin Island. I heard him. He was good!

An important camp boss was at the dance that night. When he heard the little harmonica, he borrowed it from the young man and played a rising series of rich-sounding notes. "What do you want for this?" he asked.

"Nothing," the young man said. "I like it. I am going to keep it." Many people there remember the conversation that followed.

"Will you take my other rifle for it?"

"No," the young man replied. "I'm keeping this tooth blower."

"Will you take my red canoe in trade for it?"

"No," said the young man. "Our family has a good canoe."

"Will you take some dogs?"

The young man paused before he answered. Dogs. Now dogs were what the boy needed most of all! "How many?" asked the boy.

"Two," the camp boss said with finality, for he was becoming angered and upset because other hunters were listening to him losing in this trading haggle with a boy.

The young man didn't answer.

"Will you take four?"

No answer.

"Seven?"

Still no answer.

"Eight?"

The boy opened his eyes wide meaning "yes." That was all the dogs he and his father and brother could possibly feed. "Wait!" said the boy. "I've got no sled, no wood to build one."

"Then it's eight dogs and my sled," the big man growled.

And the boy, seeming somewhat reluctant, handed over the seventy-five-cent harmonica.

Trading was sometimes like that before money came into the country. Something given for something wanted was the usual method of exchange.

The young man and his father had a good hunt that autumn, and the dogs flourished. The young man journeyed once more to Iqaluit with his new sled, his new team, and his brother. This time the girl's parents were vastly impressed with the young man and gladly allowed their daughter to become his wife.

52

Getting Married

Kingwatchiak was a dear old friend of mine who had long ago traveled to Dundee, Scotland, on a square-rigged whaling ship. He said he had lost his real virginity there to a young lady he met at a church supper who decided on her own (no language between them) to visit his room late at night. So much for Victorian morals.

The missionaries tried to enforce strict sexual restrictions in the Inuit world, but fortunately they no more worked up there than they have worked down here. When I recently asked a young Inuk friend about modern marriage practices, he answered in clear English, "But, Jim, nobody gets married here any more." Fifty years can make a tremendous difference in their society, as it clearly has done in ours.

Of course, there is nothing simple about getting married, whether you live in the Arctic or any other place. But in earlier days on Baffin Island, it seemed especially complicated!

Preparing there for marriage often started early, even before you were born. That is to say, two men who were hunting companions and their wives, if they both had wives, would agree that their children should marry. It didn't matter if one of these two children had not yet been born. These couples assumed they would soon have or adopt children of the opposite sex.

While these two children were growing up, they were taught to call each other by special names. The boy called the girl *nuliungasak*, meaning material for a wife, and the girl called the boy *ungasak*, material for a husband. As they became *uvikait*, teenagers, they both grew excited about the prospects of marriage. There is a saying in the Arctic that "a good hunter is the man his wife helps make him." Certainly, a young man could not even think of setting out from his family and joining another hunting camp with other younger couples until he had a wife.

To avoid embarrassing that hopeful bridegroom, I have chosen to call him Upik. He gave me a detailed account of how the whole business worked for him.

When Upik was aged about seventeen, he was out scanning the ice for seals with his grandfather when the old man said to him, "If you want to make a lamp for the mother of your wife-to-be, you can use that piece of pot stone that's out behind our tent. She'll be the one who will have to agree that you might soon be old enough to provide for her daughter. With her husband, she'll decide when you can live with them and try out their daughter before you marry." The grandfather also told him, "Women admire gifts. You might make the mother a new lamp. I could help you to make it."

Upik was pleased that he could use his tools and be helped by his grandfather. Working together, they made a strong stone lamp. It was small, about the length of your two hands, bow-shaped, and smoothly hollowed out to hold the seal oil.

Later when Upik's uncle visited their camp, Upik asked for a dog-team ride to visit some relatives – any relatives, for his blood was running hot and he was feeling restless. The uncle planned it so that they would visit overnight at the camp of Upik's wife-to-be. Both Upik and the girl were excited when they glanced at each other, but they were shy with others around. They did not speak that day to one another, and the girl went out of sight with a friend of hers to practice the seductive, womanly art of walking.

When Upik was alone in the tent with the girl's father and mother, he opened his sack and brought out the new stone lamp. He didn't exactly give it to the girl's mother, but he laid it down carefully, halfway between the mother and himself. He waited, but neither she nor her husband mentioned the lamp. Finally, the boy said to them, "I made that lamp, but I guess it's not much good."

"Well done, it appears to me," the girl's mother said, being careful not to touch it.

"It's good work for a boy as young as you," said the girl's father, glancing at it. "One can see that you will be able to carve well when you are older."

"I got a seal on the ice this spring," Upik told them, "and my father has already given me one of his dogs. I'm making a short sled to go with that dog as soon as I find the rest of the wood."

"I've heard about that sled," the girl's father said. "I have a piece or two of wood that I will give you."

"But only one seal so far?" The girl's mother sighed.

"Yes, only one," Upik admitted. "If I had my own rifle . . ."

"Oh, we believe that you will some day be a good hunter like your father and your grandfather," added the mother. "But it takes time to learn the ways of the dear animals." She sighed again.

"Quiet, woman," said her husband.

There was a long silence in the tent before Upik said, "The lamp is a gift for you. I have come to ask if you'll let me stay here for a while and try out your daughter."

The mother coughed. "She's still too young for that. She's just starting to learn to sew. But I suppose in time, perhaps, she'll learn. She might even make a wife for you later on, maybe after another winter or two has passed."

"It looks like a real good lamp," said the girl's grandmother, who had been sitting quietly on the other end of the sleeping bench. "You ought to take that lamp now," the old woman called out to her daughter. "That's a good young man. Let him stay. They're promised to each other."

Most grandmothers in that part of the world approve of early marriages. But what she said that day changed nothing.

Upik put the lamp back in his bag after he saw that the girl's mother refused to touch it. That meant she was not going to let him have their daughter this season or maybe even the next. Upik believed he'd be too old to get married then. He tried to think of any other marriageable girls he knew. There were fifty-eight families spread along that vast Arctic coastline, spread out into a dozen nomadic camps. All the young girls had been spoken for but two, and he didn't want to marry either of them. He wanted the one that had long ago been promised to him.

They left the camp next morning. His uncle didn't tease Upik about his problems, for he himself had suffered similar difficulties when trying to marry.

When the first moon tide of summer opened a wide shore lead through the ice, the girl's camp of five families sailed into the trading post and put up their tents, waiting for the annual ship to arrive. Upik's family had come earlier. His father went out with his older hunting companion. Sometimes, they took Upik with them, but just as often they did not, for these men liked to talk alone together.

Now Upik and his material for a wife saw lots of each other during that brief summer. It was the accepted habit of young people to stay up throughout the endless summer nights, then sleep all day. They went to the dances, which everyone attended, including the oldest grandparents and the smallest babies in their mothers' hoods. Upik and the girl, like all the other teenagers, used to run off and hide together. They were free to do anything they wanted with others of their age. Sex was never a problem. No one minded that! But just passionately rolling around on the summer tundra or in the Company's fur shed on rainy nights didn't really get you anywhere. If the girl had a child, she would have to offer it to her mother or it would be adopted by some relative or family friend. Until she had a husband, a girl could not keep a child. As for Upik, what he wanted was a proper wife so that he could quickly become a respected hunter and be asked by other young hunters to join them in a camp, and that could only happen after Upik had married his *nuli-unga*, his promised wife. So Upik was eager to move to her family's camp and begin their trial marriage while he hunted for her father. During that time, her parents would watch Upik to see if he would prove suitable material for a husband.

After shiptime, the arrival and departure of the annual supply ship, everyone went out to camp. Winter came, then in due course lost its strength as good spring traveling returned. Upik's father and one of his uncles each gave him another dog to go with the dog he had. This completed the team to pull his short new hunting sled. Three dogs would make a respectable-looking young man's team. This time he would journey by himself to visit the girl's family. Upik's father helped him lash a frozen seal onto his sled, and his mother gave him a good-sized aluminum pot. It was burned black and had a big dent on one side, but it didn't leak. It was the best kind of pot for holding a dozen eider ducks or a caribou stew. The boy's mother said she was giving the pot to him to give to the girl's mother if he wanted to. He lashed it on the sled with his tight-rolled bag and a pair of sleeping skins.

He had some trouble getting started because his two new dogs didn't get along with his first dog. They still wanted to fight or go in opposite directions. But before he reached the girl's camp, his dogs had settled down and were acting like a team. When he rode up through the tidal ice, everyone in camp was out to greet him. Even the girl's grandmother stood smiling by their entrance, leaning on her stick.

This time when Upik offered the girl's mother the big, store-traded cooking pot, she accepted it with pleasure. The seal meat he had brought they treated as a special feast. This time Upik looked squarely at the girl. She was sitting by her grandmother, carefully sewing a new, knee-length sealskin boot. A wife had to be able to sew boots for her husband. The grandmother nodded to him and even handed Upik the other boot for his inspection. The sinew sewing was quite small and fairly well spaced for a young girl.

"Hunting this spring, has it been good along your way?" the girl's father asked Upik.

"Enough," Upik answered nervously.

"Perhaps you would wish to stay down here and hunt with me?"

The mother didn't say a word and the girl went right on sewing.

"This granddaughter's going to be a real good sewer." The girl's grandmother gave Upik a smile that was evenly short-toothed, for she had spent a lifetime chewing soft her hunters' boots.

"She's getting better at the stitches now," her mother admitted, "but she's got to practice more before they'll keep out water."

Upik trembled when he heard those words, for they signalled that he was on the true path toward his adult hunting life.

On that first night, he squatted quietly just inside the entrance of their winter tent and watched as the family eased their way into the bed that was as wide as their big tent. They put their feet toward the back of the tent and lay with their heads toward the entrance as every family did. But in that bed of furs and blankets, there was no room for him. Finally, the girl's father rolled toward his wife who was lying, tending her lamp.

Upik stood up quickly, for he could see that a space had been opened for him. He whipped off his boots and clothes and slipped in beside the daughter, feeling her father's brawny back against his own.

Be careful here, Upik thought. Only later when everyone seemed to be asleep did the girl begin to squirm and Upik reached nervously over to her. As the girl responded, Upik had the sense that her parents were not asleep, while the girl's younger sister, who had been faking sleep on her other side, felt the motion and let out a giggle. No one cared. Everyone in the wide bed was aware that this trial marriage had begun.

When summer returned, they went in to the post to dance and trade, putting all their dogs out on the islands, feeding them when they could and letting them fish and fend for themselves.

All the hunters and carvers who were Upik's relatives and those who were the girl's relatives gathered to decide about their marriage which until now had been a trial only. The big gift pot was passed around, crammed with eider ducks and broth. The girl's father was the first that day to drink from the gift pot and fish out half a carcass to pick. Then the pot was passed to Upik's father, then everyone there shared, each being careful to leave enough for others. After eating, Upik's uncle, who was spokesman for this meeting, asked if anyone could say why Upik and the girl should not be married, then looked carefully at each person inside the tent in turn, seeking their assent. The youngest were teenagers, but they, like their elders, took this duty very seriously. No one made any objection until near the end when one young hunter refused to answer. When the question was asked of him again, he hung his head, but still he did not speak.

Upik's father, like the girl's, got up and strode out of the tent, not looking pleased.

Once again the uncle asked the teenager who had refused to answer what was wrong.

"*Kakivak*, fish spear," he answered. "Upik borrowed our fish spear when we were at the fish lakes. He never gave it back."

"He forgot," his uncle said. And walking to Upik, he asked him, "Where's their fish spear?"

"Oh!" Upik gasped. "I left it lying up there by the fish cache."

"Go and get it if you want a wife," the uncle told him. "Go in my canoe, but be sure to bring it back. Here's a file. When you hand the fish spear to that family, you be sure that it's well sharpened."

Upik made a swift journey and returned the spear to the young hunter. He took it without a word, but went and told his own father, "The spear is back."

Now the fathers and all the hunters related to them had to go through the whole damned ritual again. This time none of them had any objection, and now the path to marriage was truly open to Upik.

But his difficulties were far from ended. After the ship had come and gone, the Company made its arrangements with each hunting group and Upik's family, like the others, departed. Upik remained with his uncle's family, and waited. When the girl's family set out to make their winter camp, he was welcomed aboard their old trap boat with them. When Upik looked at the girl who was sitting up in the boat's bow with her younger sister, he felt a shudder of excitement run through him. If everything went as planned, she would soon become his wife. He asked a friend to bring him his three dogs and sled when the snow was right.

Life went well for Upik in that camp. He got on wonderfully with the girl and all her family. He felt he was moving closer to the kind of life he had been dreaming of. He was truly on his way to manhood.

In late spring, as Upik had hoped, his father and older brother arrived by dog team. The father was pleased to hear that Upik had done well over the winter. Everyone seemed to like Upik and the fact that he had taken six seals. But those seals were not considered his. By tradition, they all belonged to the girl's father. Of course, this man shared all the meat fairly, and the whole camp had done well that winter.

Upik's father and his brother had built an igloo of a kind only made to last a night or two, with no meat porch or freshwater ice window over the entrance. Of course, they were welcome to feast and visit the others as often as they wished. After two days, Upik's father said, "It's time for us to return to camp." He loaned Upik one of his strong male dogs.

"Shall I bring her with me when we go?" Upik asked.

"I don't know," Upik's father said. "That is up to you, and the girl, and her family. I have no objections."

"I want to take her home with us," Upik told his father. "I want her to be my wife."

"I'm leaving in the morning," said his father. "You two be ready to travel with us."

When Upik asked the girl's father, he said, "It's all right with us. She can go with you or stay with us."

Upik slept that night with the girl in her family bed. "Your family says," he whispered, "it's all right if you come with me. I'm leaving early in the morning."

When Upik woke up, the girl was gone. His back was still against her father's, and her sisters lay sleeping one space away from him. Upik panicked. Where was she? Half dressed, he slid out of bed. She wasn't in the tent. He rushed outside. She was nowhere to be seen.

Upik ran back inside and shook her sister's shoulder. "Where's your sister?" he demanded.

The girl's younger sister looked up blearily at him, then hid her head. This time Upik pulled on his parka before he darted out the door, looking carefully all around the camp and hills and sea ice. He could see no one.

A light snow had fallen in the night and in a moment he found her tracks. He followed them, breaking into a trot and then a run because they were so clear. He saw where she had stopped, turned around, shuffled back and forth as though she were thinking or dancing, then hurried on, using longer strides, probably running away from him. Why was she doing this? Why this morning, with his father and his brother watching? Why had she pretended so long to accept the marriage, then decided to run away from him?

The girl's footprints took a new direction in a wide circle around a hill, back into the valley leading to their camp. He ran along her tracks, following them back into her father's camp.

When he reached the igloos and winter tents again, the snow around the camp was packed hard with hundreds of human footprints, dogs' footprints. Where was she now? Upik went inside her family's tent. The grandmother was lying on one elbow, heating a cup of tea over the small oil lamp he had given the family. Upik was ashamed to ask her if her granddaughter was in that small space. Her younger sister was composed now, still in bed, but watching him very carefully. "Where is she?" Upik demanded.

"She's not where she sleeps," the sister answered, pulling back the covers to show him the empty place where her sister had been lying between them.

Upik rushed outside again only to see his father and his uncle with their big team already gathered. They were lashing down the load on their sled. They looked over at him, growing impatient, eager to leave. Upik was in a panic. He rushed back into the igloo again. This time the grandmother raised her head and nodded to him.

"Is she here?" he asked her.

She gave Upik her short-toothed grin, but did not answer him.

How could she be anywhere in there? Turning, he again burst out the entrance. He was so furious now that he caught and harnessed his own three dogs, overturning his sled so they could not run away. Then striding back inside, he noisily snatched up all of his few possessions and stormed toward the door.

"*Annanasiak!* Grandmother!" the younger sister called, pointing at her grandmother.

The old woman laughed and pulled the blanket over her head. Upik took two strides to reach the old woman and rolled her off her sleeping skins and pulled them back.

There lay the girl who had been hiding underneath her grandmother. Upik grabbed her by the wrist and pulled her out. She refused to look at him and started wailing. Her wails were not too high-pitched at first, but they grew louder as he dragged her outside by both wrists. Now her voice was turning into a scream. The camp dogs started howling with her, and from the winter tents and igloos whole families burst forth and began to call her name. The girl wailed, "Father, Mother, friends! Help! Save me!"

Upik's father and his brother sat in silence on their sleds, watching.

All the women in the camp were now screaming, "She belongs here with us. Upik, let her go!"

Upik looked round and saw his father and his uncle jerking their long sled hard and heard them yelling at their dogs. They took off, thumping hard through the barrier ice, then halted their dogs and turned to look back.

Upik had to drag the girl to his sled. She dug in her heels and fought so hard he had to force her onto the sled, then hold her there as he tried to guide the four excited dogs. The newest one decided to rush forward and rejoin his father's team. They made some progress, but the moment Upik bent forward to gain control of his dogs, the girl leapt away from him and raced back toward her relatives and her friends, all of whom were shouting, "Faster, run faster, faster!" urging her back among them.

Upik jumped off his sled and turned it over so the dogs could not drag it far. Then, running like a caribou, he caught the fleeing girl. She screamed out to those watching her from the camp. They yelled back, urging her to break away again. The women and children were wailing, and the hunters were pacing back and forth in great excitement.

Upik looked around and saw that his team was trying to drag his upturned sled along the fiord, but its curved runners kept snagging in the drifts. Once more he dragged the girl until he caught the sled and tried to straighten out the yelping dogs.

Again the girl gave a tricky twist and Upik lost his grip on her. She was off again and running back toward her camp with her family and neighbors cheering wildly. She quickly gained a wide lead on him. This time Upik didn't run, but stood sadly watching her go. The crying and the yelling from the tents and igloos instantly ceased. The girl stopped and looked back at Upik. He was busy righting his sled and untangling his dogs. Then, without turning his head, he started to drive his team out of the fiord.

The girl watched him as the distance between them widened. She began to walk and then to run – this time toward him! Upik saw her coming and dragged his foot like an anchor to slow the speeding sled.

Now she was running just behind the sled. He looked back at her and called, "*Atai*, come on," and she jumped onto the sled beside him of her own free will. At that moment, they were formally married. They were no longer just two pieces of material for marriage, they were man and wife. Her campfolk resumed their yelling, but now the wailing changed to cheering, this time for the two of them.

You may think this is a crazy way to get married. But I say look around you, friends, and think again!

53
Coppermine and Kalvak

On one of my trips to the western Arctic, Hudson's Bay House in Winnipeg was my first stop at the invitation of the Company to see how their new methods of distributing carvings was working out. I then flew to Edmonton, Canada's most northern major city where, if you're leaving without much time to spare, be damned careful. Edmonton has two distinctly different airports, one on each side of town. Only one leads to the Northwest Territories. I was traveling with a Company clerk from Newfoundland who was bundled in a crackling stiff, new parka. He had never ventured into this part of the country and seemed anything but keen to do so. When we discovered that we were bound for the wrong Edmonton airport, the taxi wheeled around and raced for the other one. The driver told us the other would have taken us to places like the Bahamas and Rio de Janeiro. "What's so bloody wrong with that?" the clerk grunted. "I'll trade this fuggin' parka for a straw hat any day!"

We flew north and overnighted at Yellowknife in the Northwest Territories, the home of Giant Yellowknife, North America's largest gold mine. Then we departed next day for Coppermine in a single-engine aircraft coughing and rumbling over the vast, sub-Arctic plain. The river courses in that country nurture the last outgrowth of the Land of the Little Sticks. Lakes beyond all counting shine like molten silver across the somber tundra, marked on occasion by pingos, huge frost humps thrust up like isolated Mayan pyramids in the rumpled landscape. Far before us at our destination, the vastness of the Arctic Ocean came into view with huge sheets of pan ice floating in the cold, blue reflection of the sky.

The aircraft landed and we met the Hudson's Bay man, a middle-aged Scot, who silently eyed his new clerk while the clerk eyed him, each absorbing those helpful or damaging first impressions. The Bay man took me to the store along a well-groomed gravel path bordered by whitewashed stones. He showed me some interesting-looking *ulus* made with pounded, native copper fastening in an antler holder. I felt sure there would be a market for these in museum shops along with other objects made by Inuit trading into Coppermine.

Coppermine ulu

The name Coppermine had not come from a mine, but from the fact that an abundance of pure float copper had been found in that vicinity over centuries, probably carried there and dropped by some moving glacier that had dug into the mother lode. Inuit have been able to hammer this soft metal, thus cold-forming harpoon heads, arrow heads, knives, and scrapers. They have traded this raw, pure copper west, it is said, as far as Siberia, and all the way east to Greenland. That says something for their trade routes and skills before we foreigners arrived.

Saying goodbye to the trader and his new clerk, I wished them luck. The small plane took me north across the strait to Uluksartuuq, Holman Island, on the western tip of immense Victoria Island. There the Bay man, Scotty Gaul, and Father Tardy, OMI, introduced me to the remarkable, middle-aged Inuk woman, Kalvak, who, it was said, in her earlier years tried hard to be a shaman. Tardy's collection of her carefully gathered drawings took my breath away. Finally a whole printmaking shop was built by Inuit at Holman and succeeded on the basis of her inspired work. Later, of course, other artists there created successful drawings and prints. But it is said that almost everyone at Uluksartuuq was related to Kalvak.

Much later, after I had left the North, I made some museum documentary films including one on Kalvak, with her notable facial tattoos. She had grown old and was confined to her bed at that time. When her flock of grandchildren and great grandchildren would come in to see her, she would slide open a little drawer beside her pillow which was packed full of pink Canadian fifty-dollar bills.

"Take one! Take some!" she would call to the children, then say, "It's good to see the young ones go over and trade for all the things we never dreamed of having when I was a young girl."

She did tell me one surprising story from her days as a young girl. In her part of the western Arctic, if two young hunters were courting the same girl, the girl's father would arrange to settle the matter by a sort of tug of war. Each young man would take one of the girl's arms and then pull. When I expressed surprise and wondered if this might not be kind of hard on the girl, Kalvak laughed in a way that shook her frame. "Ah," she said "a girl can always throw her weight on the side of a good man!"

54
Down at Ennadai

One of my many zigzags when I was ranging all over the North was to Ennadai Lake, N.W.T., in 1955. That's deep in the Keewatin, west of Hudson Bay, where the *Tuktumiut*, Caribou People, live. At Ennadai Lake at that time, there was an Inuit population of perhaps two hundred persons. They were a widely scattered, nomadic people who had never seen a seal. They lived on trout and caribou. There was no trading post. The government wanted me to find out if there were any art possibilities among these people who had often been difficult to find and had sometimes suffered hunger and starvation.

I flew from Baffin Island to Montreal, then Ottawa, Winnipeg, and north again to Churchill, Manitoba, a roundabout route which was the only way at that time to conquer the immenseness of Hudson Bay. I arrived at Churchill in mid-January and was impressed by the temperature. In the morning it stood at −55° Fahrenheit (about −45° Celsius), but I didn't care. I had a kit bag full of sealskin and winter caribou skin clothing: fur parkas, boots, mitts, pants. I planned to stay in that part of the country until late spring or summer, depending on transport.

Beau (Sgt. A. N. Beaumont), the Royal Canadian Mounted Police pilot, and his co-pilot, Fletch (Cpl. R. L. Fletcher), had been notified to fly me to Ennadai Lake in their new, single-engine Otter aircraft. Beau told me it would be their second flight there. Their engineer was special constable G. E. Bartlett. Also aboard was a weather station person, S. J. Sillett, nicknamed Sid, and Ataloak, an Ennadai woman, and her child, whom she called The Uncle. They were going home with us.

For this trip, the mounted police had supplied their plane with a huge, coffinlike box of survival gear that was designed to take care of passengers and flight crew for a month. The trouble with that precaution was we couldn't load anything else or move around inside the plane with this awkward box aboard.

"Awh, to hell with it!" we all agreed, and left the cumbersome crate of survival gear in a dark corner of the hangar.

When we took off for Ennadai Lake, it was overcast. Daylight at that time of year is slow to come and quick to leave. Not long after midday, it began to grow dark.

The pilot hollered back, "We're looking for a small lake we call 'the tennis racket.' It's got a handle shape that points toward Ennadai Lake. Keep a sharp eye open. Shout if you see it."

We kept looking, but none of us ever saw the lake shaped like a tennis racket. Not surprising, since the whole country under us looked like a slightly rumpled white tablecloth that stretched beyond us in all directions until it disappeared in the darkness. The pilot began turning the Otter slowly in the gathering gloom, hoping that we might see a light from the weather station. Finally, he beckoned me and I leaned forward.

"We'll never make it back to Churchill." Beau pointed at the Otter's gas gauge. "I'm going to try and put her down around here somewhere now while we can see something. We'll land under power instead of falling like a rock when we run out of fuel."

It was black above us but the gray snow seemed to unroll beneath us, rising up faster, closer, closer. What had appeared smooth from on high looked rougher now. Beau made the very best landing that could be made, but even then the plane's left wing cut a long slash in the hard snow, then bucked into the air. It landed again, twisting, tipping, turning.

I hit the bulkhead in front of me hard and at that moment thought, "We're done for!"

I must have blanked out in shock. When I started to function again, the sudden silence was terrifying. I never even thought of the risk of fire.

The weather station man across from me said, "You all right?"

I felt my arms and legs. "I'm all in one piece. How about you?"

It was pitch dark and the metal of the plane was so cold it was unthinkable to stay inside. I wanted more than anything to get outside, and so did the others. Everyone was banged up. None of us knew how much. I was trembling so hard that I had to crawl out on my hands and knees.

The first job, it seemed, was to get together and see that everyone was moving and accounted for. I found Beau, the pilot, sitting on the snow beside one ski. Fletch, the co-pilot, had his face hidden in his scarf, trying to staunch a violent nosebleed. The weather man kept shaking his head the way people do when they have water in their ears. The Inuit woman, Ataloak, was crawling around like me with her baby on her back. I felt inside her hood. The baby was naked and very much alive and kicking. I had the impression that he, The Uncle, was laughing.

God, how lucky can we be? No fire and everyone accounted for. But the thing I'd been too stunned at first to notice was the sharp wind that was kicking up the snow around us. We would quickly have to make some kind of protective shelter. The icy metal plane tipped at that angle with its doors sprung open was certainly not the answer.

Finally, Beau and I felt steady enough to stand. We fumbled around in the back of the plane until we got a grip on the new, stiff, canvas engine cover and heaved it outside. I found my snow knife and my kit of clothing, along with the sleeping bags of all the others and a folding trench shovel. I shoved everything out to the weather man. I remember that I could not get the seat cushions out.

God, how we wished we hadn't unloaded that big, awkward box of survival gear at Churchill!

Beau and I, with some help from Fletch, who had blood from his nose spread and frozen on his face, started to unfold the stiff canvas, hanging it over the plane's propeller and engine cowling, which was the purpose of the cover when a pilot needs to apply heat to start a cold engine in the Arctic.

Taking turns with Bartlett, the engineer, we dug a crude hole beneath this tentlike drapery and threw the chunks of snow outside. The wind continued to rise. Ataloak, with her child, was crouched beside the weatherman, both shuddering, their backs to the wind, just outside our makeshift tent.

When we believed the hole was large enough, I called to

Ataloak. She crawled around outside with me, helping to place the heaviest snow chunks on the fringe of canvas to weight it down and keep out the wind. The weatherman stuffed in all the sleeping bags.

Once inside, we stripped the covers off the bags and roughly spread them out to fill the hole. The woman helped. Then, fully dressed, the three Mounties and I got inside our bags and lay down. The last I had seen of the weatherman, he was having a leak against the wind. Ataloak remained kneeling beside us while she shifted her child around inside her spacious parka until she had him moved from back to front. His passage was beneath her arm so we never even saw his head. Holding the child to breastfeed him, she smiled at us, then crawled inside her handsewn, caribou-skin bag which had the hair turned in so the warm fur was against her.

We quickly settled, totally filling the space. "Where the hell do I fit in?" the weatherman demanded.

Nobody answered. We didn't care. We were so glad to be out of that rising blast of wind. It was his problem, let him find his own space.

"I'm coming in," he warned us.

I felt his weight across my legs. He struggled and with help managed to free one of the sleeping bags. He wrapped it over and around himself, then lay silent, spread across the rest of us.

I thought this arrangement wasn't going to be so bad. The weatherman had looked skinny back in the Churchill mess without his parka. Oh, well, I thought, *his weight will be spread over all of us. He won't be that heavy. Probably he'll help to keep us warm. Hell, being packed so close together, we'll keep each other warm.*

I fell asleep and woke some hours later feeling as though I were in some kind of medieval torture chamber with a cruel weight punishing my knees.

Beau next to me was awake as well. "Let's try to roll this guy over," he said. "My feet have gone numb, or maybe they're frozen?"

We couldn't roll him down, so we had to haul him up across our hips. He was like a hibernating animal, dormant, or still in shock. He didn't seem to wake.

We covered our heads and slept again.

This time, Ataloak and her child started squirming under his weight. So desperate were we this time that we woke him, made him get up and go outside. He shambled out, wearing his sleeping bag around him like a shawl. We followed, each to have a desperately needed leak, then crawled back in. This time we positioned ourselves with everyone sitting in a circle which took less space.

Beau got one of those short, fat, emergency candles out of his ditty bag and lit it. It was no campfire, but a candle's flame helps raise your spirits and it also helped raise the temperature, as did the breathing of six persons, seven counting The Uncle in Ataloak's hood. We didn't often think of him, for we couldn't see him buried in his mother's parka. He rarely uttered a sound, unless it was the one that seemed suspiciously like laughter.

With the coming of dawn, the wind died and we went out and started to poke around. We found my Primus stove in its wooden box, a brown paper shopping bag with a loaf of frozen, puffed-up white baker's bread, a bottle of rum – Thank God! – four chocolate bars, some chewing gum, and two fair-sized packages of plant fertilizer. We were temporarily delighted.

There were three radios aboard the plane and we were to find out that day that one of them had dead batteries in the cold. The plane radio wouldn't respond and the third, a miniature Japanese receiving set, crackled but had too short a range to pick up anything.

"We've got to fix this badger hole of ours," said Beau. "Let's make it bigger!"

The exercise did us good and helped take our minds off the problem. We finished our expansion in less than an hour, retied the tent corners to the Otter's skis, and increased the snow banking around our tent. Then we spread a canvas tarp at the bottom of the hole and rearranged our sleeping bags. Ataloak had a goose-wing brush inside her small bag of treasures and she carefully swept out any loose snow in a motherly fashion, which seemed to delight her son, who came halfway out of her hood to watch. She had him shake hands with everyone and introduced him as Atkak, The Uncle. Inuk children were often not given their proper names for the first few years until it was reasonably certain they would continue to survive.

Fletch managed to draw the small amount of remaining aviation gas from the engine. We all worried about using this kind of fuel in a small stove built only to burn kerosene. But in weather that was varying between forty and fifty degrees below, we had to take the chance. We carefully placed it in the center of our tent and lit it. The stove worked well for a moment. Then the gasoline flared up! A spurt of flames reached up to set on fire the leaked oil around the engine cowling!

Goose-wing brush

There was terrible confusion! All of us snatched our sleeping bags, then scrambling, rolling, twisting any way we could, we got out of there and away. The flash fire burned itself out, thank God, with no explosion.

After that event, we developed a sort of horror of the smoke-blackened interior of the tent. The two pilots and the engineer stayed there, but with help from Ataloak, I built a small igloo. She and her baby and the weatherman moved into it with me. We all had good, Arctic-weight sleeping bag canvas under us and almost enough warm clothing. I was able to share around the extra winter gear that I had brought. Beau gave us our share of the short, fat, emergency candles and we kept one of them burning in the small igloo as much as possible. Believe me, it makes the difference between a nice little home and a damn deep-freeze.

In daytime, our two main preoccupations were, first, to try and hear anything on the two radios we hoped might still work and, second, to keep the bright yellow wings and tail of the police plane swept clear of the fine snow dust that formed on them so thickly that we were sure if a plane came near us, the Otter would be totally hidden from view. Since our only hope was to be spotted from the air, we tried to keep at least one person out watching and listening for any aircraft throughout the daylight hours. None of us saw or heard a sound.

When we opened the rum after it had spent a night in the frigid plane, a thick, outer layer of ice had formed inside the bottle, leaving only a central core of alcohol. We tried to ration that, but it didn't last long. The puffy, frozen, white bread helped, but it, too, quickly disappeared. We very evenly cut up the chocolate bars. Some ate theirs quickly, others tried to save them. The great thing was we had liquid in the form of snow at all times. In the Arctic, there is little possibility of dehydration, which I have heard can kill a man after a single day of desert sun and heat. If a person acts sensibly in every way, it's been proven that they can live off their own fat in the Arctic for perhaps a month.

There was nothing to do after the igloo-building and the thrice daily chore of plane wing-sweeping, so we just trudged around the plane to keep warm, yet trying not to burn off too much body heat and energy. One of the important aspects of our plight was that we all stayed friends. There had been many warnings against downed crews disagreeing, which can lead to some leaving an aircraft to try and seek some way out. A lot of northern flyers have died that way.

The weatherman had been keen to help with the igloo-building because he was impressed that it was difficult to do. He asked me to show him how to cut and lift the blocks, a real Inuit skill. I thought teaching him would be a form of occupational therapy for both of us. We had my snow knife and a Swedish hand saw among our few treasures, so I started him on that, since using it is easier than using a snow knife. He cut straight down and sawed until he caught the trick of loosening and lifting a block without its breaking.

Instead of forming the blocks in a circle to create a dome, I thought it would be easier to start him off by building a straight wall. We took all the time we needed, hoods up tight and warmed by the exercise. Ataloak showed him how to mortar each block together with finely chopped, shaved snow, then lent him her *ulu*.

When we finished the wall that evening, it was as long as a stretched limousine, but was only two blocks high – meaning about crotch-high. But Sid, the weatherman, was proud of the job and we were both warm enough to push our hoods back for a while to listen in the cold and deadly silence. We heard nothing. I had a bad night, and in the morning still we heard no sound.

We leapt out of our holes and danced around near midday when we heard a plane. It was a military twin-engine Dakota. We prayed that it was out on search for us because it appeared so low above the horizon. Beau got out the flare gun and fired twice into the air, but told us he thought the pale, sunless afternoon would make the flares impossible to see. The Dakota slowly disappeared, into the south.

The plane we had seen belonged to the Navy stationed in Churchill and was out on search for us. They had about a dozen spotters in the plane watching on both sides, but they did not see our plane, or our igloo, or the flares. The one thing they had seen was a long, straight blue shadow that began and ended sharply. The men peering out of the plane's starboard windows insisted that what they had seen must have been manmade. That was all they saw, the shadow of our practice wall.

The Dakota was already short on gas and forced to continue south to Churchill, but they sent word ahead of them that they believed that on the featureless white plain, they had seen a sign from us.

That night, out of the blackness in the southeast, we heard the roar of a large aircraft. All of us ran out. Beau fired three flares into the air. The aircraft's pilot saw them and tipped his wings. We let out wild shouts as we saw the big military plane without skis swoop toward us, red and green lights flashing. It turned and circled low over us, though we knew it could not land. We heard their radio calling to us on our small Japanese shortwave receiver that unfortunately had not been built to transmit. We could hear the pilot telling Churchill radio that it was difficult to give our exact location and that he would remain over us until another plane came in to replace him while he returned to refuel, that he would not leave us until some other aircraft had found us and could keep us in sight. Such a plan seemed like life's blood to us. The big plane continued to make long, thunderous sweeps over us, so low we felt we could reach up and touch it.

That day we had been reading the fine print on the fertilizer bags and wondering if the contents could possibly have any human food value. The fact that we had no supplies had been our fault. But three long days and nights of waiting had worn us out, from the relentless pressure of the fifty-below cold and the uncertainty of our situation. I went into our igloo with the plane above us, and fell sound asleep, lulled by its reassuring roar just above our heads.

I awoke in the igloo and listened. Silence. My God, where were they? Rushing out, I could only hear the throb of engines very faint and far away, wrapped in the snowstorm that was filling the air. Had the rescue plane lost us or gone back to base for fuel? Soon there was no sound at all except the moaning of the blizzard. The snow was growing finer, driving harder.

When light returned, it marked the fourth day of our predicament. The bright blue and yellow colors of the police plane had disappeared. Ataloak climbed up and did a super job with her goose-wing brush on the wings, tail, and top of the fuselage, but the driving storm whitened it again almost before she could finish the job.

Would they find us again after this storm? Certainly, the whole country around us would have formed new drifts and taken on a different look. In summer, the many lakes in this part of the Arctic would have helped locate our position, but in this season everything looked like freshly whipped cream on a pie.

Beau had been a Canadian Air Force pilot flying Hawker Hurricanes during the North African campaign. There he had picked up the habit of smoking a pipe that smelled like a burning rubber boot. Sometimes we could see whiffs of blue smoke come puffing so heavily out of the tent that we thought it was on fire again.

The infant, Atkak, had remained in a jolly mood throughout this whole event, and he had taken a fondness to the pilot's awful pipe, reaching endlessly for it when he was near. Finally, Beau said, "Hell, go ahead, kid, take a puff."

The mother seemed delighted, but when The Uncle drew on it, the pipe made a ghastly sucking sound and Atkak disappeared inside his mother's hood and let out his first real wail. His mother retrieved the pipe, smiled, and took several deep approving puffs herself before handing it back to Beau. She eased The Uncle around under her arm and onto her chest and we heard him sigh contentedly.

"What kind of a plane do you think they'll use to try and take us out of here?" I asked Beau.

"Probably another Otter on skis. But, Jesus, it will take someone who really knows the country and has had experience. Not just anybody should try a landing around here!"

"Who might try it?" I asked nervously.

"Well, there are a few around, but if the search is centered out of Winnipeg, through Churchill, I'd guess they'd get Bounce Weir. He's a good old rough-style bush pilot who's in the Air Force now. But I've heard he's retired, gone to Victoria where he's going to grow roses."

"I hope he hasn't done it yet!" said Fletch.

"I don't know how or when he or anybody else could get here," said Beau. "Who knows when this mean bitch of a storm will blow away?"

Next morning it was gone, and we saw not a plane on skis that might land, but a large search plane coming in above our heads. The men in this aircraft tossed out an empty tin can with a note inside. "Are some of you hurt? It's reported in the South that only three of you have been seen. At least we know you have lots of food and survival gear. An Air Force jock has volunteered to fly in on skis to try and pick you up."

"That'll be Bounce Weir!" Beau laughed. "I'll bet anything he's the man."

With our "lots of food and survival gear" stored in the hangar at Churchill, we all ate handfuls of snow. The weatherman got up and brushed the hell out of the Otter's blue body and its lemon yellow wings until they shone.

Then we saw it, smaller than a mosquito, then heard it, as the rescue plane zoomed in low over us and turned.

"There he is! Look! Thank God it's him!" Fletch shouted.

We could see Flight Lieutenant (Bounce) Weir and his engineer unbelievably close and waving at us. They studied the surface during two more turns, then made a landing that was rougher than a bear. In no time we were all huddled together, shaking hands.

"Beau, this is one hell of a place you picked to set that Otter down." Bounce laughed.

"We didn't pick it," Fletch told him. "It picked us."

"I'd be overweight if I tried to take you all out at once. Who's going first?"

Beau said, "Jim and Bartlett and I are going to stay. Take this weatherman and the Eskimo woman and her kid and Fletch, whose nose is probably broken. We'll stay here until you get back if you'll leave us something to eat."

"Sure," Bounce answered. "We've got an emergency pack in here somewhere. Take what you want. We thought you had a bloody great survival box stuffed in that plane."

"We did, but it was so bloody great we pitched it out at Churchill."

The three of us watched Bounce gun the engine and start his take off, the sturdy Otter bouncing and bucking across the drifts like a rodeo horse.

"There's not many like him," said Beau. "On skis or floats, he's the best bush pilot ever. The amazing part about Bounce is that he's been pulling off awful landings and take offs like that for years. The trick is that he's still alive."

We were so delighted to have been found that Beau and I lay back and watched Bartlett prime and light my Primus from a proper tin of kerosene. We boiled the coffee black and loaded it with sugar, and ate half-frozen jam with a spoon and soaked our sea biscuits. We stretched out in our sleeping bags inside our tent igloo and waited, laughing uproariously at each other's jokes, not giving a damn how many sharp, dried crumbs or half-frozen crumbles of Australian bully beef we scattered inside our bags. We three felt like we'd been born again.

Ennadai Lake in fifty-below weather would have made a miserable walk, even if we had been able to find it, thirty-five miles, about fifty-five kilometers, away.

On the fifth morning, the weather was still murderously cold but clear and we were delighted to see Bounce in his Otter reappear. We crossed our fingers inside our mitts as he circled us twice before his landing, this time just as rough and successful as his first.

"I'm taking you three in to the weather station right now. Then maybe I'll bring Beau and Bartlett and another engineer back here tomorrow and see what can be done about the plane. Maybe you can gas it up and get it out of here. Who knows."

Our takeoff was as rough as skiing in the Bugaboos, but when the right time came, we bounced into the air in that grand, wild style that had given Bounce his name and reputation. In no time at all, we were over Ennadai Lake. The country around it was so flat and featureless that we might have missed it except for the countless empty fuel drums that were scattered across the snowy surface of the lake. The search for our single-engine police plane had been much more intense than we had ever imagined, with many larger planes from as far west as Edmonton landing on the lake's smooth, hard surface to refuel and take off again. Everyone was eager to help rescue the Air Division of the police, for they, with the Air Force, were the ones others could count on in a rescue mission.

The weather station crew and a crowd of local *Tuktumiut*, Caribou People, met us at the plane along with the smiling Ataloak, her husband, and Atkak, who was laughing at us from his mother's hood. It was the custom of Inuit women there like Ataloak to wear oval bands of brass on their hair above their foreheads, as women today wear their eyeglasses, with dangling strands of beads over their double braids of hair. In summer, to cool themselves they wore the brass bands on the bare brow.

Brass band headdress

This was a new part of the country for me, with a strange dialect difficult to understand. Almost everyone in these families was wearing caribou skin clothing, sometimes with an army blanket added against the cold. I could scarcely wait to get my sketch pads out and start drawing them and find out what kind of carvings or drawings these nomadic caribou hunters and their wives would do.

55
The Other World

The Caribou People, *Tuktumiut*, around Ennadai Lake and Garry Lake had a different way of thinking, which had a great effect upon my drawings and on me. These isolated, central Arctic people had relied for generations upon the hypnotic pounding of a drum and the monotony of their songs to induce their entry into another, magic world. People around the world try to achieve that now with drugs.

Inuit also used the hypnotic power of their age-old art of story-telling, which can involve the breathtaking excitement of changing pitches in the human voice, mixed with animal sounds and shouts. This performance was often accompanied by dancing, the rhythm of the drum, the accordion, or howling Arctic winds. In some places those strange rhythms were sung by one young woman into another's throat to make an entirely new sound, a ghostly wind out of the past. Sometimes the storyteller's assistant clicked a goose quill against his teeth to help build excitement and suspense. I remember those times in the igloos and dance houses when we swayed, sweating, trying to enter the world of dreams.

I recall the words of an old hunter and kayakman, a famous singer and dancer. He had seen the lives of Inuit change. "When I was a boy," he said, "I knew a shaman who still possessed the ancient power. He was a man who at a seance could leap astride a single drumbeat and rise up through the nose hole of the dance house and ride it into those other worlds beneath the sea or in the sky. We ordinary humans may only hope to see those places now in dreams."

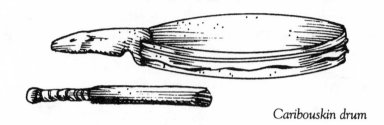

Caribouskin drum

Shamen are the only ones who say they have been able to enter the other world and return alive to tell us of it. But some ordinary people who have been sick, or perhaps have lost their way in trances, claim to have visited the entrance passage to the other world. In that strange place, they say, it is neither bright nor dark, warm nor cold, nor did they feel well fed or hungry. They felt neither happiness nor sadness. While waiting in that passage, they could see through a hole large enough for a human to wiggle through. They say it is lined around with warm, gray eiderdown. And inside that, they can see a much larger place with humans walking around. All seems calm and well in there. Although some Inuit have been to that smaller entrance place to look through the hole into the other world, no ordinary person they know has been able to go through that hole and then return to tell us of those things we cannot know.

56

A Guest for Dinner

"I am leaving now, returning to my family," said the dog-team driver who had been visiting in our igloos beside the frozen lake. "Do you wish to come with me?"

"Oh, yes," I said as I snaked my way off the sleeping platform from beneath the blankets and the sleeping skins I had lain on.

The winter light was failing, but we could see the white line that marked our destination at the far edge of the frozen lake on which we traveled. The driver jumped off the sled and ran for a while beside the dogs. Suddenly, he darted away from them, moving sideways, then back to them. This he repeated several times. Then, jumping over the traces of the dogs, he made elaborate gestures on the opposite side.

"What are you doing?" I asked, for I feared that he had lost his mind.

"I am signaling to my wife," he answered. "I have told her that one *kalluna* is traveling with me and that she is to thaw a lot of caribou meat over her lamp. I told her we are hungry."

57
Wife Changing, Old-Fashioned Style

Wife changing, old-fashioned style, usually started like this: The children rush into the igloo and announce that a dog team is coming toward the camp. "It's coming from the east," they say.

"How many dogs?" their father asks.

The sharp-eyed children run outside again and after a while leap through the igloo's entrance, claiming there are seven, no, eight, no, seven – well, lots of dogs.

"Someone important," says the husband to his wife, then he will list the successful hunters who might be passing from that direction in this season.

The wife's brother comes over from his igloo nearby and mentions who he thinks the traveler will be. "He's the only hunter around here with a team like that. One small dog on the outside has a white head."

He looks at the team with a long glass.

"Oh, yes. And someone's with him, probably one of his sons." The husband sits for a while pondering on the sleeping bench. "I will be the first to shake hands with him."

His wife makes no reply. She knows that if he shakes hands first, it is an invitation to the visiting hunter, who will be obliged to sleep that night in their igloo. She makes no comment in favor of that, nor any objection. Now comes the critical moment. There is a silence.

"Where is he going to sleep?" he asks his wife.

She may say, "*Isumunginipalo*, it's up to you entirely." Or she may remain absolutely silent, going on with her sewing.

"Did you hear me?" her husband may ask if she fails to speak.

"Yes," says the wife. "It's up to you about him."

The hunter goes outside to welcome this distant neighbor.

The wife and family follow him outside. Everyone shakes hands.

Then the wife darts inside first and takes her place, crying out, "*Taktualuk*, dark it is in here," depreciating her ability to keep a lamp flame long and constant in her igloo.

The husband sits to the left next to his wife, with the best space kept open in the middle of the bed for the traveler to eat, then sleep there. When the food has been passed around and eating is finished, the two hunters go outside to look at the sky, together thinking about the weather, but being careful not to make any wild guesses, the way we foreigners so often do. These hunters are cautious not to make wrong weather predictions, which next day might make the one that spoke a liar.

Just before they go back inside the igloo, the husband asks the guest, "Where do you wish to sleep?"

The guest could say, "Tired am I."

The host would say, "*Opinani*. No wonder. You've traveled far."

But if the guest says, "*Isumunginik*, it's up to you," exactly as the hunter's wife has said, the guest will then sleep between the hunter and his wife. It is understood that the guest and the wife will have sex together.

The principal difference between their way and our way is that all three persons involved have had their say and are totally aware of what may happen, so there is no secrecy. That takes the danger and jealousy out of the whole wife-changing act. Of course, as wives in those days would quickly say, it's not just wife changing. It's husband changing, too, and what's so wrong with that?

58

Star Shit

The French archaeologist was very excited. "James, I've made a find," he said. "*Oui*. These people took me straight to it. Four house ruins. Just a border of stones now, and the sleeping platform. You know the hole in the center where they sometimes hid their little treasures, well, perhaps not to them treasures – magical, shaman's things, perhaps."

He brought a tin tea box out of his pack, handling it very carefully. The old man beside us watched him in an amused, quizzical sort of way, studying both of us from head to foot with his deeply hooded eyes. Not because we wore foreign clothing from outside, but because we both wore Inuit clothing strangely cut from distant, Arctic places. Points on our hoods, front splits in our parkas, no sun marks sewed into the fur, strangely constructed sealskin boots. He sighed, but said nothing, nor did he miss a move.

The Frenchman carefully laid out the small artifacts in a neat, straight row. They had all taken on that gorgeous, honey-brown patina of age that enriches ivory. Most of them were smaller than the first two joints of your index finger – a walking man, a bear, a bird, a fish, and wolflike teeth.

"God! Where did you find these?" I asked.

"On the high ground, blown free of snow, across the lake," he pointed. "Tell him where I found them." The archaeologist looked at his *tusaaiji*, his interpreter, and motioned toward the old man.

The interpreter asked the old man who nodded, saying, "Yes, over there."

Shaman's teeth

"Did your father or your grandfather make these pieces?" He picked one up and examined it in the light.

"No." The old man shook his head.

"Who made them?" the Frenchman asked.

"*Kauyimangilunga*, I don't know."

"When were they made?"

"I don't know," the old man answered.

"What are they?"

The old man turned to the interpreter. "Tell them these are *uluriak anaktok*, star shit fallen from the sky. Tell them that's what they are."

59

Arctic Vintners

I am not one to make judgments about various kinds of missionaries, though, in my experience, their talents differ widely. Many Oblates have the advantage of coming from the wine regions of France and Belgium and have passed along their treasured vintner's knowledge to the other fathers.

In the startlingly shabby Oblate missions, the fathers wore long, black robes that failed to hide their hairy, sealskin boots. They were pious men, some of their piety caused, perhaps, by violent actions some had experienced in war. Many had grown rough beards reaching almost to their waistbands and some had maybe twenty years of service in the far North. In their dark brown rooms, if their stove did not function well, there were those among them who would fetch it a violent kick and in their native language shout, "*Marchons!*" It was noticeable the care they took to protect a tall cupboard not too close to the only heating source.

If you entered with your parka bulging, the fathers would swiftly rise to greet you. Then they would open the cupboard. Inside that warm, dark nest would be a clutch of bottles of every size and shape – catsup bottles, whisky bottles, vinegar bottles, sealing jars – any glass container that would hold liquid. At that time in the Arctic all bottles were hoarded. In among the forest of odd-shaped bottles, standing upright for fear they might leak, would stand a kerosene lantern burning low to maintain the exact cave temperature the vintner desired. There was nothing casual about these fathers when it came to the sacred art of making wine.

The father would pause and stare at you, carefully disregarding your questionable Protestant learning, then slowly select a vintage that he thought would reflect your worth. The character of each bottle was so well known to him that they had no need of labels. How long these fine wines had been bottled, only God and these Oblate fathers knew – a year, or two or even three. These were quiet, reflective men of endless patience, not like those wild Hudson's Bay traders with their twenty-four-hour Christmas punch. After you had spent a while in the country, most of the Oblate wine seemed a triumph with a splendid bouquet, full-bodied, and a smooth aftertaste. The miracle of faith was that not one drop of their homebrewed Arctic wine had ever seen a grape.

When the tasting was ended and your seal or caribou stew had been devoured, it was mandatory that you produce the second part of your treasure: dried prunes, dried apricots, dried apples, or raisins. These were the vineyard harvests of those fabulous Arctic vintners.

Sometimes, in other places, we had visitors by dog team or small plane in the early spring – biologists, mammalogists, zoologists, whatever. They quite often brought with them, for scientific purposes, several gallon tins of pure grain alcohol. Those were the glorious days when the government wanted to assist medical science by collecting and preserving polar bear livers to determine how the white bear's liver stored such massive quantities of Vitamin A that it would kill man or dog. (Some Inuit say the fear of eating bear liver was because shamen forbid it; I wonder if science knows the answer yet.) All you had to do was offer bed and board to one of the scientific men and rattle a tin of dry grapefruit crystals at him. They would sometimes make a shaker full of cocktails that would spin your head!

The trader and I went over to visit two scientists one evening with the grapefruit crystals and heard one call out to the other, "Who the hell threw out that alcohol I drained off the bear's liver? I was saving it until that government guy and his friend came visiting." After that, we changed our tactics and returned to the Oblates and gladly shared their delicious apricot wine. It was not nearly as potent as the bear liver preserver, but it let you go home under your own steam and with that joyful peace of mind that passeth all understanding!

60

Fast Tracks Inland

Osuitok (now the famous artist Osuituq Ipellie, R.C.A.) was a best friend with whom I worked and traveled for nine years. He was a short, lean, muscular man with a narrow, dignified face, prominent cheekbones, and a fine, hawklike nose that clearly distinguished his ancestors from other more recent Inuit immigrants to the Baffin coast. Like all Inuit and most others in the North, his face turned a dark mahogany brown from the Arctic sun that reflected off the snow with an intensity that could snowblind a person during a long day's dog-team travel.

Osuitok was almost constantly good-natured, and had a rich abundance of patience, which he needed to train me. From him I learned a lot about human life in general and about some of the ways of Arctic animals. We traveled a thousand miles together by dog team, and more by small boats along Hudson Strait, in ice-choked fiords, and up north along Foxe Channel as far as the ice or open water would allow. I learned most about Inuit life in the Arctic from his careful teachings.

On one early spring morning, he was half running and half being hauled toward me while he held two of our biggest, strongest male dogs by their harnesses. He was hitching them into their positions in our team of twelve dogs. Our smart little bitch, Lao, was on the long line in the lead.

I was helping to load our sled. First, it had a sturdy, wooden grub box with a hinged lid on top that was the narrow driver's seat. Inside, it was a catch-all for our food, ammunition, knives, spare mitts, binoculars, and any other odds and ends that we might have. This box Osuitok had lashed firmly to the sled with strong sealskin line. Such a line can stretch slightly to allow the sled going through rough ice to writhe like a serpent. If a sled is nailed, bolted, or screwed rigidly together, in rough ice it will tear itself to pieces.

On top, across the grub box, was a hardwood steering bar to push or pull to guide the sled. Tied next to it were two boxes, upside down and sometimes empty, to keep us up out of the water in late spring and early summer. On top of these were lashed our sleeping skins and sleeping bags. Behind that, our tent was tightly rolled. And last of all, our blackened kettle, beside a box charred black inside, that was especially made to hold a small Swedish Primus, a tin of methyl hydrate to start it, and a two-gallon tin of kerosene. In addition, Osuitok had snaked in beneath the lashing our two tent poles, our two fish spears, and last of all, our rifles in their homemade canvas cases, sewn exactly to size with one end open. The muzzles were always carefully pointed toward the rear of the sled. Nipisa, Osuitok's wife, had sewn a small design on each case so that we could instantly distinguish his rifle from mine. These rifles would always stay outside the snow houses on the trail: the warmth inside would cause the metal to sweat, and then to freeze and jam in the colder air outside. So we kept our rifles on the snow house roof, where they would be handy if a bear came by.

In the grub box, there was a battered leather case with my

binoculars. There also was a book entitled *Icelandic Sagas*, protected by a folded paper bag, a tin of roll-your-own tobacco and cigarette papers, a good-sized can of tea. There was a used cotton flour sack containing half a dozen unleavened bannocks. Also, there was sugar in a baking powder tin and two tin mugs, two plates, a pot, four tins of bully beef, a tin of jam, a large butcher knife, and two rolls of toilet paper.

Ours was thought by Inuit to be an elegant travel kit, and I came to see that there were few ways to improve upon it. On top of the whole pile, we placed two caribou skins tightly rolled with the hair side on the inside. Spread over almost the entire load was an old polar bear sleeping skin with the hair side out for protection against splashing water. Osuitok and I thought this gave our sled a touch of grandeur when we were on the trail.

In the later 1940s and early '50s, the price for dog-team travel had been firmly established by the traders – ten cents a day for each dog and one dollar a day for the driver. A day sometimes amounted to fourteen hours of hard travel (achieving approximately one hundred kilometers, or about sixty miles, in distance if the going was good). But a hunter thought himself lucky to get a job like that. He could buy tea, tobacco, and cartridges, enough to last a whole year, out of a single trip of any decent length.

Sometimes the driver supplied the dog food, walrus, sometimes the traveler did, depending on who had it. And, of course, everyone brought along a packsack. After the war, none of us dreamed of carrying packsacks in a city – too many could remember the forty-pound military packs they were required to carry and wished to God they could forget them. But in the Arctic, however, you carried them, though not on your back. There was nothing grand about staggering between two camps with only a dog or two and little burden. Inuit believed in showing a good load. Who wanted to be a person or a family that looked bone poor?

Once when I mentioned to Pitseolak that Osuitok and I planned to go inland in late winter or early spring to count caribou for the government and eat a few while doing so, he immediately said that he would meet us there.

"Where?" I asked, knowing the vastness of Baffin's inland.

"There," he replied, pointing north in a sweeping gesture. "We'll meet up there."

So with no month and no point of location agreed upon, we parted. I set out as planned with Osuitok. The weather was troublesome and held us up for a day or so here and there. We saw not a single human being during our journey. The Baffin caribou population, like the people, was then much smaller, less than one third the number counted today. Those figures have been dramatically on the rise elsewhere in the eastern Arctic and Ungava.

Not long after we had left our disposable nightly igloo, the dogs put down their tails and lunged forward, eager to sniff the tracks that a dog team had left, crossing just ahead of us.

"Whose tracks are those?" I wondered aloud.

"Pitseolak's," was Osuitok's answer.

"How do you know that?"

He sighed the way a mother does when explaining something to a very young child. Then bending over the tracks, he pointed. "Look at the narrowness of those sled runners. See the way they both edge outwards. That's Pitseolak, all right. He builds a sled for speed. And look at the number of dogs." He waved at the tracks. "Pitseolak, like his two brothers, always travels with a good-sized team. Look how deep his tracks are," Osuitok said. "He's taken probably eight caribou."

Proud of all this hunter's intelligence about both humans and animals that I had gathered on this inland journey, I said to Pitseolak when I caught up to him a month later, "We crossed your sled tracks near Kakitawak on the inland."

"Yes," he agreed. "I saw several igloos you two had built but had already left."

"How did you know they were our snowhouses?"

"Because," he said, "no one around here needs to build an *iglookotak*, a tall igloo like yours."

"You had eight caribou," I told him, taking a chance, but wishing to sound wise.

"No, only seven," he said, then paused. "One was very heavy."

A skillful Inuit hunter closely observes all the signs in his own country. The understanding of such details has sometimes meant a lot to their ability to survive.

Consider this: if you are hungrily following the snow tracks of an Arctic hare and those tracks suddenly disappear, will you think that it's some shamanistic trick? Don't worry. It's much more likely that a snowy owl has winged up silently behind its prey and scooped it away into the air instead of killing it on the snow.

61

The Mace

In the early spring of 1956, we were invited to Government House in Ottawa for a dinner that turned into a discussion with His Excellency Vincent Massey, Governor General of Canada. He believed some piece of Arctic symbolism should exist to represent Inuit, and this should be presented to the Northwest Territories Council. It was decided that a mace might be appropriate, one vaguely similar to that used in the Canadian Parliament.

After making some preliminary sketches of what might possibly be suitable, using materials native to the Territories, we two made plans involving a narwhal tusk, muskox horns, a piece from an ancient shipwreck, Inuit whalebone carving, Dene porcupine quill weaving, gold from Giant Yellowknife mines, and native float copper from Coppermine in the central Arctic that would form an Edward's crown.

My improved drawings of such a mace were quickly approved. A somewhat similar circumstance had occurred when I made the original drawings for the crests of the Northwest Territories and the Yukon. Both had to be tightened and approved by the College of Heralds in Britain before coming into being.

The actual shaping and making of the mace would fall to Inuit artists and craftsmen of west Baffin Island. I gathered together those

Arctic materials that I knew we would not readily find near Cape Dorset and flew north. In particular, we had great help from Superintendent Henry Larsen, RCMP, in supplying muskox horns and the piece of oak from HMS *Fury*, commanded by Sir William Perry, which went aground on Somerset Island in 1825.

Mace for Northwest Territories

During the making of the mace, I slept in Felix Conrad's little abandoned house. We used it as a workshop when it snowed or rained, but usually we worked outside. It was difficult to explain a mace. Tomasi Manning helped a lot with that. I asked Pitseolak to be the head of all the craftsmanlike efforts and Osuitok to be head sculptor of all the whalebone carvings, with their friezes of humans and sea and land mammals that would appear upon the mace.

As soon as the Inuit grasped the idea, they went quickly to work. They are ingenious at performing clever and relentlessly steady progress. They set to work with bone chips flying, native copper being pounded, narwhal tusk and muskox horns being smoothed and polished until they seemed glazed with ice. Curiously enough, the old ship's oak gave us our greatest problem. No one among them had ever carved hardwood. We decided to incise the lines of a ship on it instead.

Pitseolak was a wonder when it came to working copper. Some experience in his life had caused him to know all about it. I was most worried about the crown, for we did not have welding tools and none of us had any welding skills. Pitseolak solved this by taking our laboriously shaped sheet of copper and pounding confidently downward at its center with a ballpeen hammer while I hopped around him nervous as a flea, terrified that the copper would crack. But no! He caused the metal to sink slowly in the middle until its sides stood upright, forming the band of the crown. It seemed pure magic to me. (Try it with a thinnish two-inch square of copper. You'll see how well it works.)

Pitseolak, Osuitok, Lukta, Tauki, Asivak, Nuvusuitok, Kovian-atiliak 1, Kovianaktiliapik 2, and Kavuvawak formed the team of artists and craftsmen. At first they referred to the mace as *ping-warktok*, a plaything. Then, as it took further form, they spoke of it as *anoutuk*, a club, and when it was almost finished, they called it *anoutualuk*, the great club. Actually, they had that exactly right. A great club or mace had been laid down in the French and English parliaments, a threat that the king's champion, the sergeant-at-arms, would use to defend the kingdom against disorder. The core of this mace, the unicorn horn, that great symbol on the British coat of arms and in French tapestries, was born into ancient myth when early Vikings first traded live polar bears and the much rarer Arctic narwhal tusks to European rulers.

Throughout the creation of the mace during April and early May, radio messages were sent asking when I could bring the mace with me from Dorset. We had had an early spring that year, and pilots with planes on skis were understandably reluctant to try a landing on our slush-covered ice. *Damn*, I thought, for I had hoped to be outside for the birth of our second child in June.

Pootoogook, Pitseolak's brother, offered to take the completed mace and me aboard his still winter-beached Peterhead, *Ivik*, and to try to reach the military airbase at Coral Harbour, a place where none of them had been. I studied a map. It sounded almost impossible to me, but we decided to try it. The mace, as tall as most Inuit who had made it, and weighing seventeen kilograms (thirty-five pounds), was securely fitted into its custom-made box.

"*Nakoamiasit*, thanks a lot," I shouted, waving a temporary goodbye to everyone ashore.

The *Ivik* encountered little ice at first until we came almost to Seahorse Point (Sea Unicorn Point) and there we saw enormous herds of walrus and endless masses of house-sized blocks of ice grounded along the shore. At one point, standing at the bow, I shouted, "*Nanuit!*," pointing out one bear on our port bow and a mother and cub off our starboard bow.

Pootoogook, at the helm, shouted back, "*Nanuitpuukpeet*, forget the bears! Look at the ice!"

A moment later, we suffered a mighty blow which stove *Ivik's* bow. I'm grateful to say the damage was well above the water line.

We managed to snake our way along that ice-bound coast to Coral Harbour, a place named by early explorers. *Sadliarmiut*, Inuit people, came out to greet us on their flat island, saying they had never seen a Baffin Peterhead in their part of the world.

A Jeep bearing the mace took me up to the base where I explained my problem to the American commander.

"Easy," he said, looking up at his chalked schedule board. "We've got a kite flying out of here tonight. We'll drop you off at Winnipeg or Westover, Massachusetts – take your pick."

I went back to *Ivik*. The local people were talking to these visitors from distant lands while it was being repaired. I heaved a sigh of relief and gave my thanks to Pootoogook and his crew. I was going to get the mace out on time and I'd be out for the birth of Sam.

At about midnight, I climbed into the back of a huge, empty, four-engine military aircraft. It took off and I lay on a folded tarpaulin and went to sleep. A little later, a crewman came back and shook me awake.

"Jeez, sorry, buddy," he said in a southern accent. "We forgot you were back here. There's no oxygen. You were out! Come on up into the cabin. I'll turn a bucket upside down so you can rest your lucky ass with us."

62

Unicorn Horn

Kallunait, white people, have always been eager to collect the horn of an *agalingwak*, narwhal. The longer it is, the greater their desire for it and the more they will trade for it. Some here think they must use these unicorn horns for some magic purpose of their own.

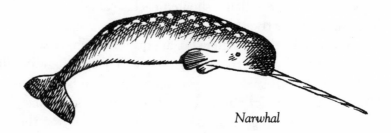

Narwhal

Many believe that the narwhal's long front tusk was formed one summer when a girl was out clamming and did not notice the tide coming in up to her knees.

Two gulls soaring over her said, "What a careless girl. Let's play a double trick on her."

They swooped down and each snatched one of her hair braids in their beaks. Then they began to fly around, twisting them together. At first, the girl did not notice, so hard was she digging for clams. But when her hair braids tightened, she shrieked in surprise and the gulls let go. But the long, tight twist of her hair remained straight up in the air and the girl fell forward into the water and became the first narwhal to swim the seas.

63

Building the House

Until I was appointed the first Administrator for west Baffin Island, I continued to live in my double-walled tent with snow-blocks built around it in winter. Then I moved into the newly built government house. In it we cut several unauthorized wall niches for carvings. I painted the living room walls a warm, golden yellow. A good many Inuit, when seeing the room, would go near and pretend to lick the walls, some saying the color looked like *putik*, that delicious caribou marrow. Women said the walls looked like summer Arctic poppies. I hung lots of prints, of course, and many artists for the first time saw how their works would be used, because at that time few of them had any place to hang a picture. But when I visit them these days, I see lots of wall hangings, posters, and blown-up photos on the walls of their permanent houses.

The government house at Kingait was built tight against the hill, a hiding place from the worst of the violent, northwest Arctic winds. Our east window looked down the fiord toward the rising sun, which meant that on winter days I could watch the rare arrival or departure of dog teams on the ice. During the long, morning light of summer, I could sometimes see pods of white whales rolling over the shallow reef at low tide. I called it our house because we lived there as a family, Allie and me and John and Sam when they were young, when all of us were young.

It's true that it had been located in a good place. I only had the knowledge to do that because I had gone to Pootoogook's tent one morning and asked him, "Where shall we have this new house built?"

"I'll think, and let you know," he answered.

Next day when I came out of my tent, I saw him sitting on a soft, thick caribou skin that his wife, Ningiukaluk, had spread for him. He was resting, his legs straight out in front, Inuit fashion. Beneath him was an enormous sheet of solid granite, for it is true there is no soil at all on Kingait Island.

I went and squatted by him, waiting.

"Build it here," he said, then seemed to draw a circle around himself. "There is never too much wind here," he added. "It's solid." He thumped both heels.

Just right, I thought. And we did. Later, with Inuit help, we erected a flagpole inside a whaler's old iron trypot by packing it tight with boulders. We flew the red Canadian Armed Services flag, for it was in those years between the Union Jack and the Canadian maple leaf flag that we have come to know, its image first drawn by Prime Minister Lester B. Pearson on the back of an envelope.

64
Letters That Hurt

Letter bombs can kill, and so can letters carrying viruses. Such germs were basically foreign to the Arctic, but we in the South had hardened ourselves against them over centuries. Inuit had not. Beyond question, the mail that we received in those days sometimes brought death with it.

We would have an autumn and almost a whole winter where the entire area would be virus-free of common colds or flu. Then the Royal Mail would come over on a dogsled or in a small charter plane and suddenly contact would be made. The sacks would release a small white flood of letters, bills, late Christmas presents, rifle parts, repaired false teeth, new rolls of film and magazines. The mail and parcels had scarcely been ripped open before someone became ill with a cold, or worse, the flu.

"I hope to God it isn't flu," the resident male nurse, with a thermometer in his mouth, would warn us, his hand on his own forehead, then on ours.

Too often his hopes were not enough. Inuit would soon begin to show the symptoms. But before they could be caught and treated, some would leave, carrying the virus away with them on their travels to other vulnerable camps, some a week away by dog team.

We speak openly now of the small pox, measles, and whooping cough that ravaged the Indian tribes of North America as we made early contact with them, often reducing native populations by 70 to 80 per cent. The plague by mail may not be over yet. I was personally in the middle of it all, and lay blame on no one more than I do myself and those who corresponded with me.

65
Round Dancing

At a typical shiptime in August or September, depending on the ice, the Hudson's Bay Company ship or the government ice-breaker would bludgeon its way into Kingait fiord beneath the mountain for their annual visit to deliver supplies to our small settlement. That caused perhaps 300 to 400 people to be drawn in from the surrounding area to help unload, then trade. These Inuit, numbering usually fifty-eight families, remained widely scattered along the coast, sheltered in small bays or moving to the fishing places through most of the year. They would only reappear as families during the brief and joyful summer season. Then their canvas tents would spring up all around the post, not too close, mind you, for the traders greatly discouraged that, although it was all Crown land and no one had any real right to restrict the use of land from others.

After shiptime, before families left for the camps, it was the traditional time for a big dance. Inuit in the eastern Arctic are, like most people, very fond of dancing. By the time I arrived among them, they had largely discarded their old devotion to the pagan drum and had learned during the whalers' time to do their wild sea chanteys, sailor's hornpipe reels from the Scots, and breathtaking, double pigeon wings from the Americans. And, believe me, Inuit were keen on dancing, including the old folk who had themselves danced with the whalers on the decks of their square-rigged ships.

66
Cross Dressing

There is a hunting family that lives on Baffin Island who immigrated there more than a century ago. They may have carried a rare, shamanistic practice with them across Hudson Strait.

One daughter from this family was raised as a male child. She wore male clothing and was carefully taught to hunt and take part in life as a man until she married and once more took on the female role. Then she in turn brought up her son dressed in female garb, wearing an *amautik* instead of a parka, and taught him to carry smaller children in the hood instead of hunting.

This is not an event from long ago. I knew well both that woman and her son. Locally speaking, the whole event as far as I could tell was socially acceptable.

67
Baldy Turner

The wind blew an early winter shudder along the fiord that set the storm windows on our house rattling. I heard a knocking on the door – or was it some frozen rawhide line smacking against the wall? Nobody knocked on a door around here. Inuit came inside on their own, then sniffed and coughed to announce their presence. The whites usually sent an *uvikait*, a teenager, with a note announcing that they planned to make a social visit. Who the hell could this be?

I waited until it happened again, then went and opened the door. A tall, lean man with hollow cheeks and no expression on his face said, "Turner here." He had gray eyes and pursed lips.

"Come in," I said, and as he stepped through the door, he thrust back his parka hood. This could only be the legendary Baldy Turner, a former mounted policeman. Some said that he only lived for gold, others that he was trying to emulate some medieval, northern monk. Rumor had it he had gone far beyond all that.

The skin on his head was tight-drawn over a high-combed skull like someone from the distant past. He was so slow pulling off his moosehide mitts that you felt he was thinking twice about shaking hands or touching you.

"Cold out there?" I asked.

"No," he shook his head, "a bit fuggin' breezy."

"How'd you come here?" I asked.

There was a long pause.

"Along the coast."

This was going to be a measured conversation. "Want some coffee?" I asked.

There was a long pause, with more gruesome staring.

"Tea," he answered, then grasping the point of his hood, he hauled off his parka with that smooth, single motion that made you know he'd done it thousands of times.

"How did you come into this part of the country?" I asked.

He gave me a squint-eyed glance. "With that shaggy mining outfit that tried to set up near Akiaktolaolavik. Oh, I paid them for the sea lift, and my toboggans and my kit. They knew I wasn't going to stay with them. I traded stuff enough to get nine dogs from the locals."

Turner drew a chair into the corner of the room farthest away from the space heater, although I purposely kept a cool house, rarely over fifty degrees Fahrenheit (ten degrees Celsius).

"How long do you plan to stay?" I asked.

"Year, maybe two or three, unless I have quick luck."

"What have you got to eat?"

"I'm living off the country," he said, "like most around here do it."

"You did quit the police?" I asked.

"Yeah, I'm an ex-cop. I quit when they threatened to send me to Yellowknife. Have you seen it lately? That place is turning into a bloody city. I wouldn't stand for a posting like that. The cops drive around in squad cars. It's as soft and plush as Moose Jaw or Saskatoon."

I admired his almost knee-high, elaborately beaded Indian moccasins from the McKenzie Delta where he'd spent a lot of time.

"How are the toboggans working out?" I asked him.

"Toboggans are good. It's just these Baffin hounds don't like a tandem hitch and they can't get the hang of pulling a toboggan."

"Government could lend you a *kamotik* until you find the wood to build one."

"Hell, no! I've used eastern sleds and western toboggans plenty. I know that toboggans are the best. You got mineral claim stakes here?" he asked.

"Sure. Have you got a prospecting license for the Territories?"

"No, but they say you can make one out for me."

"For an ex-cop," I said, "you're doing a lot of things ass backwards. You must have been down there prospecting for two months without a license, and you've been hunting and fishing without a license. On the inland, caribou are scarce and you living in there with dogs will make them flee the place. Inuit here worry about that and so do I."

"Who can prove that?" He frowned at me.

"I can," I said. "You're alive and your dogs are alive."

"Read the Queen's rules and regulations in the blue book." He quoted the page number. "It says, 'A person is allowed to hunt to feed himself and his dogs while traveling in the country.'"

"That doesn't mean for years and years while that person is prospecting to enrich himself."

Turner gave me a disgusted look. "You must live off the country when you're traveling."

I nodded. "But that's not the same," I told him. "I'm going somewhere for the government and then I'm coming back. But you?"

He drained off the last of his tea. "I'm self-employed," he said, and got up.

"You're welcome to sleep here," I told him.

"No, I've got my tent put up and blocked at Oupaluktok. I'll settle for the license and the claim stakes now. I'll be gone before you're up in the morning." He slipped back into his parka. "I got my tea and lard at the Company."

"I want you to buy one helluva lot more food than that. Just because you used to be a cop doesn't give you a license to live off the country forever. We've got to settle that. You want another cup of tea?"

"No," he answered, and putting on his big, decorated Indian mitts, he pulled up his hood and stalked away in the blowing snow.

Some months later, I heard Inuit calling, "That man from the *policikut*, police family, he's coming. His dogs are all hitched wrong."

Baldy was back. He unhitched his dogs, turned over his nearly empty toboggan, and walked up to the house with that loose-kneed hard snow walk humans learn to develop that will let them down easy if they slip or fall.

"Come in for a cup of tea," I called to him.

He shook hands more readily this time as he perched upon an unfamiliar chair.

"I'll take you up on that loan of a long sled," he said, resuming the conversation we had had months ago.

"Fine," I answered.

"I'd forgotten," he said, "how hard the snow gets driven by those goddamn winds back on the inland plain. You can't even make an impression in the snow when you drive down hard with your heel. Low sleds clog up with soft snow in the bush, but they're sure the best out here."

"You're looking skinnier than when I saw you last."

"Yeah, well, I'm back here to buy some food. I've moved down near the coast again."

"I'd heard that from some hunters down your way. They'd seen your tracks and your tent."

"I didn't move off the inland because of you or them," he said. "I just came out because I thought the prospecting would be better along the coast."

"Found anything?" I asked.

Baldy, for the first time, smiled at me. "Hell, you're the Mineral

Claims Officer around here. You should be smart enough not to ask a prospector who's buying claim stakes a dumb question like that!"

68

Wife Seekers

The children started screaming, then the women calling to each other. Looking out, I saw people scurrying in every direction. I scanned the inlet, expecting to glimpse a pod of beluga whales as they surfaced, then hear the echoing explosions of heavy rifles. But no. I could see no whales. Shading my eyes, looking out over Malik Island, I waited to see or hear the mounted police float plane coming into sight. But no. The whole clear bowl of sky remained empty. I looked behind me at the land, hoping to see a polar bear rambling fast across our island's red-brown rocks and tundra. But the dogs remained silent. There was no bear.

Around the headland that protects the bay, a battered old Peterhead hove into view. This sturdy, square-sterned, native boat was coming slowly to us under a gray wedge of much-patched sail. The boat flew no flag. Its hull was painted pea-soup green with a feverish, yellow trim. A skin kayak lay crossways on its deck.

"I've never seen that boat before," I said to Joanasie, one of the local hunters, who stood shading his eyes as he studied this phenomenon.

"No one here has ever seen it," said the hunter.

"Who are they?" I asked.

He made a face. "They're not from Baffin Island."

"Where are they from?"

"*Achooli!* Across from the straits, perhaps from Ivuivik. Maybe they're *Sadlirmiut*, those from the big, flat island to our west. We don't know them."

I looked along the inlet. No canoes were putting out to greet the strangers. "Why?" I asked him.

"Because they've got their own kayak. They'll come ashore soon enough."

"Why have they come?" I asked Joanasie a little later.

"They've come here hoping we will give a dance for them. They must be looking for young women to marry. No one would make an unknown crossing like that in moving ice unless – yes, I'd say they're looking for wives."

"Will they get a few from us?" I asked him.

"No, probably not." He laughed.

Oh, the Baffin Islanders did give these visitors a dance that lasted until sun-up. We discovered during the dancing and the talking that these visitors were all good, friendly men. In the end, they were given gifts of Arctic char, eider eggs, and fresh seal meat, but not one family promised any of our girls to any one of them. We suggested that they go and ask the *Ivilingimiut*, the Walrus People, saying they might have some to spare. But when you're short of girls like that and living on an island, it can be an awful problem. We know that.

69

Man Without a Grave

We were on our way to hunt for walrus. At dawn, Pudlat called into the fo'c's'le. I sat up in my sleeping bag as he climbed down and in his usual style flung aside my caribou skin covering. For he wished to encourage me to climb up and see the sights with him. Pudlat had bright white teeth and a dark-tanned face. He was a good friend. His nature was wild and quick and full of jokes. He accepted taming only from his father, Pootoogook.

Foolishly going on deck without my parka, I stood shivering at the bow of the Peterhead while Pudlat pointed out the entrance to Amadjuak. It was so large it seemed like an inland sea. I got my parka and the Primus stove and we boiled tea on deck. I sat there in the early morning, watching as the sail creaked and tugged at its lines and we moved slowly north. As the morning light grew stronger, I could see the abandoned trading post and fur shed in front of us like a pair of red and white children's toys, tiny in the vastness of this silent landscape. Even at that distance, we could hear the nervous tap-tap-tapping of the wind charger's dangling wire cable.

Pudlat at that time owned a cheap .22-caliber rifle. It was single-shot, but he was fast. He kept his ammunition inside his mouth when he confronted game, and had trained himself to spit the bullets into the breech the instant he hauled the action open. He didn't need to waste money on a repeating rifle. He was absolutely the best offhand rifle shot I'd ever seen.

Now he pointed up at some herring gulls that were flying not far from us. Most were still brown-feathered, marking their immaturity. "*Nowyat kayuk kisiani mumuktopaluk!* Gulls, the brown ones, you'll like them best to eat!"

I had taught a marksmanship course in the army, but before I could get my .22 out of its sleeve, he had fired eight shots, dropping five birds from the sky.

"*Namuktuk*, enough," he said. "That's all we need to eat right now."

He quickly gathered them, and wasting no time with plucking, he skinned them and stuffed them all into the large pot. When they were boiled, we all had breakfast. They were exceptionally good!

"We don't like this place," Pudlat warned me, looking suspiciously at the cliffs around us. "Rocks fell with snow one winter and killed a family in an igloo over there near that cliff. This place has *tornait*, spirits living here."

We anchored the Peterhead and paddled ashore in the small canoe we carried or towed. The five of us walked up together to the Hudson's Bay post abandoned perhaps twenty years before. The door was unlocked but had a stone to hold it in place. I reached down to remove it.

"*Ajaii!* Don't touch it! Don't go in there! Come with us, you can see through the window."

When I looked in, my first impression was yellowed ledger pages scattered everywhere. The table was roughly set with chairs around it, a teapot, cups, plates, knives, forks, spoons. It was hard to imagine all that left there by Inuit in need.

"I'm going inside," I said.

None of them would step across the threshold. They turned their backs on me and the house and stared out to sea as they rolled thick cigarettes from their large, shared tobacco tin.

Inside, there was a bedroom with a tumbled, unmade double bed, half covered by a once-bright homemade quilt and plump eider-down pillows turning gray. An ashtray advertising the Fort Garry Hotel, Winnipeg, and a hairbrush were on a wooden bureau with the empty drawers half pulled.

Hudson's Bay men must also have passed here by boat or by dog team in winter. Perhaps they had rightly taken anything that they thought useful. But what about the things left behind? Was it ghosts who had protected this place from any vandalism for all those years, or was it some kind of powerfully enforced rules of honesty demanded by Inuit society and the Company that had pre-served these valuable, wooden building boards, this cutlery, these English china plates with "HBCoy" decorating their red rims? The trading records scattered on the floor were written in a spidery, somewhat elegant hand. Faded handmade draperies hung tattered on the bedroom window only. Why? Some coal was still left in the scuttle by the long-dead stove.

I must admit that the house gave me an eerie, lonely feeling, thinking of the several thousand bleak, winter nights and days that it had stood alone, listening to the tapping of that damned wire against the wind charger, its black windows looking out like empty eyes at the bay.

When I rejoined the others, Pudlat said, "There's a dead man in a barrel near here. They say his head is sticking out."

We went looking and soon found not one but several wooden barrels, but nothing was inside of them. I sort of smiled and snorted at them, meaning, "Now you're putting me on."

They hunched their shoulders without saying "Ayii, yes" or

"*Aggai*, no" and we got into the canoe and departed in the Peter-head. We had not gone far when the sternman caused us to turn sharply and we landed again. This time we crossed the beach and climbed up into a tumble of large, fallen boulders. Pudlat pointed between two of them and there in the crack lay the body of a man. His head was a bleached skull that still retained some hair. He wore the remnants of a parka open to show his rib bones. The most inter-esting thing about the dead man was that he still held a rusted rifle.

"Who was he?" I asked, grateful that he had died well before my time and was not my responsibility.

"*Achooli*, I don't know," they answered, pleased to see my look of surprise.

When we returned to Dorset, I asked the trader. He said it must have happened too long ago to interest him. The police from Kingmerok, when they came over late that winter, said they hoped the dead man had died of old age, that they had no record of him. Later, I saw other dead men, whalers on Blacklead Island in Cumberland Sound, who had been buried on that rocky island lacking soil by having their ship's cooper encase them in wooden barrels. Bears had rolled those barrels around, eventually breaking them open and exposing their last remains. A body covered tight beneath the ice and snow for nine months out of every year can sometimes last for centuries.

Peter Pitseolak knew most about the abandoned post at Amadjuak. He said that when he was younger (no Inuit bothered to keep track of birthdays or of years in those old days), a remark-able thing had happened to the only two families living near the Amadjuak post that summer. One night, they had heard rattling sounds. Then in the early morning fog, they heard the splashing and snorting of caribou swimming to them from the south. This was unthinkable to them. Caribou should be inland, not coming in like seals. Soon they could see the animals herding toward them up the beach. The hunters ran for their rifles and began to fire.

The Company trader who was then living in that house came running down to shore. "Don't shoot! Don't shoot!" he yelled at them.

Don't shoot a caribou? Why not? The trader didn't own the animals. How else could hunters feed their families? Now here were the very animals they wanted clattering ashore.

"Wait! Don't shoot!" He waved his arms. Behind the caribou, they saw two boats rowed by foreign sailors.

"What is happening here?" they asked the trader. "Are these not *tuktut*, caribou?"

"These animals are from a long way off," he told them. "You're not to kill these. You're going to take care of them."

Who had ever heard of anything like that? But stranger still, these Amadjuak families found themselves shaking hands, not with just sailors – they knew all too much about sailors – but with two short, strange men wearing curled-up boots and with those men's wives and children all dressed differently than any people they had ever seen. Who were they?

It took some time to understand. These were northerners like themselves, but people from the other side of the world. Lapp Sami, they called themselves, and they set up two strange-looking tents beside the post. The *tuktut*, caribou, that had come ashore were just as strange. They didn't run away from men, but they hated Inuit dogs, and were nervous until the hunters took their teams away to forage on a nearby island.

These Baffin Islanders could scarcely believe their eyes when the younger of the two Lapp Sami cast a looped harpoon line and caught one of these animals that had come with them around the neck, while one of their women took the teats of the animal and got out what only calves could get – milk!

The Lapps did not remain long in Amadjuak. They trekked inland, following the animals they'd brought with them. They were not seen much after that, Peter Pitseolak said, but in the spring they returned to the coast. They reported that when their reindeer had met wild *tuktut* on the inland, they mixed with them and ran away forever with the wild ones. The Lapp Sami admitted that these two related animals look almost the same and they never saw their domesticated herd again.

I heard much later that Vilhjalmur Stefansson, the famous

explorer who had been born in Manitoba's Icelandic colony, had been asked by the Canadian government and the Hudson's Bay Company to advise them of solutions to the future problems of the Canadian north. He suggested that Inuit should be taught to herd reindeer as is done in northern Scandinavia and vast tracts of Siberia. But in my time, where this experiment was being tried in our western Arctic, Inuit were said to have cooperated at first, but it was too much for them. Apparently, hundreds if not thousands of years are needed to turn a hunting family into a family practicing animal husbandry. Inuit in the McKenzie Delta finally told the government, "We know how to hunt *tuktut*, we eat them and we use their skins. Why should we walk around after the same kind of *tuktut*, trying to get a cup of milk away from their young ones?"

Pitseolak said he and all other Inuit liked the Lapp Sami very much. He was proud of a large, strangely shaped, copper kettle that they had given him as a gift when they had departed. Pitseolak offered us part of that same kettle. He donated it to complete the making of the crown for the mace of the new Council of the Northwest Territories.

Primus stove and kettle

Just east of Amadjuak, we discovered a rich deposit of jade green stone which surpassed in quality the darker, coarser stone from around Kiaktuk, which carvers had used earlier. The stone near Amadjuak was perhaps the finest found in the Canadian Arctic. It had a deep green lustre and would polish beautifully. All the large early stone blocks used for printmaking came from this deposit which, sad to say, is now believed to be all but gone.

70
Traveling with Ian

In the mid-fifties, various persons engaged in Arctic research occasionally came into our part of the country. Ian McEwen, a mammalogist from Edinburgh University, had been flown from Frobisher to Kingmerok and then been brought over by dog team to Cape Dorset. In those days that took seven sleeps. He described the journey to me as "a real bitch." I knew just how he felt, for the early March weather had not yet lost its winter's sting. Right away he proudly produced what was left of a bottle of whisky. "I had intended bringing you this gift full," he said, "but that trip overland was hard." He eyed the bottle, then sighed and gave it to me. "The missing half of that whisky saved my life!"

I helped Ian take his grub box and his sleeping bag into the house, which at that time could only be described as bachelor digs, Allie being outside on a visit south. Ian showed a letter to me from my government department suggesting that I, as game officer, would accompany him on a survey of west Baffin Island caribou.

That evening, Ian put me off a bit by saying, "In Ottawa rumor has it that you and your friends live rough when you're traveling in the country."

"Never believe what you hear in Ottawa," I warned him.

"Well, let me tell you this," said Ian somewhat primly. "Whilst we are journeying together, I intend to wash all my parts each day in clean hot water and brush my teeth and change my socks. I do not believe in going wild."

"Fine!" I said. "I'll learn a lot from you. Most Canadians see nothing wrong with being clean."

"And furthermore," he said, "I am going to prepare good, hot cooked meals."

"Lovely!" I agreed. I'd never traveled with a serious cook before. "But even so," I said, "it might be best if we took two dog teams into the country – one for you and one for me. That way we can stay a bit apart, if need be, and survey twice as many caribou. Who knows, during the time away we might even share an igloo. Once or twice."

Next day, with help from Osuitok and his brother-in-law, Etungat, we started preparing our food for the journey as Ian watched in surprise. First we cut some young seal meat into mouth-sized chunks, simmering them in a big pot until it started steaming. Then we added a few leftover tins of lima beans, half a bag of rice, some ancient sticks of dried spaghetti, and anything else we found on the food shelves. When this was done, we washed off the floor of the outside porch and spilled the mixture over it.

We had Ian stand guard with a dog whip while dozens of sled dogs gathered to enjoy the rich aroma and see if they could trick him into giving them a turn at it. In less than half an hour, the whole unattractive mess was frozen solid.

"Why are we doing this?" Ian asked us.

"You must never have tried to get food out of a tin can when it's really cold," I told him. "With this stuff, when we're hungry, we can throw a chunk into hot water – or even gnaw on it as if it were frozen haggis."

Ian brightened at that thought and defended the second batch on the floor until it froze. Then using a hatchet and an old snow knife, we broke the stew up into hand-sized chunks and stuffed them into old government pillowcases. Ian tried to pick off the bits of gray enamel floor paint, demanding that everything be clean.

When we went back inside, Osuitok's wife, Nipisa, had the house filled with the delicious smell of hot bannock from an open frying pan. When you're running hard beside a dog team, the seal fat and excessive baking powder in an unleavened bannock is guaranteed to give you awful heartburn. But when you're young, it's worth it!

"We'll take about twenty bannocks with us," I told Ian. "They save time on the trail. I'll have Nipisa spread them now with jam and honey."

"Don't forget the pickles," Ian urged me. "Give her these. I can scarcely live without coffee and pickles." And it was true that he had brought in almost no supplies but coffee and pickles.

I told Nipisa to spread half the bannocks with jam and honey and the other half with mustard, bully beef, and lots of sliced sour pickles.

By that time, it was dark and cold and blowing hard. We went over to the Hudson's Bay and drank coffee with Ross Peyton, one of my best friends and a Newfoundlander who was also batching it. Ian and I went home late and fell into our sleeping bags. We did not wake until we heard someone rattling the frying pan and making the little Primus stove roar. Nipisa didn't trust our larger government stove.

In the early dawn, we pulled on thick caribou stockings over duffel socks, caribou pants over woolen pants, and heavy duffel parkas and double mitts. We carried out grub boxes, sleeping bags, rifles, Primus boxes, sleeping skins, snow knives, and carefully lashed everything onto two 14-foot sleds. On top of the load, we tied winter-thick caribou pants and parkas to go over the top of our usual pants and parkas in case the weather turned nasty.

Many Inuit came out to see the four of us – Ian, Etungat, Osuitok, and me – depart. They waited, smiling from their hoods and puffing steam like locomotives in the icy dawn. We left in a rush of excited, yelping dogs. A dozen children leapt aboard and clung to our sleds as we went thumping at breakneck speed through the rough barrier ice, then out onto the snow-covered ice of the sea. First the little kids, then older ones would drop off and wave. "*Tavvauvusiit!* Farewell!" they called to us.

When conditions are good and the snow is hard, a pair of dog teams in competition with each other make better time than one traveling alone. In favorable weather you can do as much as a hundred kilometers or sixty miles a day. We stayed out on the frozen sea and followed the Baffin coastline eastward until we reached Sorbuk, a long fiord cutting inland. We only left the ice at nightfall to build our first snowhouse in a hard-packed snowbank on the edge of the land.

Working quickly together, we built our igloo just big enough for four. Etungat cut snow blocks and spiraled them upward from the inside, while I knelt chinking on the outside. Osuitok and Ian unharnessed the dogs and fed them pre-chopped chunks of frozen walrus meat. It took us about forty-five minutes to complete our tasks.

We lit two fat emergency candles inside our sparkling new igloo and spread old polar-bear sleeping skins hair down on the snow so that they covered the rear two-thirds of the house. On those skins, we unrolled caribou skins hair up, then our eiderdown sleeping bags. In a moment, we had the Primus going and from the inner walls Osuitok shaved snow into our kettle: snow will scorch and steam away to nothing unless you heat it cautiously. It was not long until we had water boiling and were flinging in our hand-sized chunks of frozen seal stew mixture. We soon bolted this down with quick-scorched, frozen bannock and mugs of tea. Ian admitted that the stew, though very greasy, tasted delicious!

When our low snow door was wedged in place, we snuffed out the little Primus stove. I removed my soft skin boots and climbed deep into my bag where I finally chucked off all my clothes except my woolen hat. A naked body allows one's heat to circulate and get the sleeping bag truly warm.

Eskimo hunters being nomads are quick in everything they do. Before I could settle down, both drivers were asleep beneath their homemade eider robes, one snoring quietly. They had left one candle burning to keep out evil spirits and to take the chill off the glittering house.

In what seemed like a very short time, Osuitok was up cutting a huge new exit in the side of the igloo. "What's he doing?" asked Ian. "I haven't even had the chance to wash and shave my face and rinse my teeth."

"Well, go ahead," I said. "There's no wind. For hot water you can fire up that Primus and cut all the snow you want. There's plenty of it right here on the inside walls."

Ian fiddled with some matches for a while, then rolled a cigar-thick cigarette and blew smoke at the igloo dome. "Awh, to hell with it! I won't bother with the washing until tonight."

I saw him rub a square of toilet paper across his teeth before he rushed into his clothing and we were off and running beside the teams. We traveled inland all that day, not expecting caribou, but hoping perhaps to see some tracks. It was another long, hard day on the trail.

Next morning, Ian swore he'd wash up when we'd finished traveling that night. We packed up, gulped down boiling tea, then wriggled out of the low entrance and helped sort and harness the nineteen dogs that went with our two separate sleds. Our dogs at night were never tied. They had enough sense not to run away, for they seemed to understand that they weren't wolves. Alone in that bleak country, they could never have survived.

Oh, yes, I have a confession to make about the bannocks. Nipisa was at that time completely unfamiliar with sour pickles, though she said later that she thought it strange to mix the strawberry jam and the clover honey and the bully beef all together in each bannock, but she insisted she was only following my instructions. Jam, mustard, honey, and sour pickles – if that sounds like an unpalatable mixture, you're wrong! You're just not hungry! Even Ian, the gourmet pickle-eater, finally admitted that those frozen mixtures came to have great appeal. That's what a few days on the trail will do for you.

During our week-long search for caribou beyond the mountains on the great plain of the Koksoak, we zigzagged back and forth across the flat snow plain, building a new snowhouse every night. We saw no other humans and few living creatures, though on the sixth day we did see the tulip-shaped tracks where a small herd of perhaps a dozen caribou had cut a long, elegant trail across the hard-packed drifts. We turned and followed sharp hoof cuts and small brown droppings scattered here and there like delicious-looking chocolate drops, but by dark we had not found the herd.

"This is turning into a poor bitch of a survey," Ian grumbled.

When I told Osuitok that, he laughed. "Tell him not to worry. We should find them . . . maybe."

Next morning, Etungat was the first outside. When he came back into the igloo, he said, "There's a herd of them lying down on the far hillside." He nodded to the west. Ian and I hurried out with the binoculars. I searched the snowy hill. I saw nothing and passed the glasses over to Ian.

"We're going to harness the dogs," said Osuitok. "How do you want to go up on them?"

"That's up to you, Ian. How do you want to do it?"

"I hate to admit this to you," Ian said, "but I can't see any of them."

"Etungat told you they're right there," I laughed.

"You point them out to me," said Ian.

That forced me to admit to him that I couldn't see them either.

"I'd like to have that prime white fox that's wandering around among them," said Etungat as he handed back my binoculars.

It took me quite a while, but finally I saw one, then the dozen, caribou lying quietly. They were not brown the way caribou ought to be, but pale silvery white because their backs and sides had been frosted by their breathing. This seems to me to be nature's ultimate camouflage.

Ian had government permission to collect six specimen heads for biological research. We were eager to use the rest of the meat instead of our mixture of frozen bannock, jam, and pickles.

Crouching, we walked upwind and easily shot the six animals he needed. When all the others had fled, we severed each of the heads and quartered up the meat, then lashed it all on top of our sleds. During the butchering Ian did as we did, wiping his bright red hands on the snow. I noticed that he had still not practiced any of his rigid rules of cooking and cleanliness. There was never any question of our using two separate igloos. We all liked Ian more each day we knew him.

That night, we stuffed ourselves so full of tender, uncooked caribou that we decided to take the next day off and lie around in the igloo sleeping, digesting, reading, talking, or just thinking. Ian would brew hot tea and we would eat more meat. There was no need to worry about getting fat. We were both slim at that time and we each ran off lots of pounds on that journey. That day I noticed Ian for the first time hurriedly writing notes in his day journal while I lazed inside my sleeping bag, reading my pocket book.

When we left early on the following morning, Ian still hadn't shaved or washed or done any of those niceties he'd sworn to do.

The wind rose at noon and it blew hard for two days and nights, making travel a misery. At noon on the third day during tea break, with the bannocks now gone, I saw Ian crouching on the opposite side of his sled, hacking with the snow knife at the frozen cheeks of one of his specimen heads. When he saw me staring at him, he said, "The biology department requires only the skulls for study. They don't need this meat." He handed a piece to each of us. "It's a real bitch," said Ian, "our having no real lunch at all!"

After that, he never failed to offer us a share of his specimens' cheeks or necks. You could take your choice. Yes, Ian was changing. In the beginning, Osuitok and Etungat had treated him with little regard. But now that they saw him running hard and trying his best to handle dogs, they took turns teaching him their most useful words in Inuktitut. He raced with new agility across the hard-packed snow and leapt on the sled beside me as we tried to make jokes about the stinging wind and cold.

Next morning when we went outside, the wind was gone. We all four stood looking up, listening to the silence. The blizzard had carved sharp drifts that curved away from us like long blue snakes.

Even as we hitched them, the dogs seemed to sense that we were going home. You could tell that by their tails, which they held out flat, pulling hard. Taking advantage of the wind-packed snow, we made our way south toward the coast. Plump white rock ptarmigan appeared in numbers following the storm, popping up out of their own igloos.

Two sleeps later, we reached the coast and stayed that night in the Eskimo camp at Egalaksak, meaning ice window material. We must have forgotten our extra tin for we had been out of tobacco for the past four days until a kindly old lady in the camp shared with us the last of her strong, dried-out pipe tobacco. Ian borrowed the old lady's pipe and smoked it while we three rolled fat cigarettes using paper I provided from the early pages of my book. These so-called cigarettes burned very unevenly and tasted awful. But I still remember them fondly though I haven't smoked now for more than thirty years.

Next morning, we lay on the wide family igloo sleeping platform we had shared and all drank tea, ate seal stew, and admired their nearly naked children as they joyfully tottered across the bed wearing only caribou bonnets. We were in no hurry, for there was heavy ice fog rolling in along the coast, the kind that makes you hate to even think about confronting it. We left mid-morningish, I think. Ian's watch, like mine, had stopped. We didn't care.

In the late afternoon, the ice fog flew away in patches, giving us a long, blue-cast view of Kingait Mountain.

"Do you want to build an igloo and sleep here?" Osuitok asked as Jupiter flashed and the moon began to rise. "There'll be a lot of rough, broken ice ahead."

"No," we agreed. "Let's try to make it into Kingait."

He wasn't fooling about the rough ice. It was velvet black with endless stars when the two dog teams turned into the fiord. The local teams sent up a welcome howling that set our sled dogs tearing across the hard drifts on the sea ice and up through the tidal barrier so fast we had to cling to or jump off the sleds. I could see the warm glow of a lantern shining from my window. Seventeen hours makes a long day's traveling, but it was worth it. We were home!

We cached the meat and five partly gnawed lunch heads where the dogs could not get the last of them, then we stacked our rifles in the corner, hauled our sleeping skins, grub boxes, spare skin boots, and outer parkas inside the *pingwavingme*, catch-all playroom. Osuitok and Etungat, whose wives had come out to greet them, said good night and hurried home to their own beds.

"Let's go wake the Newfie and tell him that we're home," said Ian.

"He'll love this!" I said as we went along the trail to the dark Hudson's Bay house and hammered on Ross Peyton's window. He opened the door looking like a ghost in his long, woolen underwear. His kitchen seemed intolerably hot and his clock read 3:00 a.m., but good Newfs are social at any hour. Ross cracked his last eighteen processed eggs into a huge, iron skillet and, while they were cooking, he proudly unscrewed the lids of three sealing jars, releasing the pungent odor of his justly famous, forty-eight-hour dried-apricot punch. It was so delicious it made those ancient eggs taste new-laid.

"How was the trip?" he asked us.

"Well, it was a real bitch about half the time," said Ian, "but the rest of it was grand!"

"I see you've grown a sort of half-assed beard," the Newfie told him.

"Here's to you, Ian," I said, raising my sealing jar, not wishing to dwell on the subject of how often he had washed or brushed his teeth or how many well-cooked meals he had prepared.

7 1

Dog in a Bullet

In the Inuit world, a man may possess a story. I mean, a story he can tell that belongs to him alone. Of course, there were common myths and legends – like Robin Hood or Robinson Crusoe, or Sedna, or Kiviok's magic journeys. Those were in the public domain and belonged to everyone. But Inuit were always very careful about local tales or stories based on personal experiences, which seemed to have some special type of ancient copyright. It was a personal violation if you told another person's story. Yes, you could ask permission and try to trade the rights to someone else's story. Then you could tell it if you wished.

When I was trying my hardest to increase my understanding of Inuktitut, I felt that I needed a story. I hoped that I could sit with cultured people, listen to their stories, then come zinging back with a fabulous story of my own. Oh, I tried making up several of my own, but my understanding of the language was too weak.

Finally, I broke down and traded not for one, but two stories, to be safe. The first one came from a clever woman. I parted with a pound of tea, a packet of needles, and two yards of Scottish duffel cloth. It seemed to me well worth it. The second story came from an old man, and that one cost me one closed fist full of 30:30 cartridges, a warm, worn, woolen sweater with the elbows out, and a much-sharpened hatchet used for chopping frozen walrus meat.

I hate to admit this, but neither of those stories worked for me, although I had heard both owners tell their stories successfully to a crowd of persons in a tent. I failed miserably. After that, I withdrew into my shell, continued studying my word lists, and tried hapless rhymes on children.

In the middle of all this, my government department warned me that the Canadian Wildlife Service were sending in a mammalogist to do another caribou survey. The Chief of the Arctic Division suggested in a letter carried by this biologist that it might be prudent if I, as Game Officer, would accompany him. And so I did.

We went inland first, then arched eastward in a great circle, arriving at a small post manned by a lone Scot. He was holding the fort since the mounted policeman was away on patrol and the missionary, too, was elsewhere. When we entered the little post house, we felt blinded by the intensity of his electric lights and immediately peeled down to our underwear, struck dumb by normal heat. After we had each consumed several cans of tinned pears, a luxury we'd been dreaming of, we heard the radio receiver crackling in his bedroom just before the eight o'clock sked.

"Have you heard any news?" I asked him.

"Well, yes," he answered. "There're quite a few foxes east of here, and old Kipernik's still holding up after his bout of flu, and the widow's been getting some fishing through the ice."

"No, no, not that kind of news," I said. "I mean, news from the outside. Anything going on in Ottawa, London, New York, anywhere?"

"Not much," he said. "Let me think. Oh, hell, yes, the Russians . . . they've done something. They sent up a kind of rocket. They call it Sputnik. It went sailing all around the world. It had a dog inside of it called Laika."

"Sputnik! And a dog named Laika!" I thought both words sounded vaguely like Inuktitut. "Well, that's worth telling. I'll remember that."

When we were traveling again, heading back toward our home base, Osuitok asked me if I'd heard anything interesting from the trader.

"Oh, yes," I said. "They're getting lots of foxes over east of here."
"I heard that," he answered. "I mean, did you hear anything on the *naloutik?*" That's Inuktitut for radio.

"Oh, yes," I said, pausing for a moment, trying to organize my words. "*Unikaktovingaluk* . . . a big story!" Then I told him somewhat proudly that the *kallunait*, white people, had fired off Sputnik. It being in the middle of the Cold War, I did not admit it was the Russians who had fired it. I called it *sekoaluk*, a great bullet, showing with my mitt how it had soared all around the world. I made my gesture sunwise east to west. "*Silingwak avata, avata!* World around and around!" Then as a final punchline, I told him that Sputnik, this bullet bigger than a dog sled, had a dog inside whose name was Laika.

"Laika! The dog's name was Laika? *Wakadlunga*, I can scarcely believe that," he gasped. "Do you mean that dog was just sitting there driving that bullet sled?" He sat dumbfounded on the sled beside me, looking out over the landscape, his lips moving thoughtfully as he retold my incredible story to himself. Suddenly, he turned to me and said, "If anyone on this coast wishes to trade that story from you, you make them trade a lot for it!"

I did try to tell this true story in the best way I could until one night an old man stopped me as I waved my hands describing the dog Laika's journey in the bullet around the world. He called out to my small audience, "This Left-Handed thinks the world is round. Let him believe it!"

72
The Egg Boat

From a catalogue I had ordered a paint box, which was delivered to me on the annual supply ship. It unfolded into a well-designed, compact easel, springing into position with legs beneath a clever seat. I thought it perfect for my purposes. But it never really worked, for my traveling was just a bit too rough, and it was never handy to carry or tie on a sled. Of course, I removed wet colors that would freeze, replacing them with dry block colors. I reinforced the box with tin can corners so that it would withstand the hard knocks of winter sled journeys. But I rarely took it with me, for I was discovering what in that simpler life was best. I usually only carried sketching paper and rugged books, my small watercolor box just a little longer than my hand, pens, pencils, and brushes.

I can scarcely tell you how eager I was to get away from the tiny settlement and go out onto the land. I took my light and heavy rifles and my three-star, Arctic sleeping bag, a tent and Primus stove, and my art kit, piling everything onto the sled with Osuitok. We headed north up the long, frozen fiord to Tessiuakjuak. My mind was trying to grasp and hold the images of the far, blue hills laced with long, white snake designs and the new, spring glare bounding off the snow, burning our faces coffee-brown. I looked forward to this spring break out in the middle of nowhere with only me, the fishing, and the birds. Osuitok helped me set up camp beneath the granite cliffs of Pokaritaktok on the edge of the frozen lake before he left with all the dogs. I was truly alone. What a break!

Later, after fishing, when I came back to my tent with two big, red-bellied, Arctic char, I saw upturned sleds and lots of dogs lying on the snow. I opened the entrance flap and found my tent full of people sleeping. There were seven men, women, and children of various ages, sprawled comfortably every which way. I found a place to sit down among them in the sun-warmed tent and sharpened a needle's point against a stone, using it to remove a sliver from my hand. Then I eased a young sleeper closer to his mother, curled up on top of the government mailbag, and went to sleep.

When I awoke, I saw that the tent flap was wide open and the old grandmother was sitting out in front. She had lit my Primus and had it roaring as noisily as a waterfall. On it was her own black iron kettle off their sled, filled with snow water that ran down from the mountains in this season. She did not know that I was awake, and I saw her look into my little sack and examine my tea box, then carefully put it back. She reached into her parka hood, removed her fish jig, then brought out a damp twist of silver foil. When she opened this carefully and dumped its contents into the pot, I knew it was trade tea that had been used once or twice through their kettle, then mixed with some leaves of wild Labrador tea. It would take a long time to darken the water, but she was in no hurry and prepared to wait. The steam of the kettle rose and partly hid her wise, brown face, as though she were already on her way into that other world.

I lay there and wondered at the power that lay hidden within old women such as she, with their narrowed eyes beneath their epicanthic folds as quick and bright as wild animals' eyes, their dark, tanned skin tight over wide cheekbones and large jaw muscles. I asked myself, what was my visitor thinking now? I watched her as she squatted, rocking back and forth on her heels, staring out at the frozen lake, humming a song that may have come with her ancestors out of Asia a thousand years ago.

Next day, they were gone and I lit the little Swedish Primus, filled a pot with snow, melted it, then carefully poured in the porridge from its sack. I waited until it cooked, then ate it without salt or milk or sugar. It can taste all right that way, but only if you're hungry – not starving, mind you. Starving is too terrible to talk about, but being really hungry is a good, healthy situation that most so-called civilized folk in North America have never come to know. Try it. It helped me to look at life in a different way.

I folded back the flap of my small tent and watched the three teams coming across the huge, white birthday cake of floating lake ice. They looked at first like small, black ants spread out and pulling in the blinding white spring glare. I could soon make out the figures of men, women, and children running or sitting on the long, sleek sleds.

The island on which I camped stood in front of a breadloaf-shaped hill of granite, a nesting place for a pair of rough-legged hawks that showed the greatest zeal as defenders when one or the other flew screaming from their rocky nesting place to drive off a marauding raven. Osuitok had long since departed with our sled and team, traveling throughout the bright, white night in search of geese. Since I had reached this camping place, a fifteen-foot moat, about five meters, of water had formed between the floating surface of the lake ice and this island's near shore.

I had returned to this place at this precise time of early summer because of the candle ice. When ice starts to rot, water runs down through it and forms millions of thumb-sized candle shapes that are as long as the ice is deep. On summer evenings, if there is the slightest breeze, you can hear the crystal-clear forms breaking off with a sound that is like no other in the world. The ice at the edge of the gap between the giant floating icefield and the shore was incredibly slippery. I knew, for I had taken an unexpected bath some days before. Now I was eager to learn how these visitors would manage to navigate ashore. When they were in front of me, the lead driver gave a single grunt, which halted all three teams. The dogs lay down and licked their paws, enjoying the sunshine and looking across the moat between us.

After we had greeted each other, Pitseolak, the important man from Kiaktok, asked me if I wanted some eggs. I answered yes, wondering how he would ever get them across the gap of open water which was as wide as a city side street. Pitseolak turned and spoke to his wife, Agio, who came forward carefully carrying a bulging sealskin bag. Pitseolak pointed to a place on the broken ice edge. There Agio squatted down. Smiling across the open water at me, she spread a nest of their gathered eiderdown on the ice beside her feet. She placed about twenty large, olive-green eider eggs in the nest.

"*Namuktuk*, enough?" she asked.

"*Namuktopaluk*, enough indeed," I answered.

Using the small iron chisel on the other end of his harpoon, Pitseolak neatly cut the ice around the eggs into the shape of a small boat with a pointed bow. He aimed this ice boat at me and gently pushed its stern.

The ice boat with its gift of eiderdown and eggs moved smoothly across the open water and I caught it on the land side. I gathered the eggs and the soft, gray eiderdown into the apronlike shape that

I had made with the front of my parka. I carefully deposited the gift in my tent and brought back about a third of a pound of tea. Placing it on Pitseolak's same ice boat, I pushed it back to them.

"*Nakoamik*, thanks," he and his wife called. "We're going further up the lakes to the good fishing place. Do you want to come with us?"

"No, it's good here," I answered.

He called out to his dogs and they jumped to their feet and started moving northward up the lake. The children called excitedly to me and waved as they left. I waved back, then went inside and brought out my small Swedish Primus stove and frying pan. I rubbed some grease in the pan as it heated and cracked in three eggs, then as an afterthought a fourth to fill it evenly. It was good to be here, alone, alive in spring. I stayed squatting rock-still as a large flock of snow geese passed low over the tent with their wing flaps down. They landed less than a stone's throw away from me. As I started to count them, I remembered the words from an old Inuit song:

Ayii, Ayii,
Glorious it is
to follow the ebb-marks of the sea.
Glorious it is
when wandering time has come.
Ayii. Ayii.

73
When Wandering Time Has Come

There was not a breath of wind when we halted our sleds at sunrise. Knowing that the day-long heat of the spring sun would soften the trail, we planned to rise when evening came and the trail would harden again.

We humans and dogs were tired, stiff, cold, ready to stop moving, and wanted to build a place to sleep. I was thinking about sleep when I stared across the flat ice at the clouds' shadows as they moved like great blue elephants in a slow slow-motion film. We would build an igloo here and sleep throughout the day, but first a mug of tea.

I leaned against the sled in the dawn light and watched the thin veils of snow that had begun to drift as languidly as windblown curtains gently overlapping one another. All sense of home and time had gone, leaving me with these Inuit friends, this country. What more could I ask of life?

74

Friends

In the summer of 1958, two very important persons visited Kingait. One was Charles Gimpel, the famous international art dealer and Arctic photographer, nephew of Lord Duveen, who had helped the Mellon family build an art collection, which was the foundation of the National Gallery in Washington, D.C. Charles immediately took up the cause for Inuit art, both carvings and bold, meaningful drawings. In 1953, during the Queen's coronation, Charles had arranged the royal exhibition of Inuit art in London. That was the first strong European impression of contemporary Inuit art.

The second person was Terry Ryan, a graduate of the Ontario College of Art. He had been in Clyde River working on a weather station. I showed him our early efforts at printmaking and he declared he would work without salary if we could find him a job that might be helpful to the printmakers of Cape Dorset. Terry did exactly that for over a year. Beginning in 1960, he helped manage the many details of buying drawings, selecting and buying paper and inks, organizing the orderly shipping-out of the collected series, and helping to prepare catalogues. Terry Ryan has been wonderful at the job and, perhaps best of all, he has had great staying power.

For the past thirty-five years, he has worked steadily both in Kingait and at the West Baffin Eskimo Co-op sales outlet in Toronto. That's a long time in Arctic terms. And he has encouraged Jimmy Tigugligak Manning, a younger Inuk, to take over as the Manager.

75
La Petite *Yellow Monster*

Ice was forming in the saltwater bays and the freshwater lakes had long been frozen when another hunter named Osuitok (we called him "Oshaweetok A") came in from along the coast to Kingait to do the last trading for his camp before real winter set upon us. I happened to be near the store when he arrived and went in to see him.

"Any sickness down your way?" Tomasi, the Hudson's Bay interpreter, asked him.

"No," Oshaweetok A answered.

"Anything changed down there?"

"Yes, something's different. We've got *kallunait*, white men, down there with us now."

"When did they come?" Tomasi asked.

"I don't know. For one moon they've been there with us."

"Who are they?" we asked. By now, I was keenly interested.

Oshaweetok A shrugged his shoulders. "There are five of them. They came in a *tingmisuu*, plane. It left them there. We can't really understand them, but they're good *kallunait*. They give out lots of tea, coffee, tobacco, biscuits. Generous, they are. Laugh a lot. They play good football, too. They like our little kids, our old folks, too. We helped them put up their tents."

"What are they doing?"

"Making holes in the ground. They drill deep, wrist-sized, noisy holes right into the hardest rock. We've never seen that before. They bring up long, round, solid shapes," he said. "Straight as gun barrels they are. Stone from underneath the world. There's a bearded man with them who peers at each rock center very carefully with a strong bring-near glass. He lets me look through it sometimes to see the different layers in the rock."

"What else are those men doing?" I asked in amazement.

"Waiting for a little ship to come. They're going to build a house, we think, before the thick ice appears in Sorvak. The 'oui, oui miut' [Frenchmen's] ship came not long ago, and they got us all to help them haul a lot of stuff above the high-tide mark. Then right away these five men, with us to help, started to build a wooden house, a long one for them to live in and keep their food and all their long, round stone pieces inside. They got a yellow *nunatsiuit*," he said, meaning something that rolls over the ground. "It's strong," he said, "pulls like twenty dog teams, makes sparks when it strikes against big rocks, then rolls them. They're making a flat place."

"Where did they do the drilling in the ground?"

"Right in the middle of our camp," said Oshaweetok A, "we had to move two of our tents. They have a big *ajiluwak*, a picture that they roll out. It was taken, they say, from high up, from a *tingmisuu*. On the picture they showed us our own five white tents, they look like little splats of gull shit from up that high."

"I don't understand how those men managed to arrive down there without the government sending me some kind of message," I told Oshaweetok A. "I'll go back with you and ask them what they're doing there. They certainly don't have any right to be drilling in the middle of your camp."

"They're good men," said Oshaweetok A. "We like them. We're glad to have them with us there. Don't you tell them to go away."

He took out a package of cigarettes of a brand we'd never seen before and offered us each one. Traders in the Arctic didn't carry anything as fancy as tailor-made cigarettes, only coffee-sized tins of loose tobacco and thin rice papers to roll your own. But as Inuit had discovered, any kind of paper would do, though the glue that held paper labels to tins and boxes tended to make the flavor strange.

"You don't have to go down there to see them," he said. "We told them you lived here and their boss, the small man, told us that they were going to come up here to see you. The little ship left them a good new boat and two new kickers. They'll be coming in that soon. You'll like them."

"Not if they're not asking anyone's permission. Just sneaking in and drilling in the middle of your camp, the government doesn't want them doing that."

Oshaweetok A sighed. "They're good men. Don't say anything bad to them. We like them. We hope they'll stay with us."

Three days later, I saw a strange, new, red-orange boat with two 35-horsepower outboard engines, bigger than any we'd ever seen, on its stern. They dashed grandly up Kingait Fiord, then stopped near my place. I could see an Inuk and several strangers in the boat. The tide was high as they came paddling in to the beach.

I hurried over to the little office that Oshaweetok and I had built from the wood of packing boxes. Inside I quickly spread out my official government letters showing me to be the Administrator and the Mineral Claims Officer, Explosives Officer, Fur Officer, Game Officer, Fisheries Officer. I put the one that said I was the Dog Officer back inside the drawer, not wishing to impress them too much. Then I went down to shake hands with these new men and walked up with them. They followed me inside. Three of these oversized prospectors had to stand because there was so little room inside for them to move.

I, too, stood behind my desk and asked, "Where have you come from?"

"Montreal," their boss said. "Well, most of us are from there. We chartered a plane and flew to Noranda, gassed up, then landed again at Fort Chimo. From there we angled west across Hudson Strait to Sorvak, that's east of here along the coast."

Before I could get the chance to chew them out for drilling in the middle of an Inuit camp without letting anyone know that they were even in the country, their boss quickly told me that they had heard that they were to close down their operation and leave as soon as a plane could come for them. He said they would take out the best core samples but had given up any real hope of discovering a major iron mine. Or had their whole exercise been simply to promote the stock?

In due course it became clear that their small company was eager to make a deal. If we could help them by bringing their new bull-dozer, the smallest and lightest made, to Dorset where the icebreaker could pick it up for them next summer, they would turn over to the

West Baffin Eskimo Co-op everything else they would leave behind. Among those many treasures at the abandoned mining camp we discovered a new, twelve-quart pressure cooker. My eagerness was to help the West Baffin Eskimo Co-operative legally acquire all of the abandoned mining gear, including the pressure cooker, a special treasure far beyond our means.

We could not see at the time how the little yellow tractor could be of any use to us. But because of the deal, my Inuit friends were determined to bring it in. I wondered how we could move it west along the sixty miles of coastline to Cape Dorset before late summer when the icebreaker should arrive – you can never say will arrive when you're talking about heavy ice. We were excited and went back to the deep fiord at Sorvak to revel in all that remained. We shoveled out the precious tractor, which had been buried beneath a snowbank all that winter. It emerged looking fresh and violent-yellow and new.

Enter Paul Charbonneau, a great bull of a man who had been sent in on the police plane to install Dorset's noisy new government diesel generator. Ottawa had retrieved this large, muscular Québécois when he returned off a huge bulldozer in the French-speaking Congo where he had been busy helping clear that part of Africa. He was a hearty, good-natured man, hard-drinking sometimes when he got the chance, which wasn't often. He was ecstatic when he heard of *la petite* cat, as he liked to call it. Charbonneau was absolutely in love with the cats – bulldozers, large or small – and he was a genius with them. He refused to recognize any climactic distinctions between the steaming River Niger and a raging Baffin winter.

A pilot had once described Charbonneau to me as tough. To explain tough, he said that he had tented with Charbonneau, who never bothered to untie the canvas tent flaps when he had an urge to rush outside. His forward-thrusting weight would tear the tent ties off – now that's what I call tough!

Charbonneau went down the coast by dog team with a group including Pingwarktok and Bill Berry, my new government assistant from Ottawa. The weather was forty degrees below. Bill told me that during that extreme cold, Paul tinkered happily with that untouchable steel. He and Pingwarktok were amazed when Charbonneau built a fire out of broken boxwood beneath the engine, then tried to start it. They were even more amazed when they heard the thawing engine shudder, then groan and slowly cough its way to life.

Charbonneau had even stood up on the moving sled, Bill told me, so anxious was he to look over the country on our way east. "No cat is ever going overland there," he told Bill, "not over them goddamn rocks. They would tear the tracks off. But don't worry, I'll take her back on the sea ice."

"You keep off the ice," Berry told him. "Inuit say Sorvak is a dangerous place with narrows and huge, fast-swelling tides that cause weak places in the ice. They say a hunter and his family on a dog sled were drowned down there a few years ago. I warned him," Bill said, "not to try and drive over unknown ice with a heavy monster like that."

Later, when the engine was running and they were debating the route back, Bill repeated his warning about the cat disappearing through holes in the ice. "Fock d' holes in d' ice!" said Charbonneau, who was nothing if not bold. "I got a special way. You hand me that long coil of sealskin line they got tucked on that dog sled."

With it, he made some complicated loops and hitches and attached them like long reins to the accelerator and the steering mechanism. He kicked the tractor tread and yelled, "*Marchons!*" jerking back the clutch. The heavy little tractor snorted and moved forward. Charbonneau jumped off, paid out thirty feet of line, then walked behind, steering with his reins, geeing and hawing like a farmer guiding his horse and plow. He followed behind the tractor down the bank as it headed out over the various unknown thicknesses of ice.

"If this son-of-a-bitch goes through," Charbonneau shouted happily to Berry, "she's going to do it by herself. *Venez à droit comme ça.*"

Singing "*La Rose aux Bois,*" he followed *la petite* yellow monster over the ice.

Pingwarktok later said of Charbonneau, whom he admired,

"That man thought of nothing except getting his little yellow cat to Kingait."

Charbonneau never seemed to tire, he said, walking mile after mile behind the roaring, puffing piece of iron. One dog-team driver would go ahead each day and build a snowhouse for them. There was a great deal of shouting when the little yellow monster appeared at the mouth of Kingait Fiord. Everyone was impressed by this little snorting giant that could be driven like a dog team. Charbonneau waved to all of us in triumph, like a ringmaster guiding his plump, feather-footed circus horse up through the jagged piles of barrier ice.

That summer, Charbonneau showed Pingwarktok how to drive the yellow cat from the shore onto the ramp of the icebreaker's largest barge. The Co-op's bargain with the mining company was now settled. All valuables from that camp belonged to the West Baffin Eskimo Co-operative. They made me a present of the pressure cooker and always gladly helped me eat the contents.

76

Dynamite

Our main sea ice in Kingait Fiord that year had been firmly in place since October and now, in late July, we were tired of it. We wanted it to go. The warm July sun that brightened our world through midnight finally had its way. With the help of a big moon tide, the ice broke and was carried beyond our view. The fiord sparkled and danced free, blue as the Mediterranean. We were more than ready for our brief summer, but we were not ready that day for the slow-rolling thunder of the large, twin-engined flying boat that circled over us, then set its wings for a landing. Lord, we thought, our ice has been gone for less than a day and here comes civilization.

I went out in our twenty-two-foot Cree-built canoe with Osuitok and pulled up beside the grand old "pig boat," which had been designed and used as a submarine hunter during the war. It had the unusual capacity of being able to stay airborne for more than twenty-four hours – the only plane, they said, that could take off on a Monday and land on a Wednesday.

When they opened the rear door, which was almost at water level, Bill Mair leaned out and said, "Hey, Houston, aren't you even going to ask us in for a cup of tea?"

He was head of the Canadian Wildlife Service and had with him John Findlay, head of the U.S. Fish and Game Service.

"Sure, I'll ask you in," I said, looking nervously out at the entrance to the fiord. "Did you see much ice coming in?"

"Yeah, but it's way off to the east. We're not going to stay forever, you know. Tomorrow, we're going up to Koksoak River. Do you want to come with us on this wildlife survey?"

"You bet!" I said as they, with the pilot and co-pilot, piled into our canoe.

When we were inside the house and Allie had met them all, we looked out the window and could see the big silver plane riding on the fiord like some serene summer dream.

"You're worried about the ice?" I asked the pilot, an old friend of mine.

"Hell, no, not if it stays down where it is."

"We should keep a watch on it through the night."

I got Kiaksuk to do this. He's an old man and wise about ice, but unfortunately not wise enough about the takeoff time for flying boats.

Kiaksuk came into the house about 3:00 a.m. and called, "Saomik, *ayii, sekoalooktikiniarkposi,* the ice, it's arriving!"

I leapt up and rushed to the window, then in a panic woke the pilot.

"We're bloody late!" he roared as he pulled his pants on.

We rushed our canoe into the water and paddled hard, watching the white line of ice being forced back in by the tide until the pilot judged it was too close to risk a takeoff. All we could do now was to try and save the plane. That would be no easy trick. Some of the broken pieces of sea ice were as big as a half-sunk 18-wheeler truck, and they were moving in fast on the tide.

I asked the pilot if there was any way he could start the engines and drive it up on shore.

"Not on this beach," he said. "We'd never get her turned around again."

"Could we pull her back ashore?"

"We'd have to, her engines won't reverse. We could try," he said, "but we've got nothing here to help, and this big piece of war surplus weighs more than you'd believe. I'll run it in as close to shore as possible, then we can turn it around, and if you get every last person in this settlement to come and haul on the ropes, and I mean every man, woman, and child, we just might be able to ease her up the beach a little."

"Sure," I said. "The next tide will probably carry all this incoming ice away for good."

All the muscle power of every soul nearby did almost nothing to move the sea plane once her steel hull grounded on the gravel. We all watched the incoming ice with horror, imagining how it would crumple the plane like aluminum foil unless we could drag it up the beach to safety.

Bill Mair, who had been a colonel in the war and a Saskatchewan farmer as well, said, "I know a trick we used to do with a tractor mired in mud, and that same thing worked with a weapons carrier rolled off the road. Houston, have you got anything like a good, strong, leg-thick fence post?"

"I've got a ship's timber that we found floating off the coast."

I asked Lukta and he went running for it.

"And cable?"

"Yes, we've got some light ship's cable left here after the Nascopi sunk – in the Arctic, we never throw anything away."

"Then all we need is two of your longest, strongest crowbars."

Under his guidance, we assembled it all together and hitched the cable onto the steel eye at the rear end of the Canso.

Bill held the post free, standing on the gravel beach, and we tied the crowbars crossways at chest height to make a primitive capstan. First eight, then twelve men started turning the post, which steadily wound the cable on itself. It seemed nothing short of a miracle that when the strength of eighty persons had failed to do anything, suddenly the strength of twelve started to move the aircraft. The

Canso came grinding up across the gravel just in time to escape the ice. The line slackened and the thick, white slabs stacked up on the beach stood still, waiting for the tide to rise twelve hours later. The worst ice remained grounded on the beach. What would the wind do next time? How were we ever going to save this aircraft? No plane could come in or go out to help us now. We'd have to wait and fight.

The wind controlled our lives for the next thirty-two days, even when in our protected fiord we could not feel it. Most days the tidal ice went out, then came back in at us. During all of this, I didn't really believe we'd be able to save the plane. I know we never would have succeeded without Inuit ingenuity. While we were sitting around in front of my house discussing how we could save the Canso, Inuit were sitting around in their tents discussing how they would do it. Always as the tide was starting in, we'd get together and hear each other's ideas.

Canso in ice

Inuit had long known that if you had a canoe with a five-and-a-half-horsepower outboard engine, with one man to run it and another out on the ice to hold its bow, you can move ice weighing hundreds of tons. We did this daily to protect the plane's hull. In fact, we wore out both government outboard engines and five others belonging to the local hunters.

When the big tides began to build again, they left several enormous pieces of ice on the beach dangerously close to the plane. If the wind was wrong, these would certainly cause damage.

All this time, we'd been sending radio messages in and out from the Hudson's Bay Company, which operated once daily every evening at 8:00 p.m. The airline based in South Porcupine,

Ontario, understood our trouble as did the Canadian Wildlife Service. But the U.S. Fish and Game service in Washington, D.C. sounded furious. They finally sent in a message to John saying that they did not believe there was any place on earth where he could not call in some kind of boat or plane, and that he was to leave Cape Dorset next day, for it was essential that he be in Washington to settle the game openings and closings on a number of hunting seasons in various states. John rolled his eyes.

There was nothing anyone could do but wait, and above all try to safeguard the position of the still imperiled flying boat.

Then the Inuit think tank came and asked for dynamite. Inuit did not have a word for "dynamite," but they knew what it was and what it would do. The post manager, Bill Hall, said yes, that there was a case of dynamite up in the powder shed that looked like an outhouse way off on the distant hill. He advised us not to touch it since the last time he'd looked, he said, the gelignite was running out of it, which makes dynamite very dangerous to handle. No, he said, he didn't have any dynamite caps.

"What are you going to do with it?" we asked the hunters suspiciously.

"Blow up the ice," they said.

"You'll blow up my plane as well," the pilot told them.

"We'll show you what we'll do on that piece of ice way over there."

They sent someone running for my long ice drill and my rifle with a mounted telescope. At waist height, they drilled a hole in the ice and shoved a stone inside, then we oh so gingerly eased a stick of dynamite inside, and they covered it with a stone the size of the hole.

They all moved well away, then said, "Go ahead, Saomik, hit it."

Not a long shot. It was easy. First, the sound of the rifle, then a dull thump and the whole car-sized piece of ice shattered and collapsed completely.

"That shouldn't hurt the plane," the pilot said. "Try it."

We drilled the biggest of the threatening ice slabs and set our stones and dynamite. We went back and I fired again while everyone stood close by me, watching the ice completely disintegrate as if by magic.

Ikaluk and Uvilu, who had been looking after our sons, John and Sam, said that while they were watching, the disc-shaped stone I'd fired at must have gone hurtling back two hundred yards or about 180 meters because it smashed through our front window. The stone must have cut all too near the people around me to have broken that window at that distance. We cleared everyone out of sight before we broke the other slab.

The wind changed on the big tide on the thirty-first day and the ice moved out to jam in a rough barrier across the entrance to the fiord.

"It's far enough," the pilot said. "I've got room for takeoff, maybe. I'm going to try it, but I'll only do it alone."

With even the children pushing and shoving at high tide, we managed to float the pig boat again. The pilot made his heart-stopping run and got it safely into the air. With a cluster of Inuit beside us, I walked with the Wildlife people around the hills behind Kingait Mountain to the west inlet, a few miles away, which had recently blown clear of ice. I was glad to see the Canso sitting there, clear at last, but sad to think that these visitors of ours were going. We'd all of us in Dorset been through a major daily struggle to keep that plane alive. And now the main characters in the play were leaving. Allie and the boys cried, and so did the departing Wildlife men and that ace pilot, Jimmy Bell. You don't have adventures like that happen often in a lifetime, adventures that bind everyone together in a common cause.

Our annual summer icebreaker had been delayed by the ice, so when the Wildlife men were with us, we had been reduced to seal meat, Arctic char, eider duck eggs, and lots of leftover dried spaghetti. None of the food part was any hardship. Allie cooked it wonderfully. Like us, the kids preferred country food, and the guests soon got the hang of it. We heard from them for years following that experience. I know we'll all remain the best of friends for the rest of our lives.

77
No Need for Maps

A group of scientific people came in with a large, military helicopter, which was based on a vessel anchored out somewhere on the Foxe Channel, well beyond our view.

"We're going to do some measurements," they said, and showed me on the map the route that they intended to follow north across the Great Plain of the Koksoak, a place where few had ever been in summer.

"You want to come with us?" they asked.

"Sure," I said, and when I told Osuitok, I could see a look of longing in his eyes.

"Can Osuitok come, too?" I asked.

"It's okay with me," the head geographer said. "We should be back tonight or tomorrow. Believe me, we're in one helluva hurry to get this done before the snows start to fly. Cold can play hell with these choppers."

We took with us binoculars, a sketch book, a thermos of hot tea, a tin of bully beef, and a heavy-caliber rifle. On the first landing, the scientists jumped out and set on the ground something that looked like a coffee grinder and started rapidly taking notes. We left in a few minutes and landed perhaps five minutes later not far from the only irregularity on that whole, flat, inland plain. The small Kikitiwak Hills are an easily identified place. I had come there each year to survey caribou for the government and while doing so I ate a few. At that time, it was called legally living off the country. I was the Game and Fisheries Officer for the area, but I had yet to issue my first hunting license. That's how few tourists ever came into the country.

"Are you coming back this way?" I asked the helicopter pilot.

"Yes," he said. "We're only measuring the earthen folds and magnetic variations. Nobody really knows exactly how large this world is with all its complex wrinkles. We need to find that out – and fast!"

"If we stay near here," I pointed to a pile of rocks, "would you be sure to pick us up again?"

"Yeah," the pilot said. "Here, take one of these," he said, handing me a colorful signal cloth. "Spread that out on the ground where you want me to land, but be there! We've got to get this part of the job wrapped up today or at latest tomorrow."

The helicopter vibrated upward with the usual pulsing rush of wind as we walked over to the slablike hills and climbed them. We were only about two stories high above the level of the plain, but it seemed to me like the top of Kilimanjaro as I looked around and could see the vastness of the land spreading out and disappearing into distant mists.

Osuitok pointed without speaking and I saw the distant flash of white – a snowy owl out hunting against a clouded, autumn sky.

"Where's south?" I asked.

"Difficult," said Osuitok. "Otokie got lost in here during bad weather and they went round and round with the dogs until they almost starved to death." The sky looked evenly gloomy and did not indicate east from west or north from south for me.

Osuitok got up and started walking. I followed behind him, Inuit fashion, not walking side by side as we do. One man should break trail, the other follows – a habit learned during those weeks in spring when the snow is softening and the going is hard.

Osuitok seemed to be looking for something on the ground. He was not walking head up like a man looking for an *inuksuk*, which is a kind of stone scarecrow used to guide travelers or cause caribou to follow a given path to a river crossing. Caribou have the habit of following one another, leaving a deep, narrow rut worn through the tundra. Some of these trails are old and deep, but they often lead in the caribou's direction of that day. Caribou do not like to feed with the wind blowing up their noses.

Osuitok seemed to be carefully searching the ground when, suddenly, he stopped.

"What do you see?" I said, after looking carefully ahead of us.

"Look at that rock. What do you see?"

"*Petaungi*, nothing," I answered.

"See the white patch on that stone?"

"Yes," I admitted.

"Dog teams have been traveling this way for years. As they passed this stone, all of them were eager to sniff, then cock their leg against this rock. So often have they done this that they have worn away the black lichen that once clung to this stone." He began looking for the second sign. "We need only spread out and walk until we find another cocked-leg rock and we will have set the line that we should travel to the coast, then home."

When we did find a large, man-sized *inuksuk* in the country, we approached it.

"Why did they build that?" I asked.

Inuksuks

"Maybe hunters waited here for caribou with nothing to do but find good stones, then carry them back and build this likeness of a man for pleasure. See the small space left between the rocks? You're supposed to look through this hole."

He tried from both sides of the man-shaped stones, then said, "There it is."

I looked through the hole and could see two smaller, standing stones lined up.

"There's the way to go," he said. "That would lead us to a camp."

We started back when Osuitok pointed to a small dot low in the sky. "*Kungatasu*," he said, meaning the helicopter.

A breeze was beginning to sweep across that lonely plain as we unfolded and spread our bright orange ground flag, weighting it with four fist-sized rocks.

The helicopter landed and we climbed in.

"We're finished for today," the U.S. scientist told us. "It will be getting dark by the time we get back to your place."

He took out a Canadian government survey map that was 1 over 250,000, a relatively small map of a segment of the Great Plain of the Koksoak, the inland area of Foxe Peninsula, an unpopulated patch in the second largest country in the world.

"Have you got a map or compass?" he asked.

"No," I answered.

"Would you know how to get home?"

"Yes," I answered proudly, and pointed at Osuitok. "My friend knows everything I need to know around here. Why are you doing your measuring?" I asked.

"Because these maps are only nearly accurate. We want to know the exact measurements so that we could fire a missile and guide rockets anywhere on a foreign target or later maybe to fly to the moon."

"What does he say they're doing?" Osuitok asked.

"They want to fly to the moon."

"*Wakadlunga*! Imagine that," he said. "Some people at Akiaktolaolavik camp say they got an old shaman down there named Aluriak who can fly there any night the moon is full."

"What did he say?" the scientist asked.

"Great that you're going to fly to the moon."

"Yeah, well, a lot of our reasons are from worries a lot closer to home. That's why we're trying to get all these distances just right."

78

Banished

The second difficulty with Pitseolak came some years after the costume contest. A hunter and his wife came to me and demanded that I do something about the fact that he, their camp boss, had taken their underage daughter without asking their permission, and now planned to keep her as his second wife. According to the laws of Canada that I was to uphold, this act was classified as statutory rape.

Pitseolak readily admitted to me that he had taken the girl without her parents' permission, saying that he loved her and would not give her back. The girl assured me she loved him, too. What to do? The age of consent in the Northwest Territories was sixteen years of age. My duty as administrator, in the absence of the police, was to uphold the law.

I warned Pitseolak of the trouble this would cause, and I all but begged him to return the girl to her parents. He refused.

I sent a radio message to the two-man police detachment at Kingmerok asking that one of them come over. He set out next day by dog team. His journey took about a week. Pitseolak assured the policeman that he had no intention of giving up the girl. I advised the government of this, as did the young policeman, and it was decided by Ottawa to fly in the territorial circuit court on the police plane during their rounds that spring.

Court was held in the small schoolhouse, with the judge and crown prosecutor splendidly attired in their black and scarlet robes, plus a canny lawyer to act in Pitseolak's defense. The girl's parents' point was argued by the prosecution. Pitseolak insisted on his own interpreter as well as the one supplied by the court. At the end of the daylong trial, the judge found Pitseolak guilty, and the weeping young girl was returned to her family.

The judge decreed that my often good friend, Pitseolak, should be banished from west Baffin Island for a period of ninety days. He was to be flown by the police next day to Kingmerok where his movements were to be unrestricted in all social and hunting matters, except that he would not for those three months be allowed to return to the Kingait area. Nothing like that, so far as I know, had ever happened in the Canadian eastern Arctic.

Next day when it was time for the plane to leave, Pitseolak had been instructed to meet his police escort at the government flagpole. He stood there alone, head held high, staring defiantly at the world. My wife and young sons went out to shake his hand and say goodbye to him, while I stood weeping out of sight. I felt awful! Pitseolak wrote me a letter from Kingmerok, saying that my wife, Arnakotak, had acted properly, but that he was ashamed of me for not coming out to say goodbye to him.

79

Printmaking

Printmaking began among the people of Kingait (Cape Dorset) in the early winter of 1957. This is how it started:

Osuitok sat near me one evening casually studying the sailor head trademarks on two identical packages of cigarettes. He noted carefully every subtle detail of color and form, then stated that it must have been very tiresome for some artist to sit painting every one of the little heads on the packages with the exact sameness.

I tried to explain in Inuktitut, as best I could, about "civilized" man's technical progress in the field of printing little packages, which involved the entire offset color printing process. My explanation was far from successful, partly because of my inability to find the right words to describe terms such as "intaglio" and "color register," and partly because I was starting to wonder whether this could have any practical application in Inuit terms.

Looking around to find some way to demonstrate printing, I saw an ivory walrus tusk that Osuitok had recently engraved. The curved tusk was about fifteen inches long. Osuitok had carefully smoothed and polished it and had incised bold engravings on both sides. Into the lines of these engravings he had rubbed black soot gathered from his family's seal-oil lamp.

Taking an old tin of writing ink that had frozen and thawed many times, with my finger I dipped up the black residue and smoothed it over the tusk. Then taking a thin piece of toilet tissue, I laid it on the inked surface and rubbed the top lightly, then quickly stripped the paper from the tusk. I saw that by mere good fortune, I had pulled a fairly good negative image of Osuitok's incised design.

"We could do that," he said, with the instant decision of a hunter. And so we did.

The concept of printmaking as a method was new to Inuit, but the images and ideas they created were firmly based on centuries of their ancient traditions, myths, and skill of hand. Four young men, Kananginak, Iyola, Lukta, and Eegivudluk, soon became interested in a printmaking project, and we all embarked on a long series of tests. This led to the development of limited Inuit print series, a practice that is still in progress not only in Cape Dorset, but now in a good number of Arctic settlements, extending across Canada and into Alaska and Greenland.

We gathered other examples of flat, incised, low relief carvings done by Inuit on stone not intended for printmaking, and we printed them, but with mixed results. Printing ink was not available, so we tried making ink by mixing seal oil and lamp black. It was awful. We tried schoolchildren's poster paints with better luck. Since there was only one official mail a year, at shiptime, government correspondence was not a large feature of my life, so I borrowed almost all of the official supply of government onionskin stationery, which proved to be excellent for proofing prints.

We soon discovered that the close-grained carving stone, steatite or serpentine, so named for its rich, serpentlike green color, reacted best to ink. This stone, which was abundant on west Baffin Island, provided for our needs, as it had done in the case of the carvings. It was semi-soft and not too porous, a perfect texture to chisel and carve like the best quality of marble, and it had proved hard enough to take a fine polish. Inuit had traditionally hand quarried this stone at low tide during the summer to use as material for making their lamps and pots, and had even traded it with other Inuit. Much of it tended naturally to cleave away from the rock face in large, flat sections several inches thick, too thin for most carvings, but perfectly suited as stone blocks for printing. We prepared the stone by chipping the printing face flat with a hand ax, then filing and sand-polishing it into a smooth, even surface. Onto this level face, a low relief design could be cut, the basis of the print. Some of the best blocks were very large, two feet long and as much as six inches thick, often weighing more than a hundred pounds.

Good stone was plentiful and we decided to use it. Walrus ivory, by way of contrast, has serious size limitations and requires the killing of those animals. When arts and crafts depend on wild animals' tusks, bones, skins, or feathers, that will – and should – cause trouble. However, caribou antler is a wonderful material and the animals shed their horns naturally every year. Any whalebone the Baffin Islanders use is well aged, since the oil-rich blubber was taken off the bones by the American and Scottish whalers much more than a century ago.

It was a time of high excitement for Inuit trading into Kingait. Everyone was aware that something new was happening. Indeed, it was for them the beginning of printing, that first thrilling step that Gutenberg had made for us into the age of printing.

But the whole question of printmaking hung in limbo, no one knowing whether the idea would be accepted by west Baffin Islanders. We worked to gain support from Pootoogook and Kiaksuk, those two important elders of the Kingaimiut. I got up my nerve and went and asked Pootoogook to make me an illustration of something he had been trying to explain to me. He did this and sent the results next morning. I asked his son, Kananginak, to help print his father's drawing of two caribou. Kananginak gladly did this, helped by Eegivudluk and other relatives. Pootoogook greatly admired the result, and after that the whole stone block and stencil printing project was off to a powerful start. Now, after the creation of more than 300,000 drawings and the development of an important and prosperous co-operative, printmaking is run by Inuit, and has been for almost forty years.

West Baffin Island has always had an abundance of uninhibited artists and craftspeople eager to express themselves in a variety of ways. The main problem of developing printmaking, therefore, was technical. These potential printmakers needed a small, heated building in which to work and a system of creating and pulling limited series of prints from the blocks that they were making.

In the early days, there were some problems. Snow-white paper seemed impossible to keep clean. Fingerprints were everywhere. In the morning cold, ink stuck and came off the stone unevenly. At times, there seemed only to be a few good single impressions pinned to the walls around us, but far more important, we always had the skills, patience, and basic Inuit good nature to carry us through.

By the spring of 1958, we had laboriously assembled small series of prints from a dozen different artists. We tried for numbered series of thirty, after which we cut the image off the stone block or destroyed the stencil. Examples of the prints were sent south and the Government of Canada, the Guild, and the Hudson's Bay Company helped arrange exhibitions of the prints. The first, I believe, was at the Stratford Theatre in Ontario during the annual summer Shakespeare festival. This exhibition was in every way successful and all the prints offered were sold. Other prints of these series exhibited by the Guild and the Hudson's Bay Company were also quickly purchased.

80

Rabbit Eating Seaweed

The old trap boat came in at low tide and touched Kingait's summer beach, a vast, dark stretch strewn with slippery, skull-sized rocks woven over in places by long fronds of seaweed. I saw Kenojuak climb out and help several of her younger children down. She had that familiar bump of another infant in the back of her parka. Two of her older children followed her out of the boat, while two others stayed with their father, Jonibo, to help anchor the boat.

I continued along the beach toward Kenojuak, a bright-eyed, cheerful woman whom I had always liked. She seemed remarkably young and healthy with a great deal of bounce considering that at that time she had already borne eight children – she was to have sixteen in all.

"*Kunoipiit?*" she called in greeting.

I noticed that she was carrying a sealskin bag on her shoulder. It was not unlike other bags I had seen Inuit carrying, but hers had something on it. I asked Kenojuak to show me. The bag had a dark, scraped outer sealskin image carefully cut and sinew-sewn onto the bag itself which was sealskin reversed, the inside being light tan in color.

"What is this?" I asked, listening carefully to hear her answer.

"*Okalik isumalook kikkoyuk memuktualuk*. Rabbit thinking of eating seaweed," she said in a way that she knew I would understand.

Kenojuak went out into the tide and showed me one particular kind of seaweed. "*Mumungitok!* Not good eating. Here, this kind," she said and gathered some. "Take this with you to Arnakotak. Get her to cook it for you. It's good. Rabbits come down to the shore to eat it."

I wasn't so interested in the seaweed as I was the startling image on her work bag. Why had she gone to that trouble?

*Rabbit Eating
Seaweed bag*

After Kenojuak and her family had set up their summer tent, we all went a few nights later to a large dance. It was one of their typical, mid-summer pleasures where the families ate, then slept and rose refreshed and ready to start the dancing at about 11:00 p.m., and could carry on until they tired, when the morning sun came up again.

I purposely took a pencil and two rolled sheets of paper to the dance and gave them to Kenojuak, asking her to make a drawing of her rabbit eating seaweed. She stuck the paper in her parka hood, then gave the parka and her current infant to an elder daughter when she heard the button accordion start to wheeze, then play. She leapt into the local version of a wild, Scottish whalers' reel.

A few days later when everyone had recovered from the muscular activities inherent in these dances, Kenojuak came to me with both sheets of paper I had given her. They were covered with pencil drawings of very different subjects. These were rolled for protection in the very piece of sealskin from which she had cut her rabbit eating seaweed. The images were in two separate pieces.

I asked Osuitok to join me in an experiment. First, we spread the sealskin out on a table over a piece of my own drawing paper from the school. I had borrowed an unused stencil brush that made a mark about the size of a silver dollar. Then onto a piece of glass I mixed and spread some blue paint. I tapped the brush in it until it picked up the color, then pounded the bristles of the brush through the sealskin shapes that Kenojuak had made when she had cut out her skin forms to sew on her bag.

When we lifted away the skin, Osuitok was impressed with the clear image, and believe me, so was I. Here was a new, ancient art form emerging, the main component already created by Kenojuak, one of Canada's best artists, who is now a distinguished Companion of the Order of Canada. I remember that when we showed her the first new print, Kenojuak was delighted.

A whole new woman's version of Inuit art was beginning to bloom, based on the skills of the women trading into Cape Dorset. Like Eskimo women everywhere, they are magnificent sinew sewers, and adept at the art of skin appliqué, that ancient practice of cutting silhouette forms and designs from animal hides to be sewn into clothing or carrying bags for decoration, such as Kenojuak's design on her sealskin bag, which had set me thinking and experimenting. Another time, on a visit to one of the far camps, I stayed in a snowhouse where the hunter's wife had cut a number of figures from some sealskin scraps, had wet them on one side, and had then placed them on the snow wall above the sleeping platform to freeze in place. These served, she said, to illustrate an old story she was telling. Looking at the holes in the sealskin from which she had removed the figures, I was impressed by the flat, stiff texture of the skin. I was sure that paint could be brushed through the openings to form strong, stenciled images. This stencil process was to prove an expanding method of reproduction that grew directly out of an age-old Inuit practice.

It was in the early spring of 1958 that our printmakers first experimented with stenciled prints. A number of Kingait women cut bold patterns from sealskins that had been dehaired, then stretched until they were as stiff as parchment. Trying bound brushes of polar bear hair at first and then paint-soaked wads and other successful and unsuccessful devices, the men found ways of printing those designs cut by the women.

Stenciling is perhaps the most immediate graphic art form ever developed. Perfect for schools, it is a simple medium and one can achieve direct results in a few minutes. In Cape Dorset, the skin stencil slowly evolved into a hardy type of paper stencil. This change occurred because as sealskins became more valuable, we did not wish to use them for stencils. As in most Arctic events, the change developed based on Inuit ingenuity and the available materials at hand.

Speaking of materials at hand, the seaweed was a surprise. Allie boiled and blanched it twice, as Kenojuak had suggested. It had gone into the water first as an unattractive rusty brown and had emerged on the second blanching as a glorious shamrock green. It turned out to be the only Arctic vegetable we ever knew, and it was delicious!

81

Japanese Lessons

In the spring of 1958, the government reminded me that I had a lot of unused leave accumulated. I had forgotten about all that since during the past winter we had been doing exciting tests concerning printmaking.

I had found myself inadequate to offer Inuit the help they needed to start a print program that would suit their needs. I had read an article in a British art magazine that had mentioned and shown the works of several contemporary Japanese printmakers and discussed their techniques. That was exactly what I wanted. I decided that since the best printmakers in the world were in Japan, I should go there and learn from them, and pass on what I learned to my Inuit colleagues. I went outside and sought assistance from the Japanese Embassy in Ottawa and they contacted Kokesai Bunka Shinkokai, a Canadian–Japanese cultural relations organization in Tokyo.

During the past two years, I had made enough drawings and watercolors to put together a one-man exhibition which my dealer, John Robertson in Ottawa, was keen to do. John offered me the money in advance that he felt would be earned from sales. With this, I bought a return ticket via Vancouver to Tokyo and I was off.

Very few Canadians were traveling to Japan almost forty years ago, but my whole experience in Japan from the autumn of 1958 into the spring of 1959 was completely rewarding. I was shown great kindness by the Japanese people, who were intrigued by the idea that their printmaking techniques might be of some benefit to Inuit people. During my stay, I made a number of long-lasting Japanese friendships. I was invited to live in the Japanese household of Professor Murai, who was later appointed President of Waseda University. Above all, I worked with the very distinguished, seventy-year-old Japanese print master, Unichi Hiratsuka, in his studio on a one-to-one, teacher-student basis. Sometimes I learned to cut and print wood blocks until the middle of the night and slept in his studio.

Ukiyoe was the old, world-famous system of Japanese print-making practiced by Hokusai, Hiroshige, Utamaro, and many other artists creating the design. The printmaking was done by others. *Hanga* is more modern where the artist and the printmaker are one. Because of the nomadic Arctic situation and the need for paper, and heat so that the color would print, I felt that *Ukiyoe* would prove the most successful system. I learned many invaluable methods in Japan concerning both systems. Perhaps there will be time to write again in fuller detail about that Japanese experience and what it meant technically to Inuit printmaking.

On my return to Canada, I could scarcely wait to get back to Kingait. I was eager to have the Inuit try the new tools, the papers, the techniques that I had learned. I gathered the most enthusiastic and talented printmakers together, and we started to develop a working and printing technique that would blend the wild, free talents of Inuit artistic styles with centuries of Japanese ingenuity. Inuit artists and craftsmen in the Co-op were always eager to give new ideas a try. We soon discovered that water-based paints stuck in cold weather, and the Inuit judged that Japanese rubbing tampons made of bamboo leaves were not as good as a new version made of hair sealskin which was much more available on southwest Baffin Island. The hunters in the *senlavik* felt that Japanese wood-cutting tools, traditionally made of soft metal, were not as suitable for cutting stone as worn-out file steel, which Inuit knew well and could make razor-sharp to suit their purposes. The Japanese *Ukiyoe* system of registering a print, they agreed, was marvelous and they thought the strength, transparency, and beauty of Japanese paper splendid for printmaking.

Now we started to prepare ourselves to take on printmaking in a much more competent way, blending centuries-old, Japanese wood-cut printing methods with fresh new Inuit ideas for stone blocks and stencils, using imaginative drawings that would form a record of Inuit history, a record of their lives from the past and the present, and, I trust, the future.

Imagine the thrill of seeing Kenojuak, Osuitok, Parr, Niviaksiak, Pitseolak, Kananginak, Iyola, Pudlo, and Lukta of Kingait, Ango-kudluk and Oonark of Baker Lake, Kalvak on Holman Island, Joe Tellirulik of Povungnituk, Lipa Pitseolak of Pangnirtung, and so many others all start to create drawings and make important prints.

I was also pleased when the Department of Northern Affairs told me that what I had done in Japan at my own expense was thought worthwhile and that I should not consider my time in Japan as leave, but should take additional time off later. In the meantime, they asked me to submit an itemized list of my airfare and living expenses while in Japan. I felt that was unnecessary, but I leapt at their kind offer. And the Ottawa exhibition of drawings and water-colors did sell out, which was gratifying news.

An advisory committee comprised of knowledgeable persons in the field of graphic arts in Canada and the United States was named to view the prints each year. At first, these prints came only out of Dorset, but later they began to come from Inuit at Baker Lake, Povungnituk, Holman Island in the western Arctic, Pangnirtung, and last of all George River. The committee was authorized by Inuit printmakers to reject any series they felt to be unsuitable for that year's sale. These rejected prints were not destroyed, but were held as Inuit property.

Everyone who served on the Canadian Eskimo Art Council has been helpful in the furtherance of printmaking.

Inuit everywhere have several unique and special characteristics. They do not usually view scenes and objects in the traditional western way. Their point of view may be from above, as in looking down at fish in the water, or from below, as in looking up at birds in the air. In fact, they sometimes hung bird prints on the ceiling. They are not constricted by a need for background or any of the troublesome rules of perspective. Inuit have a way of isolating images in space, giving each its own importance.

They often choose to make a single statement, and these statements are almost always about creatures of flesh and bones. They are master anatomists, possessing the keen observations of the hunter. They show us powerful animal and human forms moving in a rhythm that is perfectly understood by them. They show us how to drive the caribou and how to hold a child. They understand the patterns of fur and feathers, bone structure, the sheaths of muscle, the rolling gait of the polar bear, the great weight of a walrus, the sleekness of seals, the rhythm in a flight of geese, the nervous movements of fish, for these are all life's blood to them.

Through their prints, they often speak to us of legends and ancient mystical happenings, of great inland journeys. They reveal themselves to us. They show us a very old system of viewing and creating images. Powerful thoughts have existed in their art and their songs and legends for thousands of years. These thoughts and ideas were almost the only things these nomads could carry with them on the long trek from Asia into the wilderness of Arctic America, the lasting gifts they could leave their children.

The creation of a producer co-operative was fully discussed at Cape Dorset in the spring of 1959. Both the Canadian federal Government and the Hudson's Bay Company had been immensely helpful in supporting Inuit in a search for some new economic bases of their own to replace the fur trade in the eastern and central Arctic. In an Inuit meeting, it was decided to form a co-operative based on the sale of prints and any other arts or crafts work that might be produced. The enterprise was to be called "The West Baffin Eskimo Co-operative."

The series of prints for the year 1959 was completed and sent to southern Canada for distribution and sale in the spring of 1960. The Montreal Museum of Fine Arts held an important exhibition of the prints that was echoed across Canada and the United States, then spread widely throughout the world. Print sales were totally successful. When the news of that spring's triumph reached Kingait Inuit, they were delighted.

Terry Ryan has now been Kingait's advisor and southern sales manager in and out of the Arctic for the thirty-three years since my departure in 1962. Since its beginning, the West Baffin Eskimo Co-operative has carefully collected and catalogued more than 300,000 original Inuit drawings and stored them in fireproof spaces. I'd sleep more easily if the best 10,000 drawings were microfilmed.

Jimmy Manning, along with Terry, has done an enormous service in keeping Inuit printmaking and carving moving constantly forward. It has been exhibited and sold in almost every country of the world. Its effect on the Canadian Inuit economy, as well as on those who have dealt in their art, is now beyond measure, running to hundreds of millions of dollars – almost a half century of proof that Inuit are perhaps the most ingenious and industrious free spirits in the world.

Art was by no means the only thing the West Baffin Eskimo Co-operative produced. Helped by the money earned from their art, the Co-op ordered in canoes and nets, and parka material and tent canvas for the women to sew. The nets were set by Inuit, all expert in the art of gill net fishing through lake ice, and fish were sold to all Co-op members, meaning everyone on the Foxe Peninsula coast, at twenty-five cents apiece, regardless of size. That charge was an Inuit concept of a suitable price for a fish.

Whole grain bread was baked by two skillful women, Uksuali and Mukitu, in a new small bakery building with ninety-six square feet of floor space. It, too, sold for twenty-five cents a loaf. A sewing project was another part of the women's program. This was followed by a small, then larger, community-owned co-operative store. At its very beginning, the store was run by, of all people, the former Hudson's Bay trader. This was big Red Pedersen, who later became Speaker of the House of the Legislative Assembly of the Government of the Northwest Territories.

Their prints, like their stone carvings, are important to Inuit at this time. Apart from providing a necessary buying power for them in their swiftly changing world, the prints speak out in a language understood around the world. Their art expresses an approach to life and death.

Eskimo art must surely owe its original debt to the religion of shamanism. Little more than a generation ago, Inuit were governed by their perceived relationship to an awesome spirit world. The amulet figures of animals and humans worn in their clothing were intended to establish a sympathetic magic between the hunter and the animal. Today, the small, simply carved amulets have almost disappeared. But more than half of the prints they produce, like the amulets, still draw their inspiration directly from shamanistic sources. The printed images we see are reflections of these old traditions. The prints and carvings of Inuit are readily understood and accepted by adults, children, artists, and art critics. Eskimo art has the ability to speak to us across great gulfs of language and time.

It is difficult to imagine the future of Inuit carving or printmaking, since the Arctic world is currently undergoing drastic change. The new federal day schools, improved medical services, and the gathering of families into small, permanent settlements have already altered Inuit lives – perhaps for the better – but I fear that these changes are not likely to improve their art.

82

Legal Tender

One morning just before the West Baffin Eskimo Co-operative was about to go into full swing, I went over with two sealskins to see my friend, Red Pedersen, at the Hudson's Bay post.

"Good-looking pair of skins," he said. "What do you want in trade for them?"

"Money," I said. "I want cash."

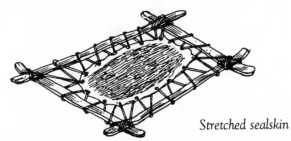

Stretched sealskin

Red leaned on the counter. "You know I haven't seen any real money since I arrived here. Neither have you."

"Well, there's the problem. Money is legal tender in Canada to be paid in exchange for goods. I want cash. Not trade."

"How can I do that?" He laughed.

Red sent a message to the Company: "Cash has been demanded."

At shiptime he received about five thousand Canadian dollars in small denominations. Inuit were then free to sell their goods and take cash away from the Company store or the new Co-operative store. This was a right that had never been put into practice since either of the trading posts was built on west Baffin Island more than forty years earlier.

83
Big Money

While they understood the idea of barter or trade perfectly – these furs in exchange for these bullets and this kettle – helping Inuit understand the use of money was anything but simple at first. Big Red Pedersen lent me a white fox pelt for a demonstration to the printmakers. Next to the fur, I spread out its current value in Canadian dollars and coins then explained denominations under the watchful eyes of hunters. I began by changing a blue five-dollar bill into five green one-dollar bills and so on.

"Only paper," they would sigh.

Paper had always been fragile and useless in their lives except to wrap a cigarette and burn it. To dispel that thought I displayed one of their prints, a stone block or stencil, printed on paper, then laid out beside it all the various dollars it would gain.

"Bigger money can be made from printmaking than from trapping foxes," I stressed.

After one of these head-spinningly clever monetary discussions of mine I slid home and slept as soundly as Disraeli must have slept after purchasing the Suez Canal for the British government on the strength of his financial prowess.

Early next morning, when I went into the *senlavik*, print shop, I discovered on the drying line the printmakers' idea of what I had meant in my demonstration. Hanging between two clothes pegs was a huge, chest-wide, stencilled print of a green dollar bill – the monarch's head in the center and a "one" on all four corners. That's big money, I thought!

Perhaps the whole idea of printmaking was coming through to them. Or was that marvelously naive piece of Inuit folk art just one of the better jokes they played on me?

84

The Bring-Near Glass

In Kingait, it was often said that the whole concept of an art co-
operative might never have succeeded if it had not been for the
mid-morning and mid-afternoon hot coffee break when thick meat
sandwiches were served on hot, homemade bannock. These were
two glorious, brief breaks in each printmaker's day and I enjoyed
them as much as anyone.

In those times, the *senlavik*, print shop, was a totally male place,
a private club where no females were invited except twice a day
when the food appeared. Nothing interesting or amazing was ever
said while those girls were present. When they were gone, the
artists and printmakers often gossiped as vigorously as any women
at a sewing bee.

I had discovered that if a person asked straight, formal questions
about Inuit life, he usually got straight, formal, Inuit answers. But
if a person kept his mouth shut and listened, he would eventually
come to understand exciting things. One conversation heard
during a break in the print shop went like this:

"*Netsisiortok uvagoot. Suitumut ouvagoot takovingaluk seakosima
wakadlunga takoalookinga kamotikik audluktok Kingaimiut semiapiani
tawavikasak . . .*

"This hunting friend of mine and I were out seal hunting on the
ice yesterday. Yes, seal hunting we went, two of us. It was not too
far away from here. He had borrowed his grandfather's bring-near
glass, that great brass one that the old man had traded from the
whalemen in the big ships long ago.

"I was searching the ice in the bay for seals with the bring-near
glass when this one saw something moving out on the main ice.
We turned the old man's bring-near glass around and saw a sled
with five dogs. It was going west. To our surprise, when we looked
closer, we saw that it was you! Yes, you!"

They pointed to a cousin who looked down shyly at his print stone.

"You were going along on your father's sled. Remember that? You can't deny it and you weren't alone."

No answer.

"Yes, you were not alone."

The young man, who was especially liked by all of his friends, hung his head and wiped something non-existent from the edge of the stone block and then started to ink it.

"You were supposed to be guiding that sled," said his first cousin. "You were supposed to be the driver. But no, even from that distance where we rested the long glass on the rocks, we could see that you had forgotten everything about your father's dog team and had left it to the lead dog to find her way along the trail. We watched you very carefully, and to our surprise, we saw you preparing yourself to mount your passenger, who was that camp boss's daughter."

There was some snorting and playful pushing in the room.

"Don't try to alter that which we witnessed with our eyes. Yes, we saw you riding on top of that dear girl like a rutting caribou, with the sled still moving along the trail. We thought certainly that you two would fall off in your excitement. But no. That friendly girl must have had a good grip on the lashings. She supported you from falling."

There was a great deal more pushing and laughter in the room and many sidelong glances at me, wondering if I was getting the drift of all this. The men took long, sugar-laden gulps of coffee from their large, enamel mugs, then bites into the thick meat sandwiched in the bannock. There was lots of grinning, chewing, and nudging at the blushing young man.

"Is that true?" I asked the printmakers.

"*Akalunapalo*, it is certainly true," said the young man's hunting companions.

For the first time, I looked directly at the accused. He hung his head, absorbed in the study of his work. Then he, too, smiled faintly and raised his eyebrows, meaning yes.

"*Wakadlunga*, can I believe it?" I said.

"Yes, believe it," the others said.

"It's not too surprising," one young hunter, a cousin, said. "What else could this good man do? He knew he could do nothing with her in her father's igloo, and nothing when he delivered her as ordered to her uncle and her aunt. For that day at least, it would have to be there on the trail, nowhere else. He feared that if they got off the sled together, his father's dogs would probably run away. If they swerved off the trail, the next hunter coming along would certainly stop and study the event and think, 'What's going on here?' and he would follow this dear man's tracks to the knee marks that he and the big man's daughter would have left in the snow. So this friend of ours did the only thing that he could do. Still," his cousin groaned, "we think it was going pretty far. I mean, riding that big man's daughter out there on the moving sled for us to see. No footprints from this sly one, no."

They all pointed happily at the culprit.

"If it hadn't been for this clever cousin and his grandfather's bring-near glass, no one would ever have known what happened on that short journey between two camps."

85
Children and Parents

Living in the Arctic, our two sons, John and Sam, did not grow up in the ways of most kids. Speaking Inuktitut as they did and disdaining English – for they played exclusively with Inuit children – their lives were different.

It was very difficult to get our children to join us in a meal because their friends' mothers invariably fed them along with their own children. With them, their food was usually caribou, raw fish, raw seal meat, seal livers, and any kind of eggs that were in season. Our boys considered this *nerilarik*, real food. The whole atmosphere in every Inuit establishment seemed home to them. We did not discourage this in any way. Inuit kids lived in tents or igloos, except in the case of Pingwarktok, Osuitok, and Tigugligak, who had small houses.

Osuitok, my hunting companion, was Sam's godfather, and Pootoogook's son, Kananginak, was John's godfather. Both men took that relationship as a serious responsibility.

I sometimes used to watch from a respectable distance as Jonasikudluk (John) and Samijuali (Sam) used to run off on the days when the weather permitted the teams to go out. They would race to stand by the sleds of their godfathers, remaining perfectly still and silent with their godfathers' sons, all of whom were trying to act like grown hunters, hoping against hope that the dog-team drivers would bend over and whisper to them, "All right, boys, I've got a rifle for you. Jump aboard my sled." Of course, the reality of this proudest moment in the life of any Inuit boy was years away from happening to them. But they never gave up hope.

They were, however, allowed to leap aboard the fast-moving sleds as they took off and made the exciting, swaying ride down through the barrier ice. The dogs always did this in a rush, as eager as the boys to be off on the hunt. Once the team and sled were on the main ice, the godfathers would look back at the boys and they would obediently jump off and run back, stopping to talk together sometimes and to watch their godfathers driving their teams out toward the open hunting waters by the floe edge. This polynya in the ice was a paradise six miles away that our sons had not yet seen. Yet, all those sons of hunters, with their overwhelming desire to grow and sharpen their skills, to run fast, jump, tie knots and hitches, handle dogs, and fire a rifle were preparing themselves for that great day when they would finally be allowed to join with their elders and with me in the hunt.

One spring day, the Deputy Minister of the Department of Northern Affairs, Gordon Robertson, landed on the ice in the RCMP plane. I don't remember now how he came to us, if he was held up by weather, or perhaps it was that he wanted to spend a few days in the country with us to better understand Inuit on their home ground. Gordon was a truly notable person, a Rhodes scholar who, I believe, did more than anyone in government at that time to hold things together during those dangerously critical years when the North was being transformed from a remote, mail-delivery-once-a-year trading post into what could be considered an Inuit world that was becoming relatively modern and accessible.

On the morning after Gordon's arrival, before anyone else was up except John and Sam, I breakfasted quietly with them while I tried to explain how important this high-level civil servant was. (He later became Clerk of the Privy Council and Secretary to the Cabinet during the memorable Trudeau years.) It was impossible for me to gather from the boys whether or not they had grasped the meaning of what I had been telling them about our important visitor.

They then rushed off to be on time for their second serious meal in some Inuit household. This makes it sound like we had a poor relationship with our sons, which we did not. It was simply that they wanted to live like their best friends, eat what they ate, do what they did, and learn along with their friends everything in the world that, in their opinion, was worth knowing.

Later that same day, I could hear Inuit children gathering in the *pingwavingmi*, a room set aside as a playroom in our house, with John and Sam warning the others to quietly follow them. Then they led their friends one by one down our short hall and encouraged them to peek around the corner at the Deputy Minister, who was having a bowl of soup with Allie and me. They looked wide-eyed at him, then ducked back out of sight. I'd heard Sam say, "*Avitilo, mukolo, siakok, atowskituinak kisiani*, a .22 bullet one only, that's all." In other words, they were charging for this rare sight.

I got up after the fourth or fifth young Inuk face had peered around the corner.

"What's going on out here?" I asked John.

"We're just letting these friends have a look at the *angiukakvingalook governmentikut*, the big government man. We told them he's the big boss of the government family."

There was a pause.

"I heard you say more than that," I said.

John and Sam proudly opened their hands. "These boys each give us a .22 bullet for letting them have a good look at the big *kallunak*."

"Wait a minute," I said. "You're a *kallunak*, too, remember?"

This did not go down well. "We're not *kallunait*, Dad, we're *Inuisi*. Don't call us *kallunait*." And John started to cry.

I told them to go outside and play. I knew they were collecting the bullets to be ready for the day when their father and godfathers would finally allow them to go with them on the hunt.

When I got back to the table, the Deputy Minister was saying to Allie, "I love the way you two and your children are so much a part of this settlement. Those kids seem to be having so much fun together."

They were! No wonder, they had all grown up in an Inuit environment. Whole hunting camps grew up together, knowing how essential everyone was as a family member. Living in the vastness of those remote regions, they all learned to care for each other throughout their lives. When Inuit children are young, they are lovingly cared for by their parents and as those parents grow old they, in turn, are lovingly cared for by their adult children.

What have we done to ourselves and to them, I wonder now. What are we doing to interrupt this ancient normality of their lives and of ours?

I once decided with a forty-year-old Inuk friend of mine to go hunting on the following morning if the weather was good. It was. In the morning light, I asked him which direction we should go to hunt.

"I don't know," he answered, "I haven't asked my father." When we finished our tea, he said, "Help me," and together we picked up his old father, too feeble to move on his own off the sleeping bench, and carried him outside the snowhouse.

The old man looked along the icebound coast to the right, then to the left, then thought a moment. "Go to the east, *uvikait*." Teenagers, he called us, though we were much older. We went east, and whether by chance or his father's wise advice, we had good hunting and brought home meat to share.

"My father knows a lot about hunting," my friend said proudly. "I'm glad to have it so. He still helps with the hunting that lets me feed this family."

86

Going Outside

The trick was to try not to think about leaving. Just imagine – I can get irritable now in an airport if a plane is an hour late in taking off, and back then I waited thirty-eight days for a flight delayed by weather. Nevertheless, I kept my kit packed and my drawings ready to go outside. On that unbelievable thirty-eighth day of waiting, I was quietly frying my last pair of ten-month-old processed hen's eggs when I heard someone jerk open my storm door.

"What the hell's the matter with you, Houston?" my old friend Fletch, the police pilot, shouted. "Haven't you been hanging around here long enough? Come on, let's go. That fog bank is rolling in like smoke from a forest fire."

I grabbed my art portfolio and bags and hurried with him down through the upheaved ice toward the blue and yellow plane. A small crowd of Inuit had gathered there, mostly small kids and *uvikait* girls. They were there not so much to see me off, but because they wanted to see that handsome, smiling sergeant pilot. He had wide yellow stripes running down his police trouser legs and he wore beautifully beaded western Arctic moccasins. They thought that a sight worth waiting for.

I noticed the pilot edging nervously around the plane, the bevy of girls following him. I climbed up into the opposite seat and before I slammed the door, I called, "Come on, you told me to hurry. What the hell's keeping you?" He had been right about the fog, it was almost on top of us.

Fletch climbed up into his seat, slammed the door, and pressed the starter on the still-warm engine. We waved to the boys and girls who were having fun, arms spread, trying to fly like birds in the Otter's prop wash. We bumped across the hard-packed snows until the plane leapt off a hard drift and soared into the air.

We were engulfed in thick white fog, but only for a minute or so before we climbed above it into a clear blue sky. "Good," I shouted, for he had his earphones on.

"Good for you, maybe," he yelled, "but I'll die if I don't have a leak."

"Why didn't you do it when we were on the ice?"

"I tried to," he said, "but those girls kept crowding all around me."

"That's the price you pay for being a gorgeous-looking pilot."

"Yeah, well, you hold Matilda steady," he shouted into my ear, "or I'm going to bust a kidney."

I gasped in disbelief but had no chance to stop him, for he had already heaved himself out of his seat and was moving back through the Otter's cabin. I held onto a plane's controls for the first time in my life. I glanced at the terrifying array of dials and switches, then back at him in horror.

He was kneeling now, pulling the felt pad out of the funnel he used to refuel the plane. He unzipped both his flies, then began to fiddle with the rear door handle. It swung open. He smiled and nodded at me. I closed my eyes, for I hated seeing him leaning out against the cold blue sky. Finally, when I dared to look again, he was readjusting the funnel's long, flexible, metal nozzle. Lord, he was taking forever! When I looked at him again, he grinned back at me contentedly. The Otter's engine was roaring a thousand times too loud, and I swear the plane was starting to veer upward or downward or left or right. Oh, God, was I alone in this plane? Had he fallen out the door? I could feel the rush of air and was afraid to look back again. But I had to know.

When I turned in desperation, he was casually stuffing the felt back in the funnel, then bent forward to look outside. I almost died. He slammed the door and, doubling over, made his way back to the pilot's seat. "Phew! What a relief! You know how bad that feels," he chuckled.

"I know how bad it feels to be flying in this plane without a pilot!" I yelled at him. "Nothing in the world could feel worse than that!"

He laughed as he straightened up the Otter, and we zoomed on, guided by the long, rugged range of coastal mountains that would lead us to Frobisher Bay.

"When you bring me back in here again, you bring an empty gallon can with you!"

"Awh, hell," he said modestly, "a half-gallon tin would do the trick."

87
Leghold

When we brought them out on a visit to Ottawa, John and Sam, my two sons, at the time about four and six, did not seem particularly pleased or displeased to have come outside of the country. They had grown up in the Arctic and still spoke to each other exclusively in Inuktitut. They did seem thrilled to encounter most of the things they were seeing for the first time: traffic lights, escalators, long bridges, manhole covers, city buses, restaurants. They ducked as neatly under the doors of pay toilets as though they were entering a traveling snowhouse.

They enjoyed the dinosaurs and huge moose antlers at that old stone fortress, Ottawa's National Museum, which was my favorite place to take them, for I felt they badly needed culture. Twenty-five years later when I asked them, they admitted that they had come to hate that museum more than any place in the world. However, I notice now that Sam is on a board of the Colorado Museum and John delightedly makes films in many of the major museums of Europe. It's hard to tell about your kids at any age.

One raw November Sunday when we were walking back from that same museum visit, we wandered toward the Ho Ho Café through the city's tiny Chinatown. There was nothing to see but a few signs that read "Chinese–Canadian Cooking," with symbols of a maple leaf and Oriental fan, perhaps, or a commercial-looking Peking screen, or tasseled lanterns displayed in half a dozen windows.

I was holding onto both boys' hands because they had no fear of traffic at that time. Lord knows there was practically no traffic in sight on that Ottawa Sunday morning, but I was cautious anyway. Suddenly, they both gave a violent jerk and, breaking away from me, they ran wildly down the street until they could each lunge and grab a surprised Chinese man around his right and left legs. He looked down at them and struggled, but they wouldn't let go, each looking up and calling out to him in rapid Inuktitut. When I caught up to them, the plump Oriental man in his gray fedora, gray necktie, and gray topcoat stared at them, then me, in amazement.

"What are these two boys saying?" he asked me.

He tried a little Mandarin, or perhaps Cantonese, on them, but they continued to hug his legs in desperation, fearing that this one great treasure of Ottawa might get away from them.

"Where are the other hunters?" John asked in Inuktitut. "Where are the children and their mothers?"

"They've made a mistake," I said, smiling at the man. "They think you're an Inuk."

"He is an Inuk," John told me very positively.

"*Atai Inuktitut okakniarkveet*, go ahead, speak Inuktitut. We understand!"

He smiled down at them when Sam gave him another shake. "Talk, you, want you to talk do I!"

"He doesn't speak Inuktitut," I told them. "He's from China, another part of the world."

"Awwh!" they answered, full of disappointment. Then reluctantly letting go of his legs, they stepped back to stare at him.

"He looks like a real person, *Inuklarik*!" said Sam, "one of the real people."

"Oh, he's real, all right," I told them.

The man patted them both on the head, then turned and went inside the Ho Ho Café. They insisted that we follow him and then stared at him with pleasure throughout lunch.

Both John and Sam have since been to the Orient. But Ottawa was one of their first encounters with other people, other cultures, and, to their delight, with chopsticks.

88

Inuit Art

When we first went to Kingait in 1951, I found a certain fiery spirit among Inuit men and women trading there which I think has served to drive a special sense of life into their carving and print-making. In Dorset, there have been, and are, so many truly notable carvers still alive and with talented children and grandchildren following in their path. There is no need to name them, for many are sculptors and printmakers well known to Canadians.

You may not see many carvings displayed in the Cape Dorset houses if you go there, for these people are artists and sculptors, not collectors. Collecting art is a different passion.

There is little evidence that Inuit have ever had competitive feelings among themselves about their art. Certainly, they rarely seem to imitate each other. Rather, they excel in originality. Inuit carvings have tended to increase in size over the past forty-seven years, and this has helped to change our perception of them from small netsuke-sized curios to more robust works of sculpture.

Their word for a carving is *sinunguak*, a small thing you make. A print is *titoraktok*, marks you make with your hand. Surprisingly, the Inuit have no satisfactory word for art, though Inuktitut is poetic and extensive, with, for example, dozens of words for various conditions of snow. Like other hunting societies, Inuit consider living in harmony with nature their art, and a sort of coalition between humans and animals rests at that core.

Anyone who questions the validity and importance of contemporary Inuit art as an expression of the people's true feelings would do well to recall the words of the famous artist Pitseolak, translated from a tape as part of her biography, *Pictures Out of My Life*, edited by Dorothy Eber. Of her drawings and stone block prints, she said, "I am going to keep on doing them until they tell me to stop. If no one tells me to stop, I shall make them as long as I am well. If I can, I'll make them even after I am dead."

Inuit art – carvings, prints, and crafts – forms the backbone of the Inuit-owned co-operatives. The Government of Canada estimates that sales amount to twenty million dollars a year, channeled still through the Bay, the Guild, and newer organizations: Dorset Fine Arts, Canadian Arctic Producers, *La Fédération des Co-operatives du Nouveau-Québec*. In the 1990s, some of the best-known artists earn as much as one hundred thousand dollars a year and pay their taxes. With this money they buy rifles, cartridges, warm family clothing, cameras, radios, color TV sets, household goods, tenting, boats, and snowmobiles – whatever. I'm for that. I would have done anything to spare them from the necessity of the government dole.

89
Sleeping Arrangements

The Ontario College of Art, at our request, sent in a summer assistant to help the West Baffin Eskimo Co-operative. I'll call him Randy. He came in on the icebreaker early one morning when the weather was so still you could hear the mosquito hordes just outside the window. I jumped out of bed when I heard the anchor chains go rattling down, then as I shot up the blackout blind, I saw her – all sleek seven-thousand-tons of power – riding in our bay, oblivious to all the broken ice behind her. The ship had come to drop supplies and to do an annual medical check on the families that had come in for the dancing and the trading and to help handle the supplies.

The tide was running out as Osuitok and I pushed the long freight canoe into the water. Jumping in, we took off, weaving fast but cautiously through the small ice, charged up with excitement at the prospect of seeing dozens of new faces, trying to imagine all the necessary and unnecessary things the government would have sent to us. And the mail – bags full of exciting mail – a whole year's supply of half a dozen magazine subscriptions: *Time, Life, The Beaver, The New Yorker, Maclean's, Saturday Night*. We did not wait for the ship's gangplank to go down, but tied the canoe and climbed the swaying rope ladder, immediately shaking hands with a crowd of people, some of whom we knew from other annual visits. As I was heading for the captain's cabin, a huge, gangling youth stopped me – I mean, stood right in front of me – and said, "I'm Randy."

"Randy?" I said. "Randy who?"

"You know, from your old art school."

"Oh, sure." I laughed and shook hands. "Glad to see you. We've got about a million things for you to do. Meet Osuitok."

"What shall I do first?" Randy asked. "Shall I start making sketches of the people?" He squinted his eyes and held up a pencil to measure the length and width of Osuitok's head.

Osuitok struck a pose for Randy, then smiled at me. "*Uvikikotak*," he said, meaning "Long teenager."

"Forget sketching right now," I said to Randy. "Go ashore with Osuitok." They shook hands and one medic and an ichthyologist eagerly climbed down to join them in our big freight canoe.

"What am I supposed to do in there?" Randy called to me.

"When a crate comes ashore, marked 'West Baffin Eskimo Co-op' or 'Dept. Northern Affairs,' you do the reading for those guys then help them carry it above that dark line on the beach. It marks the high tide, and it will be coming back. Be sure everything's above that. Don't let anything float away. Your job's to help organize all our stuff."

The Inuit liked Randy right away because of how he launched into the freight with them and laughed a lot in a friendly way that would make you know why he would be a big success among these *Kingaimiut*. They liked to be with someone who tried to learn and speak their language. When they heard that Randy was staying, I remember some of the teenaged girls leaned against the outgoing

Company fur bales, evaluating him as though he were some twice too long, exotic creature that had sledded down from the wintry surface of the moon.

Inside our government house at the time were three beds and two cots. I always liked to welcome some travelers from the ship to sleep ashore. When I returned to the house later that night, it was like a different place, with piles of unfamiliar, military-looking winter boots and hats and Arctic parkas. A sort of Royal Navy type of impromptu cocktail party was going on, with people clutching dozens of steaming coffee cups made rich with the aroma of grand, half-forgotten, overproof navy rum. Nipisa, helping in the kitchen, gave me the two halves of a large tin of bully beef, which she had cut in half with a butcher knife. Stuck in the meat was a pair of spoons. She wanted everything to be fancy!

Into all this wandered the long, gangling, smiling Randy, head and shoulders taller than the rest. "Some place you got up here. No wonder you're trying to keep it all to yourself. I'm tuckered out. I'd like to find a place to sleep."

"Sleep?" I said. "Oh, God! Where? There's no room left in this house. Wait – I know – I hope you've got a sleeping bag."

"Sure have," he said.

"Well, out behind this house," I pointed, "there's a little bit of a shed – no heat, no bed or anything – but it's dry. So why don't you find some floor space in there tonight and when the ship leaves tomorrow, we'll find you something better. Come in and have breakfast with the rest of us in the morning."

Finally, about 5:00 a.m., I slipped off my boots and slept like a dog on our too-small modern Danish sofa. Nipisa woke me when she heard the others rising.

Randy came in later and joined us at breakfast. I asked him if he'd had a good night's sleep and apologized for failing to give him a can of DDT to spray himself and to fill that little airless room with a strong concentration to ward off the mosquitoes.

"I made out fine," said Randy, looking around at the visitors who had decided to sleep ashore and were now seated around the breakfast table.

Henry Larsen, superintendent of the RCMP's Arctic Division, was there. Donald Arctic, the Anglican bishop (who took his formal surname from his diocese), sat next to him. Grantham, the government's head of Arctic education, was between Alec Stevenson, officer in charge of the Eastern Arctic Patrol, and Dr. Wynne Edwards, a Welsh ornithologist whom we all admired. They all listened to Randy as they ate their oatmeal and he told them of his first impressions.

"This is a really friendly place!" Randy exclaimed with schoolboy enthusiasm. He described the pitch darkness in the windowless shed, standing up to demonstrate how he removed and rolled all his clothes into a pillow, then crawled into his sleeping bag. He was awakened, he said, when he heard someone cautiously unzipping his sleeping bag, then felt a hot naked body slip into the bag beside him.

"What did you do?" the head of Arctic education asked him.

"I trust he got out of there mighty fast!" I added, before Randy could answer.

"Well, I couldn't see who it was," Randy continued, "so I felt this naked body all over and discovered that it was a girl. She started giggling when I tickled her."

"Never mind," I said. "That is sometimes the problem around here."

"What's wrong with giggling?" Randy asked me.

The bishop stared at Randy, then at me. I rearranged the porridge in my bowl, planning what I would say to Randy when I could catch him alone.

"Then what happened?" asked the bishop, his glasses shining.

Randy smiled at him and shrugged.

"I mean," said the bishop, "what did you do then?"

"Well," said Randy. "It definitely was a girl. I could easily tell that because she was warm all over, and naked like a model in a drawing class."

"Well?" said the bishop. "What did you do then?"

Randy looked at him in amazement. "Sir, I'll give you three guesses. What do you think I did?"

90
First Real Tourists

In late winter of 1959, the government sent me a radio message informing me that eight tourists had declared an interest in coming into the country as a group, and had expressed a desire to visit Baffin Island because they had heard of the West Baffin Eskimo Co-operative and wished to see its artists in action. The bizarre nature of this request meant that I gave no serious thought to it until a month later when the government sent in the foot sizes, heights, and chest measurements of these unknown New Yorkers. All this information caught my wife's attention and we realized these adventurers from the South just might be serious. Allie handed out their foot sizes, hiring some of the most skillful women to make sealskin boots, and she asked other women to make pants and parkas for them.

The New Yorkers had said they planned to stay for about two weeks. Cape Dorset itself had no accommodations for that many strangers. So along with Inuit, I began to plan a tent camp for them, still not knowing their names or whether they were males or females. I decided we should make five new sleeping tents, plus one for me, and one for their plane crew, as well as my larger, double-walled tent for recreation, and a dining tent large enough to seat twelve persons. Oh, yes, and there must be some kind of toilet. I planned to place that discreetly around the corner of the nearest hill.

I slept out in this new camp at Telikjuak, the name suggesting a big arm of the sea. It was a handsome place, utterly barren, but set in a little valley with the tundra just slightly reddening for autumn, and the ground closely strewn with large patches of yellow Arctic poppies.

The Inuit Co-operative members who were to join in the running of this camp were nervous. Nothing like this had ever happened before. Young Joanasie Salomonie was head man because he was quick, enterprising, and had learned quite a bit of English in hospitals in the south. Eisiak and Nitiani, who were given cooking experience in our house, became the chefs. Pingwarktok was in charge of our four large freight canoes and their outboard engines. Finally, the Co-op took the bit in its teeth. It chartered Joanasie's grandfather Pootoogook's Peterhead, *Ivik*, so they could do this right.

We held our breath when finally we heard the big Canso flying boat circling the camp to become the first aircraft ever to land on Telikjuak Bay.

I cannot recall exactly what I had expected, but these tourists looked surprisingly good to us as they clambered into the canoes, dragging everything behind them. They laughed and joked with each other and with us. The canoes took them ashore and went out again to bring in more new equipment than we on the beach had ever seen in our collective lives. Arthur A. Houghton, Jr., introduced himself and the other members of his expedition: a doctor, a professor of history, and a private photographer to record events. In all, four men, two wives, a daughter, and a businesswoman whom we were told was a great tennis player, and a chef who decided to take a holiday from cooking.

In the main tent, as they called it, we waded through piles of clothing and equipment searching for the jerrycans. These turned out to be a number of three-gallon, red plastic containers, some filled with Scotch, others with bourbon and gin. There were no labels. You had to sniff each can to tell!

Everyone had a cup or two, but strange to say, these people were all conservative drinkers and explained that they had thought to bring in an adequate supply of liquor just in case they were caught and held on Baffin for the winter. They had also brought every bite of food they planned to eat. We had prime lamb chops, beautifully cooked by Nitiani, the first, she said, that she had ever tasted.

After dinner in the main tent, these Harvard, Princeton, and Yale men had a long philosophical discussion about life inside and life outside the Arctic. Then there was an alarming discovery – we had provided only one toilet. What was to be done? How would they ever know who was inside? They anguished over this, then drew cards, each waiting patiently. If I had constructed separate men's and women's canvas toilets at that time, they would certainly have been the first on Baffin Island, and perhaps the first in the Canadian Arctic. Still, it would have been nice if I had thought of it.

Next morning, we took them fishing for Arctic char in the short, fast river that flows out of Tessiuakjuak. Considering the newness of it all, they did very well. When we returned to camp, we found that Inuit left behind had caught twenty others and put them live in a natural stone pond. On the following day, after naps and a hilarious evening, we took the Peterhead out hunting, but did no harm in any way to the local wildlife. The main thing I remember about our activities was that I had issued fishing licenses, Nos. 1 to 8, and hunting licenses, Nos. 1 to 8. These were the first licenses I had ever issued as Game and Fisheries Officer, the first, I believe, that anyone had issued in the eastern Arctic. The government had printed the license books especially for this occasion! At that time, tourism on West Baffin Island was not so much unthinkable as it was unaffordable.

One day when we were away on the Peterhead exploring the coast, a tremendous wind sprang up and our return to camp became very perilous. We had no weather warning system at that time and when this hurricane-force wind caught us by complete surprise, I was glad of the ruggedness of that Scottish North Sea trawler. The storm flattened every tent as well as our single toilet, blowing it away with long white skeins of toilet paper, along with other light items.

All the visitors' money was swept up by the wind and ended up plastered across the barren background. Several *uvikait* who had been visiting the camp in our absence, joined our young cook and her helper, darting out to retrieve the money as soon as the wind went down. Paper money seemed to cling like green leaves to every rock along the valley floor behind the camp. The teenagers collected it all and returned it to me in bulging handfuls to redistribute back to the guests.

In the main tent, our visitors had a merry sorting out of bills. To my surprise, every one of them had a written account of exactly how much money they had brought with them, and all could prove that the full amount had been returned. They were astonished by this, but I was not. Those Inuit were generally the most honest people I could ever hope to know.

While I was skylarking around with the tourists visiting the local sights – the best char river, the eider nesting colony, and the reversible falls – the West Baffin Eskimo Co-operative was seriously busy in Dorset building their first co-operative store from the profits they had gained from the exhibitions and sales of their carvings and soon-to-become famous Inuit prints. They were rushing to have that building's roof completed before the winter snows. After their store had been framed, Inuit invited these visitors to their celebration, asking them to dance hard to help settle the floor. The whole tourist group from the Telikjuak camp boated into Dorset to join that joyous party.

Next morning, we went into the small 512 (meaning 512 square feet), the Co-op's only building, where Inuit and Allie had laid out for display a large number of carvings, each with a price taped on its bottom. These were examined with care by all eight members of the party. But when they tried to settle among themselves about who would get the ones that they most favored, Houghton said, "Jim, just have them all wrapped up very carefully. We'll take them all. Tell me how much and we'll give the Co-op the cash. Now," he continued, "what about these prints hanging on the wall?"

"None of them are for sale," I said. "These have not been seen outside Cape Dorset. But I'll ask the government to let you know when they're exhibited for sale down south." Of course, I meant Toronto, Montreal, Vancouver, those cities which we considered inside the banana belt.

Many of the carvings purchased that day are now in New York's Metropolitan Museum of Art, for Houghton was its president. I have much later seen some of the sealskin boots from that same adventure still carefully preserved in some large New York household freezers: these boots deserve that treatment, for I doubt that sinew sewing as fine as that will ever be created again.

At the end of their visit, Arthur Houghton offered me a job in

New York with Steuben Glass, a division of Corning Incorporated. When I did not accept, he nodded, "Probably just as well. A week in New York City would probably drive you screaming back to the Arctic, a more grateful person for all this quiet solitude."

I admitted that I had told the Co-op members (in other words, everyone in Dorset) that I would leave the Co-op within three years, when it was up and running smoothly, and I encouraged them to prepare to take control. Houghton said he would wait and contact me then.

I asked him what he thought best and worst about the country. He, Professor Fitzroy, and their doctor discussed this matter and agreed that Inuit themselves were by far the best and most hopeful part of the equation, while the somewhat shabby and ill-equipped one-bed nursing station they thought nothing short of perilous. I suggested that Houghton write their thoughts to R. Gordon Robertson, the much respected Deputy Minister for Northern Affairs. Houghton did exactly that, personally offering to finance and staff a new, small hospital for the area. To my surprise, the government did not accept his offer but swiftly responded by preparing to build and staff such a hospital. I was gone by the time the construction started, but it did show the good effect that a little tourism can sometimes bring.

When these very first real tourists planned to leave, the weather turned ghastly on them. Jimmy Bell, the famous pilot, went out with Pingwarktok to the flying boat and checked the anchors, then came in with enough red life jackets for all.

"I think we ought to make a try for it right now," he said. "I went up on the hill to look this morning and this storm is moving ice in on the high tide."

The sides of the big tent blew in and out, thundering like a drum. Their one and only toilet blew away again, but nobody cared this time, not even when some of their sleeping tents went down.

"I think that we should do as the pilot says," they all agreed, "let's try it." They could see the line of white ice moving into the mouth of the bay. "Let's get going!" they said. "We've got other things to do this winter."

"Everybody travel light." The pilot smiled, and nodded at me.

You would not believe the pile of spare parkas, spare sleeping bags, fancy rifles, cases of ammunition, elaborate fishing gear, everything new from Abercrombie and Fitch, that was given away to us at a moment's notice.

"Distribute it among everyone," Houghton told me. "Keep my rifle for yourself, and, of course, those jerrycans of liquor. Don't pass them around!"

"I won't!" I promised him.

Some stayed huddled in the big tent while we paddled others out to the Canso two at a time. The wind had turned savage cold. Finally, when the pilot and all his guests were loaded in the flying boat, Inuit helped haul up the second anchor and we were driven back to the beach as the wind increased.

Everyone left in the camp stood in a huddle on shore watching with me as the Canso churned round and round to build up power before it made its long, slow dash up and over the advancing fields of ice. They made it.

"*Koviasukunga*, I'm glad," I sighed, relieved to see that they had actually come and safely gone.

"Happy? You're happy?" Inuit there asked me. "Why are you happy? Those are good people. Happy, laughing people. We're sorry to see them go."

That's the way it was in those days. The place was alive with that warm-hearted, welcoming Inuit spirit. I hope to God that it will stay that way.

91

Letting the Mail Blow Away

There are some wild acts one just plain dares to do in youth that are hard to imagine later on in life. One such act was prompted by the success our Inuit artists were enjoying in the world outside.

Time magazine sent in their reporter, Oliver Clausen, a Dane, and *Life* sent in its photographer, Carl Iwasaki, of Japanese heritage, to visit us. Both publications were interested in what west Baffin's Inuit population was busy accomplishing in art. Our total population was spread out in thirteen nomadic camps made up of fifty-eight families. Their earlier population of 341 was increasing by that time.

Because *Time* did a feature story in their international edition about the West Baffin Eskimo Co-operative in which my name was mentioned, I received four mail sacks packed with letters inquiring about purchasing prints, all inspired by the photographs of the colored stone block prints and skin stencils that *Time* had shown.

After shiptime, which had lasted thirty-six hours, I opened the sacks and started sorting through my mail. There were letters from everywhere – London, Paris, Rome, New York, Japan, lots from Switzerland, Scandinavia, Moose Jaw, Medicine Hat, South Porcupine, even Toronto – all asking detailed questions for me to answer about prints. My sampling of that mail showed me that many were asking me to send them prints. Some letters included money – marks, francs, kroners, yen. Many more suggested I take their word that they would send me the money. I could not then and still cannot type, and personal computers had not yet been invented. What to do with nearly a thousand letters in the middle of a wonderful life! Well, anyone would worry and worry I did. I tried to answer a few, but so many were in other languages that I gave up.

The printmaking continued to go well and in the spring, Big Red Pedersen said, "I hope you've answered all your mail."

"Sure," I told him. "I've got it ready to fly out of here today."

I walked along the hard snow path to my house. My mail out wasn't ready at all. A helluva storm was rising, causing great gusts of wind to hurtle around Kingait Mountain and go rushing out the frozen fiord. That day and the next, the settlement became almost invisible as the air filled with salt-fine, drifting snow of the first big spring blizzard.

That evening, the weather gave off the unmistakable signs of change. Bright, golden light came filtering out of the west and the wind, still strong, was beginning to gust again.

I dug out the short sled and hauled it to my office built of packing cases. I dragged out my four blue sacks of mail, lashed them into place, and set off. Out on the ice, the wind was strong, still whipping along the shoreline of Malik Island. I undid the lashings. *Oh, God*, I thought, *this is going to take more nerve than I can muster.* But bravely I tucked my sealskin mitts under one arm, then, diving in, drew out two fistfuls of unopened mail and tried to fling them high above my head. The second I released them, the letters were snatched away by the power of the wind. I released two more hand-fuls and watched them as they turned, flashing square and oblong envelopes of blue and white with pretty stamps, a new kind of snowstorm that went flying east, straight out over the Hudson Strait. Oh, what a sense of relief I felt!

Until I started to record these recollections I had almost forgotten that wild act of more than thirty years ago. When I remembered it again, I felt a stab of conscience, and perhaps of greed as well. How could I ever have come to treat that most desirable, always long-awaited Arctic mail, in such an outrageous fashion? And beyond that, how could I ever have been so reckless without even knowing what those letters to me contained?

That's what kind of a nut I was in those days. I cared a lot more about humans, land animals, sea mammals, birds that fly, and, above all, art. No decent civil servant would ever throw away his mail!

92

Soccer Game

Our two sons, Jonasikudluk and Samijuali, as they were locally known, had given up speaking the English language, for they much preferred Inuktitut. One of the things they enjoyed most as they grew old enough to be released from the *amautik* hoods of their mother (or Mukitu or Uvilu) were games, any kind of games. I remember that they loved the local style of soccer best of all.

In this particular year, there was a young Scottish clerk at the Company and the boys were especially fond of him. That summer he was determined to teach the locals how to play real soccer, not their kind of soccer, which consisted of everyone in the community, including the grandmothers, having a chance to kick the ball in every possible direction. He had brought with him from Scotland a regulation soccer football. Choosing the best stretch of flat, tundra-covered, open ground between our house and the old Baffin Trading Post, he and his friend Kovianaktiliak pegged in two sets of posts and drew taut some old fish net in between to make goals. No more of this fooling around!

He called out to the young people, male and female, who were watching him and laughing and casually booting the ball. Very seriously, he stopped them and chose two even sides, eleven players on each. John and Sam watched him do this with great anticipation.

To start the game he gave a blast on the whistle. Nothing happened, so he blew it again once, twice, three times more. Both sides started dancing, trying to catch the rhythm of his whistling.

"No, no!" the clerk shouted. "Dancing's something different. Here, I'll show you."

He got two young men and a girl to stand guard in front of one of the goals then he cunningly kicked the ball toward them. They stepped aside and politely let him play through.

"Hey, Tomasi!" he shouted to the company interpreter. "Explain this for me to these players – about sides, about offense and defense!"

Tomasi listened to him, then explained some game rules in Inuktitut to all those gathered. He said to the clerk, "Yeah, yeah, they know now. Go ahead!"

He blew the whistle again and the game began in earnest, but not the way he, the referee, had planned. Our son, John, who was then five years old, ran into the game and Sam, never one to wait though he was three, toddled in after him, ready for anything. The clerk, who was keen on serious soccer, threw up his hands when he saw several old ladies dart onto the field to get a kick at the ball. Then middle-aged men and wives with infants in their hoods mixed in, and young husky pups began to frolic with them, believing themselves to be the players.

I could tell that John and Sam thought that this was the most perfect game in the world. Nobody cared about having two sides, they ignored the goals. All were concentrating on getting a good kick at that new Scottish soccer ball.

If you've started to think that this game was nothing but a rough and tumble, you'd be wrong. It's true this was not a game of one team pitted against another, and certainly not one person going against another. That was not Inuit style. Their aim was to do their personal best by acting quickly, skillfully, in their attempt to kick or control the ball!. They weren't trying to beat their neighbors. Why would they do a thing like that? They depended on their neighbors, who in turn depended on them. Besides that, beating another person would be nothing but a shameful embarrassment to anyone.

So our family was like every other family playing there by Inuit rules. All through that summer night the sky did not grow dark. You could hear laughing and running, and the thump of soft skin boots against the pigskin ball. When the players grew hot and tired, they lay on the tundra, staring up at the pale face of the moon.

A week later, the first snows came drifting down like feathers blanketing the playing field. The clerk admitted that their Inuit style of gaming was not that bad a way to play.

Years later, Sam attended Fettes College, a boys' school in Edinburgh, Scotland, where they played a ball game called rugby that is about as physical, serious, and competitive as you can get. When I went to watch him playing, I could see that from the Inuit perspective, they were playing the game all wrong. I was shocked to see that in that game, Sam was the leader of the forwards, the guys who fought grimly for the ball. I sat there remembering those earlier, joyous Arctic games. But what the hell! I guess Sam was just busy readjusting himself to living in our entirely different world.

93
Losing a Tent

John was about to turn six. He was two years older than his brother, Sam. John longed more than almost anything else in this world to go out on the land, as it was called, to pitch his tent on the edge of the fish lakes. Both boys had heard about the fish lakes. They knew it as a magical place, five hours' dog-team travel north of Kingait, that was simply Paradise.

When the darkness of that winter was fading and the long white nights of spring were returning, I discussed with Allie whether I should take John with me, and we decided that he was old enough. Sam, alas, was still too young to undertake the journey. Osuitok, Sam's godfather, explained to him that he wasn't taking his own son, Tukikikudluk, because neither could safely balance on the sled.

We decided because the weather looked promising that we would try to go next morning. John woke me several times that night. "What time is it, Dad? Is it time to go?"

In the morning, I helped Osuitok round up the dogs. They had been well fed the night before. The moment of parting was tearful on Sam's part, but his time would come the following year.

John was not at all clumsy on this journey. He had been prac- ticing jumping on and off *kamotiks* all winter in preparation for this, his first real dog-team journey. I was surprised at how com- posed and adult he seemed, comfortably discussing the qualities of each dog in his preferred language as Sam's godfather pointed out various tricks of handling dogs, such as cracking the whip to the right or left of them to guide them, but not touching them with the lash, and rattling a short chain he carried against the grub box to let the team know he was watching them.

The journey was long, but not unusual until we saw the first flights of snow geese gliding down in huge flocks and landing where the tundra was bare beside the lakes. There were hundreds, perhaps thousands of them, tired after their long flight from the south across Hudson Strait. We could see that many more geese were landing north of us along the chain of fish lakes.

We found the markers for several fishing holes that had been kept open through the four-foot depth of freshwater ice. We broke away the thick skim of new ice that had formed in these holes and scooped out the broken bits, then laid down under our knees small squares of winter caribou skin that we had been given for just that purpose. I lowered my lure, a lead sinker and two brass .22 shell casings without hook. These were intended not to catch, but simply to lure the fish into our range. I had a *kakivak*, bone fish-spear, lashed onto a six-foot wooden handle. This was the way I hoped to make my catch.

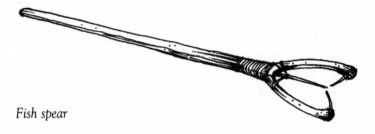

Fish spear

John peered down into the clear, blue-green water, waiting. Oh, I wanted the fish to come for John's sake, but none appeared. Finally, we gave up and went to the sled, took off the tent, and set it up near an ancient stone ring which had been placed there by some hunting fishing family a hundred or even a thousand years ago. The stones were almost black with lichen and had not been disturbed to weigh down a tent for ages.

John was excited, I could tell, but he went about the business of helping quietly, like an adult. Travelers should weigh and tie down every tent as though they expected a great wind in the night, for when a tent blows down in a really strong, Arctic wind, it can be impossible to put it up again until the wind has passed, and being without shelter in such a gale can be dangerous.

When everything was set, Osuitok said that he planned to go

further up the chain of lakes and try for fish and geese up there. He said that he would return next day.

I was pleased to get rid of the dogs, for wild animals are nervous when the dogs are free, and in those days Inuit never tied dogs – that came only after the settlements grew larger.

John and I made dinner of I don't remember what. I had promised him fresh-caught fish – never a wise idea. It was not really dark when we turned off the little Primus, although it was nearly midnight when we spread the sleeping bag, got in, and slept. What I had not liked was the ominous-looking bank of clouds I had seen gathered in front of the fading rays of sun. That could mean a change in the weather.

A violent blast of wind woke me at four in the morning. It was raging outside and the inside of the tent wall was trembling, then booming in and out. John was still asleep. Covering my shoulders, I stared up at the tent top. It had grown gray with age, a fact that made me rather proud, like a gardener or a painter who insists on wearing his old, worn-out pair of pants. Crossing my fingers, I hoped the tired old canvas would hold.

That thought had scarcely crossed my mind when an arm's length of its sewing gave way, exposing storm-strewn clouds. The first snow came blustering inside the tent. John awoke. We jumped up, afraid that we were going to lose the tent. He scrambled into his boots. In horror, we saw the old canvas rip to pieces before our eyes and flap like banners streaming away from the two well-anchored tent poles.

When the next great blast of wind came whistling across the frozen lake, the wooden tent poles collapsed beside us and the remaining parts of the tent lay flapping on the ground or blew away. There we stood, fully exposed to the blizzard. Both of us had rolled our parkas inside out to use as pillows. We struggled into these and pulled up our hoods, then searched and found our wind pants and our mitts. We both put on our small packs and I took up my rifle in its canvas sleeve.

"We'll walk over to that hill." I pointed. I knew it was there, but we couldn't see it.

John turned around and looked at our grub box that had blown over and the brown square of tundra where our tent and sleeping bag had been. It was quickly turning white in the driving snow. John started to cry and I didn't blame him. "We've got no home now." I had to bend to hear his voice. "Where are we going to live?"

"Come on, let's find some geese," I said, and we slowly made our way inland to the steep cliff that was hidden from us by falling snow. Finally, we got into its lee where the wind was broken and the snow began to angle past us. We found there a huge tumble of granite rocks at the bottom of a slide. They had formed into a kind of dark, protective cave, a cave just waiting all those years for us, I told John, as we squatted in its entrance and waited.

The wind began to lose its strength and large flakes started drifting softly down like goose feathers. We could hear the gusts go moaning eastward over the whole of Baffin Island, then over the Greenland ice cap, I told John, without, perhaps, seeing any other human beings.

My heritage is Scottish on both sides of my family. The men most often went into the quieter sport of banking. Certainly, we all learned how to pinch a penny. What kind of example had I now set for John, showing him that I was too cheap to have a new tent made even when it was seriously needed, taking him out to witness his family's hoary old tent being torn into shreds and blown away? Sometimes when I drive along the highways today and see large black shreds of tires lying on the road, I wish I had a car phone to call John and say, "Look at those tire treads worn off some cross-country nomad's eighteen-wheeler truck. They've purposely worn them until they ripped apart and scattered in pieces. It may be their economic theory, but it's mine no longer!"

We shot a goose to ensure our supper no matter what happened. We went back to where our tent had been and picked up our fish jigs and my fish spear, then went out to the fish holes on the lake. The air, or you might choose to say the goddess Sila, had blown her fury out and given us a still, clear afternoon. Nipisa had lent John her personal women's fish jig which, like so many other items in

Inuit society, was different from a man's. It was a hand-held, notched piece of wood that held the lure, two small brassy flashers, and a stone weight above a file-sharpened hook. The rig, she told him, had belonged to her mother.

Woman's fish jig

John chose to lie belly down on his square of caribou skin, his face reflected in the hole, slowly jiggling the fish lure, its bright brasses flashing in the water. Twenty paces away, I knelt on my bit of skin, jiggling my lure with my fish spear hanging an arm's length down in the water. We did not wait long before I saw a school of Arctic char moving like pale, gray-green fish seen in slow motion, drifting toward me through the water beneath the ice.

I jiggled my fish lure gently. Seeing it, the fish moved cautiously toward my ice hole, waving their side fins like pairs of Japanese fans that propelled them slowly through the water. When six of them were directly below me, I struck, driving my spear down hard into the middle of them. They disappeared in a flash. I had missed.

John looked up at me, but only for a moment, for he, too, must have seen fish below him.

I settled down and warned myself against any more overeager spearing, knowing that if I wanted to strike one, I would have to pick my fish.

A long time passed before another school approached me and I heard John call, "Dad, Dad, a fish bit at my hook!"

I didn't move or answer him because a new school of Arctic char was drifting in beneath me. I selected the largest one and waited, then aiming at it, drove down hard. I felt a lunge against the spear and hauled up the wriggling silver and scarlet-sided fish. Its length was from my elbow to my fingertips.

John ran over to admire it as I opened the spear's two springy caribou rib jaws. These contained two well-sharpened copper nails that had caught the fish in this special Inuit device that was unlike most trident fish spears.

I went over to John and waited until more fish came. Then jiggling enthusiastically, he caught his first red-bellied trout. We danced around the hole together and then went back and each caught another.

"Osuitok *tikiniarktok. Takovit.* Osuitok arriving is he. Do you see?" John called, pointing to the pencil-thin line of dogs returning along the lake.

We walked back with our fish to the place where our tent had been. John, more delighted than I had ever seen him, got the goose out of the box and carefully arranged them all, ready to show Osuitok.

When Osuitok halted the team beside us, we could see that he had a large, neatly tied bundle of white geese behind him on the *kamotik* and another large, bound bundle of fish, their sides reflecting like bars of silver. He, too, had had success. He was too polite to mention the tattered, worn-out pieces of tent that we had folded up and hidden beneath some rocks.

We carried our gear down to the sled and dogs that were lying on the ice and quickly piled our sleeping bag and caribou skin mattress on the sled with our two packs, lashing them all tight with the rifle, our fishing gear, and catch.

As the team started out across the ice, I saw John looking back at his catch.

"Do you suppose your mother will cook those for us?" I asked him.

"Yes," John answered, smiling, "but can I take one of mine over to Kananginak's tent? We'll just sort of pass the fish around and cut off what we want with a knife. I'll eat mine over there with them."

"What's wrong with cooking?" I asked.

"Nothing," he said, "Sam and I just like it the way it is."

94
Another Kind of Learning

The boys had for a while attended the one-room schoolhouse in Kingait and their mother had also taught them with Uvilu and Tukikikudluk using the Calvert correspondence system used by the diplomatic corps in other out-of-the-way postings. We felt that John and Sam would soon enough be faced with colleges and careers in the rougher, tougher world outside. We chose England for their early schooling. Allie left Cape Dorset with them in the spring of 1961. It was a sadness to see them go.

Almost a year later when I went to St. Albans to see them after spending an exciting time in Russia, neither of the boys would speak a word of Inuktitut. When I asked them why, they said they had forgotten it because they were not allowed to use strange languages in school. When I frowned and said I'd speak to their headmaster about that, they assured me that it was not his or the school's fault. They agreed it was because of the other boys.

"They don't like boys speaking foreign languages on the playing field," John told me. "Two brothers from India we know at school called out a signal to one another so no one else could understand, and the other boys wouldn't play with them after that."

"We wouldn't wish that to happen to us," said Sam. "Soccer is such a jolly good game!"

95
Russia

To my surprise while in Kingait, I received a coded message through the Department saying that I should proceed south at the first opportunity, since I had been invited to go to the U.S.S.R. to discuss their native Siberian arts and crafts. I was delighted with the unexpected opportunity to go to that restricted part of the world. Probably, I was to be part of a Russian–Canadian exchange of some sort.

Officials in Canada advised me that the U.S.S.R. had a history of suddenly not allowing their invited exchange persons enough time to reach the Soviet Union before their invitation expired. Therefore, I was briefed and told to go and wait in Paris for the exact date of my invitation to be announced. This waiting was in no sense a hardship. Almost every day, I attended my old art academy, Académie de la Grande Chaumière, but I had been advised to stay in touch and not to leave Paris.

Suddenly, I was told to fly to Finland and I did, lunching briefly with the Canadian Counsel General in Helsinki, then caught the plane that evening into Leningrad. The landscape beneath me was so bomb-scarred that it looked like the craters on the moon. In Leningrad, the Russians were pleasant to me, offered me a packet of rubles to tide me over, and took away my special passport and my return tickets. The notice on the passport said it could not be taken away for more than twenty-four hours, but I did not see my passport or tickets again until I finally departed.

I went to the Canadian Embassy in Moscow to a small dinner party. When I met the Ambassador, Matthew Smith, I started to say, "I have a message . . ."

He held his hand up in front of my lips. "We'll be in touch," he said.

Next morning, following a phone call, I went back to the Embassy. Without speaking to me, the Ambassador led me to a door, inside which hung something resembling a small, old-fashioned elevator cage. One of his aides remained outside. I sat down beside him on a little leather bench.

"Now," he said earnestly, "it's safe in here. What about the message?"

"Oh," I said, "it's from a relative of yours, a friend of mine. He says he hopes you're enjoying your posting."

"Ohhh," the Ambassador sighed, "I thought you had something more for me." He explained, "This suspended cage is about the only place to talk safely. British Intelligence comes in here every day and wave some bamboo canes around its outside to make sure that no new bugs have been planted."

My meeting with the Director of the Soviet Arctic and Antarctic Institute was equally unfruitful, and I was not allowed to go to eastern Siberia as had been planned. That's the way things went in those Cold War days. But I did see much of the wonderful Siberian and American Northwest Coast collections at the museum in Leningrad before I returned to Ottawa, then north again.

96
Arctic Life Before the Snowmobile

Isolation, or even semi-isolation, is a very special way of life that few persons have known. It is not to everyone's taste. Of course, you can easily achieve it in the Arctic or elsewhere in much of North America's vastness by going well beyond the sight or sound of any other humans or machines.

Total isolation is a special way of living dangerously. If you're all alone, of course, you are liable to curl up and die from blood-poisoning, a ruptured appendix, or even a minor injury that might easily have been repaired. Apart from this, "cabin fever" is not a joke: some persons really do develop madness during the long dark spells in total or semi-isolation. They cannot bear the winter's gloom, and may come to suffer from what has been studied and scientifically described as Arctic hysteria.

As for semi-isolation, having, say, only three or four neighbors living together in a tiny settlement for long periods can present a challenge. I'm not referring to Inuit now, I'm writing of whites. In some small communities in the North, normally decent people sometimes learned to love, hate, or ignore each other, not just because of their diverse personalities, but sometimes because of conflicting work. Missionaries have traditionally despised missionaries of another Christian faith, and vigorously opposed them. Traders often vilified other traders, and so on. Even mounted policemen in a country without horses sometimes failed to seem romantic at close quarters over months or years. Bush pilots all too often managed to leave their base just before the mail from the South arrived, or managed to bring in the wrong rifle ammunition or useless outboard engine parts. None of that was shrugged off lightly in those isolated communities in the Arctic.

Strange to say, we isolated types usually tried to hide or contain our anger and complaints, allowing them to fester during the long gloom of winter, fiendishly awaiting the return of spring. Only then would we gird ourselves for battle. With the arrival of summer and the long-awaited shiptime the whites might unleash their pent-up rage upon their neighbors, shout – raise hell! Clear all the terrible rancor from their nervous system like cleaning out a frozen food locker, then patch it up, if possible. Or, better still, greet the new replacements with new hopes, and settle back for yet another dark, uncertain winter.

97
How Snowmobiles Save Walrus

A final word about the walrus hunt – and final is a good word. Those noisy devils, the snowmobiles, started coming into the Arctic in the early 1960s and changed many of the hunting patterns. Snowmobiles required Inuit to buy gas just as formerly dog teams had required Inuit to hunt meat, with the walrus herds the main target.

Bad as some may think snowmobiles, I believe they have been responsible for largely eliminating serious dog teams. In so doing they have saved the walrus herds and allowed them to flourish.

After all, snowmobile emissions are not one half as hard to suffer as the early morning exhaust fumes from a walrus-fed dog team when you're traveling behind them on a sled.

Thirty years later, with nobody hunting them for dog food, the walrus in the Canadian eastern Arctic are nicely on the increase. I've been observing that situation during the past few years personally. Walrus on the rocks or on drifting ice in earlier days were very wary of boats and humans and quickly plunged into the water, then spread out in terror. Don't forget that toward the end of the whaling trade the Arctic whalers, unable to find big whales, started to take the small variety of whales and walrus. Now those walrus have relaxed and become almost sociable. They will allow a vessel to approach and touch their pan of ice, and a Zodiac can go among them – though I don't recommend that; you should see how fast a nervous ton of walrus can move.

A bull walrus can be immensely bold and aggressive in defense of his harem, which may number a dozen females and their young. Or he may be tired from holding several younger males at bay. These other overeager Romeos have to bide their time, eat lots of clams, and hopefully gather the bulk and strength that will allow them one day to challenge the older bull, defeating him in a day-long battle, then taking all of his females for themselves. From that day forward, the old bull walrus will wander the Arctic seas alone. Driven from the herd's favorite clamming places, he will become lean and bad-tempered, some say insane with loneliness.

In the Bering Sea, walrus are still hunted for their ivory. They say their huge carcasses are left on the ice to waste while their ivory goes to the Orient or to those souvenir carvers who supply the shops with thousand-dollar cribbage boards. Collectors worldwide in past centuries have had a passion for animal ivory and that has kept it fashionable. I now believe, thank God, those days are drawing to a close. I wish those craftsmen would take up carving stone or bone, or reindeer antlers that fall off naturally every year.

98

A Carving for the Queen

It had been decided in Canada by the powers that be that a competition should be held and a prize awarded for the best two Inuit carvings made that year, one to be presented to Her Majesty the Queen, who planned a visit to the Arctic for the first time. Part of the thrill for the two winning carvers was to be flown to Yellowknife, the capital of the Northwest Territories, to be given the prize by the Queen herself. I was on hand with others representing the Canadian government and the Canadian Eskimo Arts Council.

Eisiak, a young man from west Baffin Island, had won first prize and Lasulasii, an older hunter, had won second. They were both excited, not so much about the prize itself, but about seeing the Queen and that far-off, fabled land of Yellowknife, 3,000 kilometers by dog-team travel west if you could do it, which you could not. There was no air service east and west, so they had to fly south to Montreal, then west to Winnipeg, then north again to Edmonton, and back into the Northwest Territories.

The carvers arrived on time, but their presentation carvings, to our horror, staggered in only the day before the Queen arrived. We rushed to find a private place to open them and check how they had survived their journey. I almost had a fit when I saw that the bottom of Eisiak's first-prize carving had been knocked off in transit, and worse still, the feet were badly broken, almost pulverized.

While I was dancing around the room in a panic, Eisiak looked at me with complete composure.

"I can fix that," he said, nodding to his broken sculpture.

"How?" I asked him.

"*Niput*, glue," he answered. "Have you got any of that good glue?"

"What kind of glue would fix that?" I asked, without a grain of hope.

"Come on, we'll show you."

Eisiak, Lasulasii, and I went out onto the main street of Yellow-knife and poked along. Although I felt in an hysterical hurry, they insisted on pausing and peering carefully into every store window. They explained to me that they had never had the chance to stop in a huge city like this before.

"This store might have some glue," I said, and we entered the only real hardware store at that time in the Northwest Territories. I followed them, slowly, for everything in that store fascinated them. Finally, we came to a shelf containing glues.

Without hesitation, Eisiak said, "This is the right one." He grasped a package that held two tubes.

I paid the hardware man while the two hunters stood over-whelmed by the unbelievable array of guns of various sizes, makes, and calibers displayed on a long rack.

"Come on," I said, "you've got to get back and try to do some-thing with that carving." I didn't have the slightest idea what.

"Wait, have they *agiat*, files, in this place?"

The hardware man led them to the rasps and files.

"Take your pick," I said.

"*Amasuualuk*, so many of them," they said, and with absolute assurance as to sizes, they picked out three and some emery paper.

"More?" I asked.

"No," they said. "These are right."

When we were in the room again, Lasulasii said, "We'll need fire, something to heat the glue."

"It says on the package . . ." I read the words, "*Keep away from heat and flames.*"

"Well, you people have got that all wrong." Lasulasii laughed. "If you don't heat it, it won't work. We'll show you how."

Back inside the room, they set immediately to work. Spreading a sheet of newspaper, Eisiak started filing the bottom of one of the foot pieces that had been broken off the carving. Then Lasulasii helped until they had a pile of jade green serpentine dust mounded before them.

We found a propane stove and a small enamel cooking pot. Eisiak casually mixed all of the two glues inside and as it heated, he stirred it with a screwdriver. Lasulasii looked at me as though I were a little child when I said I was afraid the *niput* would blow up.

They confidently poured the glue in a puddle on the paper, then carefully mixed it with the pile of green stone dust – about half and half, I'd say. When it was a smooth green and just beginning to harden, Eisiak, the carver of the original piece, picked up the stone and glue mixture and began shaping it like putty, reforming the two badly broken feet that would never have been made to fit together, glued or not. I was surprised at how little time Eisiak took and how accurately he reformed and replaced the original shape, allowing his crude, hand-shaped version to harden in its place under the carving. Then he sat back, discussing with Lasulasii and me the incredible abundance in the *kallunait* world, so many guns and files, so much glue, so many *saamuts*, flags, flying everywhere. Oh, Lord, I was nervous! Eisiak, which means "pretty eyes," next took up a file and tested the bottom of one of his reconstructed feet. The two carvers, relaxed and confident, stared out the window as they pointed out the sights and waited.

Now, Eisiak tested the mixture with his finger, then began to file. He worked cautiously and gently at first, then harder, sure of his every movement, smiling, laughing, enjoying this familiar work of carving and all this foreign travel. He perfectly reformed the feet. There were no cracks, no seams, and the color matched perfectly. I could scarcely believe the splendid result. How long had this special, delicate art of restoration been going on? Eisiak said he didn't know. He said he'd learned the glue trick from his uncle, a carver I knew well.

Next morning, the Queen received her official Northwest Territories carving and gave the prizes to the two delighted winners. Later that day the Queen bought another smaller carving that Eisiak had brought with him. The money for that one came directly from the royal purse, which really does exist. I saw it happen with my own eyes. I had the honor of helping to arrange the whole transaction.

99

Liquor

I left the Arctic just as liquor was about to become legal in the Northwest Territories. "Donald Arctic," Bishop Marsh of the Anglican Church, had been invited to address the House of Commons on the subject of Inuit life at that time. He asked whether the government wished that Inuit be thought of as Canadian citizens. He suggested to the House that Inuit could not seriously be considered full citizens until they had equal rights with other Canadians, and that the most obvious factor separating them was the restriction on their right to purchase liquor. Of course, the bishop was right. His comments made front-page news.

The rule banning the sale of alcohol to Inuit was immediately lifted, causing all hell to break loose for a period of twenty years or more. Like almost all other northerners, including most Inuit elders, I thought this sudden change had torn the Inuit society apart in ways that would never be repaired. But now I hope and believe that we are slowly being proven wrong. An understanding of alcohol has come slowly to Europeans since the eighteenth-century debauchery of Gin Lane portrayed by Hogarth's prints. In the same way, Inuit have gone through an introduction to the problems of drinking, and I believe that they are now overcoming the bad effects. Drugs also have become a factor in the North, as they have throughout the world. But I hope that, too, may pass.

In the old days, there was a period of time when the RCMP was our only air contact with the outside world. They were, of course, not licensed or obliged to transport liquor to anyone on private order, and so west Baffin had the luck to be one of the last areas of the Arctic to remain alcohol-free. Ten years later when the alcohol situation got really bad, a number of Arctic communities voted to outlaw liquor from their district. That rule was obeyed with such strictness that those communities found it difficult to lure in bulldozer drivers like the famous Paul Charbonneau, who, like many other workers, wanted to power their own engines after work on a dram or two of rye or beer or ale!

100

The Paper Bag

Leaving the Arctic was about the most difficult thing I ever had to do. I had cast the die myself and had known for some time that I was going. Toward the end of April 1962, I sent a message to the Department of Northern Affairs saying that I intended to resign. I wasn't really emotionally ready for it, but now I felt I had to go.

I had been offered a position in the South as an Assistant Director of Design at Steuben Glass, with a breathtaking office on the second floor of their new building at the corner of 5th and 56th, right in the middle of Manhattan Island. I was very excited yet apprehensive about the prospects of undertaking such different work. This job offered more than three times the salary I had been earning in the Arctic. Beyond that, I was offered a wonderful sponsorship in that overwhelming city of New York. It was at a time when the Kennedy administration was just beginning and New York was a neat, clean city throbbing with life and new ideas. Living in a brownstone in mid-Manhattan after a dozen years in the Arctic did make a dramatic change. But that, as they say, is another story.

As I prepared to leave, part of me felt that after all those wonderful Arctic years, I was sneaking out on the many people who had befriended me and shown me a better way to live. I had been with the Kingaimiut coming and going for the past nine years. It had simply been the best of times for me. Terry Ryan had been with us for nearly two years and was in position to continue helping the Co-operative move forward.

Closing up the government house that I had helped to build at

Dorset was a sorrowful task. I started giving away my Arctic things. I gave the printmakers in the Co-op my big, octagonal tent, one of the hardest things to part with because leaving it seemed to cut me off forever from that joyful, nomadic way of life.

Osuitok was delighted to have my high-powered rifle with the scope, along with a case of ammunition. After that, I asked the hunters and their wives to take their choice of sleeping bags, parkas, clothing, everything, including my Primus stove. I left the dogs till last. Osuitok would take care of them, along with the big sled. Years later, I returned to Cape Dorset for a visit and said to him with the pure delight that recognition gives, "Why, there's our lead bitch." "*Kasak*, almost," Osuitok nodded. "It's her great, great granddaughter."

The Arctic weather in late May of 1962 turned fine and the RCMP flew over in their single-engine Otter on skis. We had a glorious send-off party. Big Red Pedersen, one of my best friends, was a powerful six-foot-four. He raised his arms in a farewell toast and leapt into the air with Danish joie de vivre, punching his two large fists through the plywood ceiling. The patch marks are still there for you to see!

I had a wonderful time at that party, but later I went and stood alone outside watching the white dawn rising with the moon still glowing bone-white over Kingait Mountain. *This is the end*, I thought. *It's like watching yourself die, without really doing it.* I could see the yellow police plane resting peacefully beyond the barrier ice. There was not a breath of wind. The time had really come now, no bad weather to prevent it, no excuses. I was going after all these years.

Fletch, the mounted police pilot, came out the back door in his underwear and skin boots to check the weather. He shuddered and hurried back inside, for that fine, spring weather had a sharp razor's edge that on a sultry summer's day I sometimes try to recreate in my memory.

Later in the morning, ice fog started to roll in over the hills, drifting off the open waters of the polynyas, a huge pool opening in the ice which is kept open by the winds and tidal action. Seals, walrus, polar bears are all drawn there. That is the reason Inuit hunting families chose to live near Kingait in the first place.

Osuitok came in the house and smiled at me. *"Silapeungituk watchapaopik,* weather's going to get bad soon," he said.

His wife, Nipisa, made us some coffee, and when that was finished, the pilot came into the room and stared out the window. "Well, it looks like now or never, pal. Let's go."

Now the time had really come. I thought of rushing out the door and hiding in the hills. But as I looked outside, I could see Inuit gathering near the lazily rolling flag that Osuitok had just raised. They looked to me like people assembling for a funeral. My Arctic years had come to an end, years of dog-team traveling, hunting, dancing, lovemaking, printmaking, laughing, arguing, peacemaking, crying, singing, helping the young get food to eat, helping the old get the stones put on them. All of that was ending for me. Grabbing my bags with lots of help from others, we went out the door.

"You going to lock it?" asked the other policeman.

"God, no!" I said. "There's no need to lock anything here. I threw the keys away the day this house was finished."

Osuitok was standing quietly at the corner of the building with Nipisa. "Here," he said, "It's a poor carving, but I made it for you."

It was a marvelous jade green stone carving of a walrus, the very best that I have ever seen.

"I'll carry it," his wife said, and opened her hood for Osuitok to lay it inside.

We walked in silence to the police plane – men, women, and children. I had the feeling that I wasn't going to make it, that I might collapse and die while moving with the others through the rough ice.

"*Ayii,* Saomik, hey, Left-handed," called a powerful voice.

I stopped beside the plane. The police pilot looked at me sadly, the way people do when they know you're going to have to bear unbearable news, then he climbed inside.

"Saomik," Kiaksuk said. "Left-Handed, I have a little message for you."

It was only right, of course, that he, Kiaksuk, the oldest man among them, should speak for everyone. The others stared silently at me and if I looked back at them, they smiled in a sad way that made me look at my feet. *You hold on, you weakling,* I said to myself. *These families will remember how you act right now.*

"Left-Handed, we have something for you, *tunivapiovit,* a small gift from many here."

He held out a small brown paper bag. It was old and crumpled with what looked like seal-fat stains that made irregular, shiny blotches. I wondered what was inside, thinking probably a super carving. Kiaksuk laid it in my hands. It had no weight. It was nothing like a carving. Light as a feather, it seemed to contain nothing, just a crumpled bag.

"Look inside," said Kiaksuk proudly.

I opened the bag and reached in. Inside was a clutch of small, tightly folded letters many people had pencilled in Inuktitut. I drew out a handful of one- and two-dollar bills, each one wadded up tight. There were a lot of them in that little paper bag – thirty-three Canadian dollars.

"What are these for?" I asked.

"A gift for you," Kiaksuk said. "Everyone gives them to you. You're going away, everyone says, to try and make more money."

Kenouyiat was the word he used, meaning paper with a face on it, money.

"If at first you don't have enough money in that foreign place, we thought to give some to you. *Tavvautit,* goodbye," he said, and shook my hand.

Seeing all of them only in a blur, I shook hands with everyone, including babies in the hood, then climbed weakly aboard the plane. I pulled my hood over my face and left that unforgettable place that had for so long been my home.

gathering gull eggs
off the cliffs in spring
Harston spr

Bear on shore ice
W. Baffin Is. J. Houston
Oct. 53

hunting on the ice
Baffin Island. N.W.T.
J. Houston SW

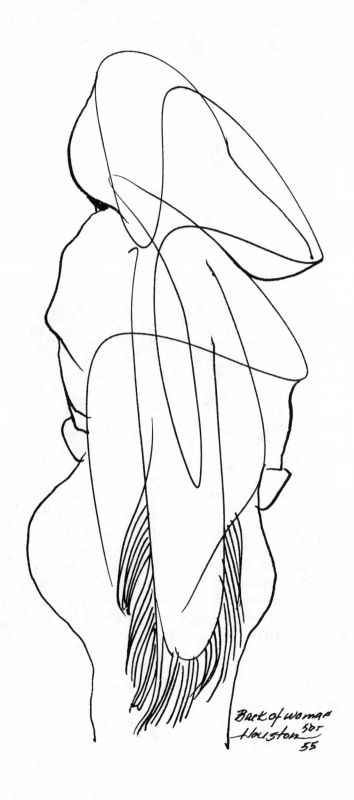

Back of woman
Houston 50¢
55

About the Author

James Houston, a Canadian author-artist, served with the Toronto Scottish Regiment in World War II, 1940–45, then lived among the Inuit of the Canadian Arctic for twelve years as a northern service officer, then as the first administrator of west Baffin Island, a territory of 65,000 square miles. Widely acknowledged as the prime force in the development of Eskimo art, he is past chairman of both the American Indian Arts Centre and the Canadian Eskimo Arts Council and a director of the Association on American Indian Affairs. He has been honored with the American Indian and Eskimo Cultural Foundation Award, the 1979 Inuit Kuavati Award of Merit, and is an officer of the Order of Canada.

Among his writings, *The White Dawn* has been published in thirty-one editions worldwide. That novel and *Ghost Fox*, *Spirit Wrestler*, and *Eagle Song* have been selections of major book clubs. His last novel, *Running West*, won the Canadian Authors Association Book of the Year Award. Author and illustrator of more than a dozen children's books, he is the only person to have won the Canadian Library Association Book of the Year Award three times. He has also written screenplays for feature films, has created numerous documentaries, and continues to lecture widely.

Mr. Houston's drawings, paintings, and sculptures are internationally represented in many museums and private collections. He is master designer for Steuben Glass. He created the seventy-foot-high central sculpture in the Glenbow-Alberta Art Museum.

Houston, now a dual citizen of Canada and the United States, and his wife, Alice, divide the year between a colonial privateer's house in Connecticut and a writing retreat on the bank of a salmon river on the Queen Charlotte Islands in British Columbia, a few miles south of Alaska, where he has written many of these memoirs.